Modern Language Association of America

Options for Teaching

Joseph Gibaldi, Series Editor

Teaching

Contemporary Theory

to Undergraduates

Edited by

Dianne F. Sadoff and *William E. Cain*

The Modern Language Association of America
New York   1994

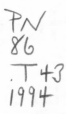

PN
86
.T43
1994

© 1994 by The Modern Language Association of America
All rights reserved. Printed in the United States of America

Library of Congress Cataloging-in-Publication Data

Teaching contemporary theory to undergraduates / edited by Dianne F.
  Sadoff and William E. Cain.
      p.   cm. — (Options for teaching ; 12)
  Includes index.
  ISBN 0-87352-368-7 (alk. paper) ISBN 0-87352-369-5 (pbk.)
  1. Criticism — Study and teaching (Higher). I. Sadoff, Dianne F.
II. Cain, William E., 1952–   . III. Series.
PN86.T43   1994
801'.95'0711 — dc20   94-20566

Published by The Modern Language Association of America
10 Astor Place, New York, New York 10003-6981

This book was set in Palatino and printed on recycled paper.

Contents

Part I
Introducing Theory

Contemporary Theory, the Academy, and Pedagogy

William E. Cain

Theory has a daunting range of meanings and applications, and it is connected to controversies not only in literary studies but also in the humanities fields in general and higher education as a whole. Some scholars define contemporary theory specifically and link it to a concrete form of practice in teaching and scholarship. *Marxist theory* or *feminist theory*, for example, refers to an intricate body of thought—marked by its own history and laced with internal disputes, contradictions, differences in emphasis— that impels different teachers to choose different styles and strategies in their writing as well as in their work with students. Other scholars, however, define contemporary theory more broadly, taking it to mean the emergence of an array of critiques of New Critical formalism and the development of alternatives: the New Left "politics of literature," structuralism, feminism, and the black arts movement in the 1960s and, in later decades, poststructuralism, deconstruction, new historicism, ethnic studies, gay and lesbian studies, and cultural studies. Still others conceive of contemporary theory in even more general terms, seeing it as implying any kind of sustained reflection on practice, any serious question asking about how teachers and critics conduct themselves. From this point of view, every scholar-teacher is a theorist to some extent and should feel no unease about the label.

Many have found theory, understood in one or more of these senses, an absorbing, challenging, and inescapable pursuit. But for others, it names an unfortunate departure from the basic activity that scholars and teachers of literature should undertake: the close, attentive interpretation of major writers. Indeed, those opposed to theory judge that it has caused literature to be shunned and marginalized. Students and teachers, it is said, are now invested in Jacques Derrida, Mikhail Bakhtin, Fredric Jameson, and Julia Kristeva rather than in Milton, Dickens, Austen, and T. S. Eliot. All this theory must be jettisoned, the antitheorists contend, so that we can return to the best texts, reading and valuing them on their own terms.

As Allan Bloom stated in *The Closing of the American Mind*, the goal should be "reading certain generally recognized classic texts, just reading them, letting them dictate what the questions are and the method of approaching them" (344).

Yet criticism has always been accompanied by theory, and there has never been a time when teachers have performed without it. The more closely one inspects debates between those who espouse theory and those who do not, the more these debates turn out to concern just what the proper procedures *are* for literary study, and thus they pivot on theoretical choices, assumptions, preferences.

Perhaps the clearest instance is the famous exchange between René Wellek and F. R. Leavis that occurred in the late 1930s. In a critique of Leavis's *Revaluation: Tradition and Development in English Poetry*, Wellek noted that the book "teems with acute critical observations and brilliant interpretations of texts" but is not sufficiently grounded in philosophy ("Literary Criticism" 23). Leavis, he maintained, fails to comprehend the "philosophy" that informs the verse of Shelley and other Romantics and consequently misunderstands and underrates their poetry. Still more disturbing, Wellek declared, is Leavis's failure to provide an explicit account of his method: Leavis displays a suggestive "practical criticism" but not the "theory" that is needed to explain and justify it (23).

In replying to Wellek, Leavis commented briefly on the point about the Romantics' philosophy, but his main purpose was to underscore the sharp difference between the tasks of the literary critic and those of the philosopher, the first of whom he views as a practical critic of texts and the latter as a theorist:

> Literary criticism and philosophy seem to me to be quite distinct and different kinds of disciplines—at least, I think they ought to be. . . . No doubt a philosophic training might possibly—ideally would—make a critic surer and more penetrating in the perception of significance and relation and in the judgment of value. But it is to be noted that the improvement we ask for is of the critic, the critic as critic, and to count on it would be to count on the attainment of an arduous ordeal. It would be reasonable to fear—to fear blunting of edge, blurring of focus, and muddled misdirection of attention: consequences of queering one discipline with the habits of another.   ("Reply" 31–32)

For Leavis, the critic's duties are urgent and demanding enough. The study of philosophy—that written either in the poet's period or in the critic's own day—and the articulation of the theory that shapes interpretation are misguided enterprises. They will, said Leavis, cause more harm than good, confusing and jeopardizing unmediated scrutiny of the words on the page.

A fair number of people remain sympathetic to the position Leavis outlined: literary critics should fasten on literary texts, reading them with intense care and enabling students to do the same. Yet one of the striking features of Leavis's many books is the sizable number of theoretical pieces they contain. He wrote frequently about the function of criticism, the nature of literary valuation, the form through which close reading should transpire, and the goals that teachers should set for the discipline of English. Leavis was not content to perform close readings and present evaluations of authors. He was staunchly committed to describing and defending the *kind* of criticism and teaching he favored and expected others to emulate. While he was not the exacting theorist and technical philosopher that Wellek wished for, he did reflect repeatedly on the processes by which criticism and teaching should be conducted. He was an anti-theorist who felt compelled to theorize.

In this respect, Leavis resembles nearly all the major figures in modernist literary criticism and reformers of English studies. Modernist criticism and the New Criticism that emerged in the English and American academy arose in large measure because of a new excitement about and immersion in theory—a recognition that efforts to dispense with theory were a mistake and had damaged criticism, scholarship, and pedagogy. I. A. Richards, for example, began his influential *Principles of Literary Criticism* by surveying "the chaos of critical theories" and urging critics to obtain at last an "understanding of the nature of experience" and "theories of valuation and communication" (2). In *Practical Criticism*, Richards restated his appeal for critical theory and methodology, expressing his frustration that "the technique of the approach to poetry has not yet received half so much serious systematic study as the technique of pole-jumping" (292). Richards was a theorist for his entire career, as was his impressively precocious student William Empson, author of *Seven Types of Ambiguity* and several subsequent books.[1]

The New Critics in America regarded theory as essential. In *The World's Body*, John Crowe Ransom declared that the "good critic" should study poetics as well as poetry: "If he thinks he must puritanically abstain from all indulgence in the theory, the good critic may have to be a good little critic. . . . Actually, it seems reasonable to suppose that no such critic exists. Theory, which is expectation, always determines criticism, and never more than when it is unconscious." In Ransom's estimation, the abiding peril for critics is assuming they can forgo theory: "the reputed condition of no-theory in the critic's mind is illusory" (173–74).

Ransom labored to devise a theory that would grant criticism the right to label itself scientific and hence to stand as a legitimate discipline and respectable academic department. "Criticism must become more scientific, or precise and systematic," he insisted in *The World's Body* (329). The foes of the New Critics agreed. Northrop Frye, though his method differed, had the same goal as Ransom. "There is no reason," he states in "The Archetypes of Literature," "why criticism, as a systematic and organized study, should not be, at least partly, a science" (7). Even as critics like Ransom and Frye disputed the ascendancy of science and deplored the effects of technology and industrialization, they sought to develop systems of interpretation as rigorous as those honed in the sciences.

Both New Critics and myth critics were rebuked for making literary study unduly scientific. Their terms and techniques were criticized and parodied, derided as jargon, and they were chastised for failing to fashion "English" into a true "corporate enterprise and a progressive discipline" (Hirsch 209). The members of these two critical schools were theorists, and, as such, they encountered the same objections to theory that were later propelled at structuralists and poststructuralists in the 1960s and afterward. Theory, it seems, is invariably to blame when the profession appears to have gone astray and abandoned its mission.

In fact, when the New Critics came under fierce attack in the late 1940s and 1950s, it was their theory that detractors found faulty. Ransom, Allen Tate, Robert Penn Warren, R. P. Blackmur, Yvor Winters, Kenneth Burke, Cleanth Brooks, W. K. Wimsatt, and like-minded new and modern critics packed their books with theoretical reflection and argument. They believed they had radically new ideas about literary criticism that had to be explained and institutionalized. Wellek and Austin Warren modified and extended these ideas in their several editions of *Theory of Literature* (first published in 1948); as Wellek observed, criticism "must ultimately aim at systematic knowledge about literature, at literary theory" ("Literary Theory" 4). But the more theory they produced, the more they spurred others to contest it and to propose different, competing theories that would repair the damage the New Critics had done to the discipline.

The defects in New Critical theory were regularly cited as the reason criticism and teaching had become subjective, impressionistic, arbitrary, formulaic, mechanical, too purely literary or not literary enough, too constricted or disturbingly open-ended. Lionel Trilling, Philip Rahv, Frye, and E. D. Hirsch were among the chief critics of New Criticism. Their recommendations varied considerably, but—and this is the key point—all four men were theorists engaged in the critique of a theory they deemed unsound. They dissented from the style of reading and interpretation that the New Critics had inaugurated, and they wrote many books and essays that advocated better approaches and methods; keener attitudes toward criticism, scholarship, and teaching; and adjustments in pedagogy.

The question, then, is not whether criticism and teaching should return to an era before theory. There has never been a moment free from theory, and the past looks to be without theory only to those dissatisfied with the theories they find in the present. It has been claimed that because critics and teachers today are saddled with theory, they know far more about it than about literature, read more critical books and journals than primary literary texts, and mimic the gestures of the currently idolized theoreticians. Yet one finds these very complaints everywhere in the annals of modern literary criticism. In "This Age of Conformity," published in 1954, Irving Howe alleged that criticism had crazily become a separate "subject," that students of literature cared only about "what Ransom said about Winters with regard to what Winters had said about Eliot," that critics were complacent "apostles of Burke or Trilling or Winters or Leavis or Brooks or neo-Aristotle," and that members of the younger generation "who have never troubled to open a novel by Turgenev" can "rattle off reams of Kenneth Burke" (43). To anyone following the current attacks on theory, this diatribe sounds familiar.

Theory, too, is often tagged as predictable, equipped only to locate in texts what it projects onto them. In 1979, for example, M. H. Abrams made just such an observation about Derrida, Harold Bloom, and Stanley Fish, remarking that their "discovery procedures" yield "new meanings" that are easy to anticipate: their methods succeed because the results are known in advance (448–49). But a similar lament was sounded about the New Critics, who, noted Elder Olson in 1952, were wedded to narrow "hypotheses as to the nature or functions of language" (40). The New Critics looked at every text the same way, Olson maintained, because they ignored genre and assumed all texts were authoritatively governed by imagery and metaphor. Others pummeled the New Critics for denying the "author"—an accusation that would be directed later at Roland Barthes, Derrida, and Michel Foucault. "The concept of the author is conspicuous in New Critical thought by its absence," said Mark Schorer in 1960 (330).[2]

The continuities of critical history are concealed by the polemics and manifestos that each new movement issues. Theorists do not always perceive such constants themselves. Deconstructionists, for instance, have proposed that their emphasis on intertextuality and indeterminacy breaks with prior methods, and it is true that they generally find meaning unfathomable whereas the New Critics worked to get to the bottom of everything. But deconstruction won converts because it took the New Criticism as its point of departure. The New Critics called for close reading; the deconstructionists utter the same plea, adding only that the New Critics failed to read closely or deeply enough. The deconstructionists describe the unstable, incoherent nature of textual meaning and the presence of conflicting elements in texts, and in this sense they do appear to move beyond the New Criticism and its belief in the Coleridgean reconciliation of opposites that literature achieves. But the New Critics were acutely aware of and focused on opposing features in texts, and they made available an understanding of literature that deconstructionists needed merely to pry apart and problematize.

When Ransom drew notice to the poet's desperate struggle to integrate logical structure and poetic texture (347–48), when Warren focused on "impurities" and contradictory terms in texts (15), and when Brooks sketched the poem's "hostility" to its own meaning (732–33), they not only announced principles for like-minded New Critics but set the stage for their own undoing at the hands of the deconstructionists. In similar fashion, Tate drew attention to a discrepant relation between literal and figurative properties of language (64–65) that the deconstructionists would later fasten on as well, but with insurgent results. The New Critics supplied their followers with terms and techniques for literary criticism and pedagogy (see, e.g., Brooks and Warren), and they also handed to their future antagonists nearly everything required to end the reign of New Criticism. They launched one revolution and then were toppled by a second they largely prepared—even scripted—themselves.

The brisk rise of new theories occurred because the New Critics furnished much theory to work with and contend against. This contention came not only from Derrida and Paul de Man, who mapped deconstructionist theory and practice, but also from Fish and Jonathan Culler, who have been concerned with the interpreter's share in constructing the meanings of the text and the conventions through which students become competent readers: their reorientations of reading strategies depend on the interest in close reading that the New Critics lodged securely in the discipline. Theorists hence are mistaken when they imply that they have outdistanced the New Criticism, just as antitheorists are mistaken when they recommend that literary study return to the New Criticism, as though it were altogether free from theory.

But while theory has been perpetually present in criticism and in the teaching of literature, admittedly there is now more of it—for several simple reasons. The first is that women and minorities, who are finally gaining entry into the profession in significant numbers, have erected a network of theories about gender, race, and ethnicity that conflict with the norms and procedures established by and within the academy before the 1960s. The second reason is the ever-increasing globalization or internationalization of literature and criticism. This change is what Geoffrey Hartman has termed the condition of "cultural translation" and "crossover" from one culture to another that pervades contemporary intellectual life (252). Literature scholars in America support their research and pedagogy through such theorists from abroad as Derrida, Foucault, Barthes, Lacan, Althusser, Bakhtin, Lukács, Cixous, Habermas, Adorno, Heidegger, Benjamin, Eco, Lyotard, Kristeva, Iser, Todorov, and Blanchot.

A third explanation for the range of theory derives from the inquiry into the category "literature" that many theorists have prosecuted. They have questioned the customary separation between literary and nonliterary texts and in so doing have eliminated boundaries between kinds of texts and between disciplines for studying them. Texts have by no means disappeared, but they are not the sole object of scrutiny. Theory now dramatizes and explores such topics as the discourses through which individual texts are constituted, the types of subjectivity they manifest, the work of representation they accomplish, the history in which they are situated, and the tactics of reading they mandate. Again, criticism today is different not because it is theoretical where the criticism of the past was not but, rather, because the multiple forms that theory has taken have made criticism into something other than what it was before.

It may seem overwhelming, and not only to old New Critics and anti-theorists. A sign of discontent within the ranks is the argument, forcefully expressed by Steven Knapp and Walter Benn Michaels, that theory has hit a dead-end and should cease. This argument is valuable in its concern for the manner in which theory is contained *within* the practice of criticism and cannot be sundered from it. But theory cannot be wished away; it never arrives at a final dead-end and is more elusive and various than Knapp and Michaels suggest. Their position, in fact, may rest on a theoretical error, an error of definition. They start by stating that for them theory means "the attempt to govern interpretations of particular texts by appealing to an account of interpretation in general" (723). But no sooner do they offer this restricted definition than they leap from it to all "contemporary theory" and then, at the close, to "the theoretical enterprise" as a whole, which, they conclude, should "come to an end" (742). They give the impression that they are presenting a highly specific argument, but they allow their conclusion to seem the necessary consequence of a far more general one.

It is possible to be against theory, as Knapp and Michaels are, but not possible to do without it. Most critics and teachers who read theory are active, adventurous users of it, mixing theories that by rights should not be joined together; trying out, like bricoleurs, a version of one theory only to abandon it or add it to a second and third, changing and readjusting its terms. There's no denying that this experimentation occasionally leads to slipshod execution in critical arguments and classroom practices. But it is the inevitable by-product of the growth of theory, its bountiful if uneven development, its scope and multiplicity, its capacity to keep its devotees alert, restless, and dissatisfied. Theory makes readers suspicious, skeptical, hard to please; it makes them admirably nomadic, unable to inhabit any single theory as more than a momentary way station. One might suggest that theory at its best creates critics and teachers of the sort R. P. Blackmur portrayed in "A Critic's Job of Work" when he celebrated the constant movement of self-reflection, "provisional, adjudicating irony," and "vivid questing" he found in Plato and Montaigne (273). Theory decrees constant experimentation, fosters change, promotes a steady degree of self-consciousness about how one performs one's work.

Put this way, theory seems eminently desirable: who could survive without it? Yet it is painted today by conservatives as the cause of a "crisis" in literary studies and the humanities. Conservative antitheorists profess that theorists have brought about a collapse of literary values, cannot distinguish a good book from a bad one, and have struck at the vital center of a once-prosperous discipline. But these charges, too, have long been a staple in the case against critical revisionists. They were deployed time and again to assail Burke and Frye, for example, whose equipment for interpretation supposedly functioned as well on a detective novel as on *King Lear*. Criticism cannot occur without theory, nor can it advance without a myth of decline that blames theory for institutional subversion. One is indeed reminded of the reiterated narratives of loss, spanning the centuries, that Raymond Williams reviewed in *The Country and the City*: the sense of a bitter fall from a better time is a permanent theme in cultural history.

Foes of theory have also seized on it as the source for something else they bemoan—the recasting of the literary canon. But it is inaccurate to claim that current theory has led to unprecedented, radical changes in the canon. Nearly all the major figures in the history of criticism— Johnson, Coleridge, Arnold, Eliot, Lawrence, Pound, Leavis—reorganized the canon, and they did so with an uncompromising boldness that alarmed their contemporaries. The best theorists and critics aim to change the order of our books and the critical terminology we use about them, and often their proposals prove strange and alienating, shocking to the system.[3]

Traditions, canons, and curricula have often altered dramatically, and many "great" texts were once regarded unsympathetically. In 1895 a young professor at Yale named William Lyon Phelps offered a course on "the modern novel" that centered on Twain, Conrad, and Hardy. His choice of syllabus was considered so outrageous that it was headlined on the front page of the *New York Times*, and it so agitated Phelps's senior colleagues that he almost lost his job. Then, too, there is the tale told by F. O. Matthiessen, author of acclaimed books on Eliot, James, Dreiser, and the American Renaissance, who in 1930 went hunting in the Yale University library for a copy of Melville's *Moby-Dick*. He found it shelved in the cetology section. To the staff at Yale's library, *Moby-Dick* was not a literary masterpiece but a catchall of information and lore about whales (Cain 136).

Complaints about changes in the canon have been part of a larger criticism of the "politicization" of literary studies that theory purportedly sustains. According to the indictment, theory is essentially an attempt to transform the academy into a leftist stronghold in which students are indoctrinated with "politically correct" texts on, and views about, race, class, gender, and sexual orientation. "Everyone in the profession well understands," states Peter Shaw, that "'theory' of any kind is at present a code word for the politicization of literature." The "deepest appeal of critical theory [is] political," reports John Gross, former editor of the *Times Literary Supplement*:

> Even the more rarified varieties of theory generally carry an implicit political message. By their very nature they suppose that traditional Western values are illusory. . . . In many respects modern theory might have been invented (and in some respects perhaps it was) in order to fill the gap left by the decline of classical Marxism.　　　　　　　　　　　　　　　　　　　(15)

In an editorial in the November 1991 issue of the *New Criterion*, Hilton Kramer tendered similar judgments about the politics of theory at an even higher pitch. He asserts that politically correct theorists and "partisans of radical multiculturalism" have ravaged higher education by their insistence "that we import questions of race, class, gender, sexual orientation, and the like into the study of the humanities" (2). Kramer's point is a common one, and renditions of it have been given by Roger Kimball, Dinesh D'Souza, Joseph Epstein, and kindred critics of the academy. It must be winning assent from many readers, for it crops up everywhere in polemics against theory, multiculturalism, and liberal-leftist influence on college campuses. Yet it is an odd point, with little real content.

The basic belief these critics share is that radicals riddled with theory are introducing inappropriate questions into their teaching and are betraying the texts that constitute the "subject" (Kramer's word) students should learn about. But is this charge accurate? Kramer does not supply examples of the practice, nor does he give any indication that he believes it is *ever* right to raise questions of race, class, gender, and sexual orientation. It is as though bringing them up at any stage, in any form, is the result of radical partisanship and ideological coercion, of importing "bad stuff" from the hinterlands of theory that defiles the true subject. This attitude is, I think, peculiarly willful—equivalent to asserting that religion should play no role in discussions of Donne, Herbert, and Milton—and it distorts the subject that Kramer intends to safeguard. What would it mean to teach *The Rise of Silas Lapham*, *Jude the Obscure*, or *An American Tragedy* if one left out the issues of social class that Howells, Hardy, and Dreiser examine? Should ethnicity be absent from discussions of *The Merchant of Venice*, *Daniel Deronda*, Saul Bellow's novels?

Perhaps Kramer might impatiently reply that it would be fine to focus on theories of race, ethnicity, class, gender, and sexual orientation in texts like those I have named. Maybe what bothers him is the surfacing of these matters when they are not explicit in the texts themselves. But this point does not have much substance either. Let us say an instructor is teaching a course on the American Renaissance. It would be interesting to consider "race" during the weeks spent on Emerson, and not simply because he is the author of many essays and lectures on slavery, emancipation, the Fugitive Slave Law, and John Brown. What would be outlandish about noticing, for instance, that Emerson presented his seminal address "The Method of Nature" at Waterville (now Colby) College in the same week of August 1841 in which Frederick Douglass gave his first public speech at a meeting on Nantucket of the Massachusetts Anti-slavery Society? One does not have to be a political partisan or radical theorist to want to investigate the ways in which the self-reliant Emerson and Douglass are similar to and different from each other; one need just be intellectually curious.

For all the aura of scandal attached to it, theory accomplishes something that is both relatively straightforward and supremely important. It enables critics, teachers, and students to illuminate anew the structure of texts, to write literary and cultural history with greater richness and depth, and to understand social and institutional relations more intricately. Theory defamiliarizes literary study, resystematizes and reorganizes it by inserting new texts among the old and fashioning inventive discourses for them.

To express the point in such general terms is to risk taming theory. But this line of response is important at the present time, when theory is repeatedly singled out as a reason—maybe the foremost reason—for the downfall and death of criticism. One could readily argue to the contrary that criticism, scholarship, and teaching have never been more exciting or healthier. No doubt some scholars are doing ineffectual, self-indulgent work, and some teachers are probably undertaking misleading experiments in their courses. But has there ever been a period when all was stable, not in need of stirring up and correction? Whatever the errors, excesses, and abuses of theory, it has greatly benefited teachers of literature and led to positive innovations in reading lists, courses, syllabi, and classroom policies and practices. What is truly worthy of notice is the amount and quality of the good work, and the improvements, that theory has generated. Theory has enhanced and enlivened the study of literature, made it more attractive to students, and preserved its value in the midst of a media-dominated society in which critical reading and thinking often appear to be lost arts.

Wellesley College

Notes

[1] It is not possible in my limited space to offer anything like a full history of modern and contemporary criticism and theory. For helpful overviews of this large topic, see Berman; Graff; Leitch; Lentricchia; and Ohmann. See also the studies edited by Natoli and by Atkins and Morrow, which spotlight recent trends.

[2] For a good survey of key terms in literary theory and criticism, see Lentricchia and McLaughlin.

[3] There have been many books devoted in whole or in part to the "canon debate." See, for example, Gorak; Lauter; and von Hallberg.

Works Cited

Abrams, M. H. "How to Do Things with Texts." 1979. Rpt. in *Critical Theory since 1965*. Ed. Hazard Adams and Leroy Searle. Tallahassee: Florida State UP, 1986. 436–49.

Atkins, Douglas, and Laura Morrow, eds. *Contemporary Literary Theory*. Amherst: U of Massachusetts P, 1989.

Berman, Art. *From the New Criticism to Deconstruction: The Reception of Structuralism and Poststructuralism*. Urbana: U of Illinois P, 1988.

Blackmur, R. P. "A Critic's Job of Work." 1935. In *The Double Agent: Essays in Craft and Elucidation*. Rpt. Gloucester: Smith, 1962. 269–302.

Bloom, Allan. *The Closing of the American Mind*. New York: Simon, 1987.

Brooks, Cleanth. "Irony as a Principle of Structure." 1949. Rpt. in *Literary Opinion in America*. Ed. Morton Dauwen Zabel. New York: Harper, 1951. 729–41.

Brooks, Cleanth, and Robert Penn Warren. *Understanding Poetry: An Anthology for College Students*. 1938. Rev. ed. New York: Henry Holt, 1950.

Cain, William E. *F. O. Matthiessen and the Politics of Criticism*. Madison: U of Wisconsin P, 1988.

Empson, William. *Seven Types of Ambiguity*. 1930. Rev. ed. New York: New Directions, 1966.

Frye, Northrop. "The Archetypes of Literature." 1951. Rpt. in *Fables of Identity: Studies in Poetic Mythology*. New York: Harcourt, 1963. 7–20.

Gorak, Jan. *The Making of the Modern Canon: Genesis and Crisis of a Literary Idea*. London: Athlone, 1991.

Graff, Gerald. *Professing Literature: An Institutional History*. Chicago: U of Chicago P, 1987.

Gross, John. "The Man of Letters in a Closed Shop." *Times Literary Supplement* 15 Nov. 1991: 15–16.

Hartman, Geoffrey. "Tea and Totality: The Demand of Theory on Critical Style." 1984. Rpt. in *Contemporary Critical Theory*. Ed. Dan Latimer. New York: Harcourt, 1989. 237–52.

Hirsch, E. D., Jr. *Validity in Interpretation*. New Haven: Yale UP, 1967.

Howe, Irving. "This Age of Conformity." 1954. Rpt. in *Selected Writings, 1950–1990*. New York: Harcourt, 1990. 26–49.

Knapp, Steven, and Walter Benn Michaels. "Against Theory." *Critical Inquiry* 8.4 (1982): 723–42.

Kramer, Hilton. "Notes and Comments." *New Criterion* Nov. 1991: 1–3.

Lauter, Paul. *Canons and Contexts*. New York: Oxford UP, 1991.

Leavis, F. R. "A Reply." 1937. Rpt. in *The Importance of Scrutiny*. Ed. Eric Bentley. New York: New York UP, 1964. 30–40.

———. *Revaluation: Tradition and Development in English Poetry*. London: Chatto, 1969.

Leitch, Vincent B. *American Literary Criticism from the Thirties to the Eighties*. New York: Columbia UP, 1988.

Lentricchia, Frank. *After the New Criticism*. Chicago: U of Chicago P, 1980.

Lentricchia, Frank, and Thomas McLaughlin, eds. *Critical Terms for Literary Study*. Chicago: U of Chicago P, 1990.

Natoli, Joseph, ed. *Literary Theory Future(s)*. Urbana: U of Illinois P, 1989.

———, ed. *Tracing Literary Theory*. Urbana: U of Illinois P, 1989.

Ohmann, Richard. *English in America: A Radical View of the Profession*. New York: Oxford UP, 1976.

Olson, Elder. "William Empson, Contemporary Criticism, and Poetic Diction." 1952. Rpt. in *Critics and Criticism*. Ed. R. S. Crane. Chicago: U of Chicago P, 1957. 24–61.

Rahv, Philip. "Criticism and the Imagination of Alternatives." 1956–58. Rpt. in *Literature* 243–57.

——. "Fiction and the Criticism of Fiction." 1956. Rpt. in *Literature* 222–42.

——. *Literature and the Sixth Sense*. Boston: Houghton, 1970. 243–57.

Ransom, John Crowe. *The World's Body*. 1938. Baton Rouge: Louisiana State UP, 1968.

Richards, I. A. *Practical Criticism: A Study of Literary Judgment*. 1929. New York: Harcourt, n.d.

——. *Principles of Literary Criticism*. New York: Harcourt, 1925.

Schorer, Mark. "The Necessary Stylist: A New Critical Revision." 1960. Rpt. in *Modern Criticism: Theory and Practice*. Ed. Walter Sutton and Richard Foster. Indianapolis: Odyssey, 1963. 328–34.

Shaw, Peter. "The Modern Language Association Is Misleading the Public." *Chronicle of Higher Education* 27 Nov. 1991: B3.

Tate, Allen. "Tension in Poetry." 1938. Rpt. in *Essays of Four Decades*. New York: Morrow, 1970. 56–71.

Trilling, Lionel. "The Sense of the Past." *The Liberal Imagination: Essays on Literature and Society*. London: Secker, 1951. 187–201.

von Hallberg, Robert, ed. *Canons*. Chicago: U of Chicago P, 1984.

Warren, Robert Penn. "Pure and Impure Poetry." 1942. Rpt. in *New and Selected Essays*. New York: Random, 1989. 3–28.

Wellek, René. "Literary Criticism and Philosophy." 1937. Rpt. in *The Importance of Scrutiny*. Ed. Eric Bentley. New York: New York UP, 1964. 23–30.

——. "Literary Theory, Criticism, and History." 1960. Rpt. in *Concepts of Criticism*. Ed. Stephen G. Nichols, Jr. New Haven: Yale UP, 1963. 1–20.

Wellek, René, and Austin Warren. *Theory of Literature*. 1948. 3rd rev. ed. New York: Harcourt, 1956.

Williams, Raymond. *The Country and the City*. London: Chatto, 1973.

Frameworks, Materials, and the Teaching of Theory

Dianne F. Sadoff

"What is literary criticism?" a young man asks me one September at course registration, voicing a question that most well-prepared undergraduates censor for fear of appearing ignorant. Unknowingly, he asks not only about a specific class he might choose to take but also about a professional practice and its institutional apparatus. I explain, simply, that the course asks why we read and how we define texts as we do, that it scrutinizes the methodologies critics apply to literature and to other texts. Surprised that such an enterprise exists, he nevertheless signs up. During the term, this second-semester freshman proves a thoughtful, perceptive student: in his sociology class, he tells other members of our group, he is reading similar texts about the problematic status of the subject. Unlike several senior English majors, he does not complain that the course fails to deliver the reading pleasure he usually experiences in literature classes, that the theory is too difficult to comprehend and—the deadliest criticism of all— is boring.

Like other teachers of theory, I had cautioned my students on the first day of class that reading is not an innocent activity. Echoing Jonathan Culler, I warned that theory does not restrict itself to prescriptive or normative commentary about literature, to exclusive strategies for interpretation, or even to the modes of producing practical criticism. Because, as Culler makes clear, theory does not "function . . . as demonstrations within the parameters of a discipline" but instead challenges disciplinary boundaries, we would read widely from the discourses of the human sciences, texts that require students to apply analytic rather than interpretive skills (8–10). The encounter with theory is necessarily frustrating and challenging, I admitted to my students, but it can nevertheless prove intellectually exciting and productive. (I had learned, as all teachers of theory do, that warnings about textual difficulty, tempered with enthusiasm, can prepare students for the adventure of discovering theory.)

I

This book became possible, even necessary, because many faculty members who undertook to teach theory—whether in a theory class or in a mainstream literature course—did not really know how to do it, despite the informal sharing of syllabi, ideas, and stories about difficulty. Although, as William Cain describes in his essay in this volume, the New Critics introduced theoretical questions into the study of literature, the pedagogy promulgated by their influential textbooks—especially *Understanding Poetry* (Brooks and Warren)—appears to us now as necessarily teacher-centered. Selecting literary texts through which to represent their political and cultural agenda, Cleanth Brooks and Robert Penn Warren hoped to reeducate readers, to introduce to literary studies a new epistemology, and so to replace the tenets of modernism with their own (quasi-religious) beliefs about literature's function as one existing outside social and historical concerns. Directing student (and teacher) attention to the imagery, metaphors, ambiguities, and ironies the authors viewed as structuring poetic texts, the New Critical textbook shaped the "close reading" strategies of a generation. Let me say, however, that despite the current critique of New Criticism, those strategies remain influential in our classrooms. Most teachers assume their novice English majors already know how to read texts; to ensure that they do, however, those who teach an introduction to literature course often use the basics of interpretation as constructed by New Criticism—for, this curricular arrangement presumes, students must acquire the skills of interpretation before they question its theorization.

The teacher as New Critic, moreover, tended to stage his reading as performance (for, as Cain argues, most faculty members in the 1950s and 1960s were men). The brilliant lecture, studded with quotations from the text, with references to tenor and vehicle, with rhetorical paradoxes, became the pedagogical norm. The successful student repeated the professor's interpretive insights on exams and papers periodically throughout the semester. Called the banking model of teaching by Paulo Freire, this pedagogical strategy—as many contributors to this volume remind us— assumed the teacher's authority, mastery of his material, and control of his necessarily passive and submissive students (50–59). But as this book demonstrates, pedagogy in the 1980s and 1990s has shifted and become more thoroughly student-centered than it was in the 1950s and 1960s. Small-class discussion has, in general, replaced or supplemented the lecture, and teachers have developed a variety of strategies for encouraging active student participation in the open-ended process of inquiry that constitutes learning. Collaborative learning exercises, small-group workshops, in-class writing and rewriting exercises, and performatory student activities require students to speak to their peers, to identify strategies for problem solving without the teacher's intervention, even to define a class's agenda.

In deploying such formats, the teacher creates a learning situation in which his or her authority is bracketed, marginalized, or interrogated. In risking the loss of professional hegemony, today's teachers hope—as the essays in this volume demonstrate—to enable rather than suffocate student energy for inquiry. Courses that teach theory, theoretical agendas, and theorized textualities, moreover, unsettle the student's writing task. No longer automatically requiring students to write the interpretive essay that closely reads a literary text, teachers represented by the authors in this book experiment with writing assignments by, for example, asking their students to compile a casebook of practical criticism about a text they have worked with, to write a concluding essay that questions the course's design and theoretical commitments, or to research a cultural artifact. These teachers also use writing to drive classroom discussion. Short position papers, informal essays written in response to study questions, student-compiled lists of comments, journal entries shared either in or out of class: all function to empower students to speak, read, and negotiate their interpretations as constructed by their assumptions and situated within a learning community.

These teachers work to introduce to students the notion that they are located within complex systems of knowledge. For, we may now teach, knowledge-producing institutions like the undergraduate college and the university are sites on which learners stage competing positions and enact conflicts rather than reproduce a bankable set of mastered facts. While acknowledging that the teacher may set a course's agenda, the pedagogical strategies sketched out in this volume challenge or redefine the teacher's automatic mastery and control and propose that students occasionally share in shaping course concerns, content, and coverage. As several of this book's contributors remind us, language, history, and culture are all sites of conflict, and the teacher who confronts literature with theory foregrounds these contested conceptual spaces, engaging students in debates significant to their understanding of issues such as canon formation, literature as social text, multiculturalism, and the English department's creation of curriculum. In teaching these conflicts, the professor asks students to question their automatic assumptions about, for example, individuality as a natural rather than class-constructed concept, the social context as a given rather than as an interested and subject-producing category, and culture as a transcendent or ahistorical realm of value.

Despite these teachers' efforts to engage students in dialogues about competing theoretical positions, however, students often resist. Many contributors to this volume report their students'—and confess their own—frustration, depression, intellectual and emotional overload; their essays share with readers their strategies for coping with, managing, even utilizing these discomforting emotive states and the transferential classroom interactions such states sometimes arouse. Yet for most of these teachers, student resistance appears healthy, even useful, in the theorizing classroom. Understanding that students will initially identify with a nontheoretical position, several contributors assign antitheoretical readings that they themselves take seriously; to represent a theorized view of such resistance to theory, they may then teach statements such as Paul de Man's. Teaching the profession's intellectual, political, and ideological conflicts, as Gerald Graff has often exhorted us to do, teachers present such dialogical strategies to interrogate even as they mobilize student disbelief. In this volume, Diana Fuss reports that her students' resistance to theory is itself already theorized; it emerges, she finds, from the political position they have formulated in opposition to already known if imperfectly understood psychoanalytic theories of gendered subjectivity. Indeed, teachers of non-canonical, marginalized, and subaltern texts conclude here that their students necessarily experience anxiety, tension, and frustration when confronting theory; to fail to do so, Simon Gikandi and Lindon Barrett suggest, would underwrite student refusal to engage intellectually their limited experiences of oppositional literatures, their often unexamined assumptions about cultural difference, and, indeed, the "situatedness" of their own knowledge. While some teachers represented in this volume, then, joyfully report their students' surprising enthusiasm for this theory about which they have heard and now want to know, most detail the ways in which they have struggled to support their students' trials with an anxiety-laden, resistance-provoking, yet still productive encounter with theory.

But teachers, too, experience theory's difficulties. Their resistance to student resistance can never win out, Fuss and John Kucich suggest, since they may thus mistake angry curiosity for petulant lack of cooperation. Patient teacher explanation, Fuss says, merely silences student dissent. Only when teaching a theory's internal contradictions and self-resistances can the teacher successfully deploy theory, so that learners about theory may see that it fails—indeed refuses—to totalize what at first appears a monolithic and globalizing position. And only when theorizing their own counterresistance, Fuss believes, can teachers mobilize theory to exploit rather than conceal student opposition; when they restructure the theory classroom "*through* rather than *around* student resistances," they ready and circulate (rather than sabotage) a productive struggle with difficulty. Still, having confronted, managed, and utilized their response to student resistance, teachers may encounter it in other faculty members as well, may discover that hard-won student acceptance of theory is withstood in another professor's classroom. Our colleagues'—and our own—opposition to theory, Susan Lanser notes, signals our reluctance to give up our classroom authority, to acknowledge our professional situatedness, and genuinely to understand ourselves as constructed by and complicit in constructing the systems of knowledge we attempt to transmit. The transferential and countertransferential relations at work in research, in teacher-student relations, and in the classroom necessitate our self-critical confrontation with our teaching of theory (see LaCapra).

As most of this volume's contributors believe, the teaching of theory raises questions of canonicity and textuality. Lanser's students simply believe in the canon as a "spontaneous occurrence," she reports; certain literary texts are naturally superior to others, they think, and such literature is objectively true and beautiful. Criticizing the concept of "literariness," Cary Nelson writes that the canon has identified working-class experience and economic exploitation as material unacceptable to poetics and has, as he and other contributors explain, excluded the subjects of female subordination, gay and lesbian culture, and white supremacy. Having never considered how texts were selected for canonical status by professional literary critics and teachers of English in the service of particular (class, racial, and gender) interests, Nelson's students do not at first wonder why John Ashbery's poems appear in *The Norton Anthology of Modern Poetry* and Irene Paull's do not. Moreover, his modern-poetry students cannot construct a noncanonical syllabus, he says, even when they desire to read poems by women, people of color, gays and lesbians, or members of the working class. Nelson discovered, then, that to demonstrate the cultural work of women and minorities, the subject positions available to writers who are not white, male, and middle-class, and the wide range of social functions for poetry, he needed to teach the canon in dialogue with noncanonical texts. Lanser likewise juxtaposes marginal and canonical, theoretical and literary, well-known and less-well-known texts, strategically arranging them so as to normalize marginality and foreground the canon as constructed. Nelson teaches the canon in a way that helps his students understand the disciplinary structures and politics of the profession, the place of literature in the dominant culture, and the social mission of English studies. As Robert Scholes reminds us in his historicized discussion of canon formation, the literary canon is a social and political construct, and "standards of literary quality," whether deemed by canon makers as "universal" or as "relative, local, and political," will continue to provoke professorial and critical debate (145–47).

Yet I should say in concluding this consideration of the canon in theorized classes that feminist, gay and lesbian, and multicultural critiques of the exclusionary practices of canon formation have altered the profession's conceptualization of canonicity and its pedagogical instruments, the canonically organized literary anthologies (see Golding). It can no longer be said without qualification that the pedagogical canon merely ratifies the status quo and "legitimate[s] an established hegemony" (Krupat 310). I imagine that Nelson's joke about leaving claims about coverage to paint companies will suit many of this book's readers, those who feel little dedication to the canon as it was conceived during the reign of New Criticism; to other readers, however, the canon is no joke in an age of "entertainment education," when English majors may graduate without having read Chaucer. Yet whether we argue for inclusion of so-called marginal texts within existing canons, propose alternative canons, or reject canonizing procedures altogether, we now know that canonicity—like sexuality after Freud or Foucault—is not "natural." In utilizing theory to critique the canon, Barrett reminds us in this volume, we must therefore situate our theories. His course thus self-consciously positions what he calls "canonical theory" in relation to both "institutional [self-reflective] theory" and "subaltern theory" to demonstrate the conceptual limitations of canonical theory. Teachers of theory, Barrett implies, must guard against fetishizing postmodernism and institutionalizing theory as an alternative canonical textuality.

Questions of textuality, contextuality, and intertextuality likewise structure the theory and theorized courses described in this volume. The study of English now no longer assigns texts to particular courses by virtue of genre, even medium. Today's syllabi may include films, advertisements, news clippings, diary entries, historical documents, and, broadly defined, cultural artifacts. Any signifying practice can be read in conjunction, then, with a variety of other such practices and their cultural productions. In considering the mutual implication of text and context, Cannon Schmitt and Donald Ulin describe the ways they teach texts as produced, distributed, and consumed within multiple and various social milieus. In critiquing the notion that historical context may be added to a course on literature—often as handouts prepared by the instructor and assigned as outside reading—Schmitt and Ulin portray the status of such contextualizing historical documents as ancillary, secondary, or extra; the idea of history as "given" is exactly, they say, what theorized courses need to call into question. Designed to make students seek theory to explain otherwise inexplicable intertextualities, their course crosses disciplinary boundaries, represents social reality as textual and texts as inherently social, and so replaces the text-context distinction with a workable concept of the "social text." As Huston Diehl demonstrates, teachers today need to acknowledge and foreground student experience of the strangeness of the historical past, the arbitrariness of periodicity, and help students experience their own location in historical temporality. Understanding the "textuality of history," students may cease to think of literary writing as a privileged, autonomous activity and its authors as creative geniuses outside historical moments and social forces and so begin to see the complex ways literary textuality relates to culture and acculturation.

Indeed, teachers of English may now find themselves teaching not "literature" but "culture." As Jan Gorak defines it in his essay for this book, culture consists of "a recurrent set of symbols and images appropriate to a certain prescribed range of social biographies" that stand for a collective lifestyle; representation of these images signifies not historical reality but a "precise, invisible decision" about historical reality "framed according to particular constructions of the world." Cultural representations serve the dominant culture's interests rather than those of emerging or subordinate groups; in the late twentieth century, Gorak and his students decide, "culture follows power" and so systematically excludes and marginalizes disenfranchised social members—even as it authorizes resistance and the formation of alternative cultures. Teaching culture, the English professor may begin to address the ways in which cultures naturalize value assumptions, as Sandra Grayson says, and in which individuals absorb ideologies as though they were facts. Empowering students to read culture as a semiotic textuality, this theorized education seeks to produce citizens with the skills to question and shape the societies of which they will soon be full members.

II

This book aims to represent the wide range of theorized courses being taught to undergraduates at the present time. Collectively, these courses can be (perhaps arbitrarily) divided into three categories: the theory course, the interdisciplinary or theoretically oriented course in culture(s), and the theorized literature course. The theory course, it turns out, can look quite different when taught in different institutions by different professors. In addition to essays that query ways of teaching the theory course (see, e.g., Donald G. Marshall), we have included others about courses that cover contemporary schools of theory, whether beginning with Romanticism, New Criticism, or structuralism (see, e.g., Kucich); that study the history of criticism through systematically arranged readings of ancient and modern theorists (see, e.g., David Downing); that juxtapose theory with an exemplary literary text or texts (see, e.g., Evan Carton); that teach theory as resistance to hegemonic cultural textuality (see, e.g., Lanser; Fuss; Laurie Finke). When these courses teach students the skills of cultural critique, they frame the social texts of, for example, Islam, Africa, England, and the New World with theoretical questions about history, ideology, culture, race, nation, postcolonialism, and the status of the subject (see, e.g., Gorak; Gikandi; Barrett). Culturally oriented courses, this book's contributors show, ask students to interrogate their assumptions about cultural, gender, and racial difference; about experience, materiality, and intellection; and to question and revise the narratives they've assumed true about their positions within a particular classroom and in an educational institution. Such classes also teach media other than literature, as David Rodowick's essay suggests; courses in film theory and texts, for example, teach students to theorize their cultural pleasures, identificatory structures, and gender or racial assumptions by addressing them through the visual medium with which their culture has made them so familiar. Having learned to read ideology at the movies, students today may interrogate, resist, and begin to shape their popular-culture texts both inside and outside the darkened theater.

The theorized literary courses described in this volume teach students the skills of textual interpretation and, variously, of reading the semiotics of race, class, and gender. When teaching students to read texts, the teachers represented here focus on the multipurpose reading-writing-research course, the general studies course for students not majoring in English, the "genre course," and the introductory or upper-level literature course, usually concentrating on texts of a particular historical period. Each kind of course, widely taught at undergraduate colleges and universities today, offers a variety of ways to introduce theory into the mainstream English course, and, as these teachers show, each benefits from the inclusion of theory in its once "purely literary" syllabus. Theory, for example, may situate realistic narrative by posing for students the questions that novelistic genre asks, elides, and represents (see Grayson); may demonstrate to students that literary texts solicit multiple rather than singular (and "true") readings (see Carton); that different approaches to texts address different questions about the categories of author, text, reader, and social world—categories students may not know about or understand as structuring their reading experience, as positioning and constructing themselves as subjects (see Lynette Felber). In addition, these courses may introduce to students questions about why they read, about affective, formalistic, and social responses to literature (see Jonathan Arac); questions about reading and writing as complicit with class or gender privilege (see Beverly Lyon Clark et al.). Experimenting with material classroom structures, pedagogical strategies, and course content, these classes address not only literary questions, it turns out, but social and cultural ones as well.

The materials available for teaching the courses represented here are legion. Rather than survey these materials, I indicate the kinds available on the book market, a market that currently commodifies and fetishizes theoretically oriented textbooks, anthologies, readers, casebooks, and introductory handbooks. For a comprehensive listing of such texts, readers of this volume might want to consult Donald Marshall's MLA bibliography of books on theory; here, I suggest possibilities rather than strive for coverage. When choosing a particular reader for a particular class, teachers of theory need to confront the problems each book poses about, for example, the status of theory (or history or culture) in the English studies course, the pedagogical approaches each kind of text implicitly solicits, and the blind spots each asks the teacher to maintain when introducing theory to students.

Different texts serve different classroom needs. The anthology of critical theory—whether organized historically (Con Davis and Finke; Richter; Adams; Kaplan and Anderson), according to contemporary critical schools (Latimer; Lodge; Con Davis and Schleifer), or cultural "kinds" (Leitch; Selden)—presents and arranges theoretical statements in a convenient package ready for student consumption. Yet these texts raise philosophical questions about the status of theory that often themselves escape theorization. Has theory become another "subject area" the student must master?

Should theory be studied in isolation from other cultural documents? Do theoretical texts appear canonical because selected by an editor and published together? Practical problems emerge as well when a teacher previews texts for inclusion in a theoretically informed course. Does a specific text falsify psychoanalytic theory, for example, despite its wonderfully representative sample of poststructuralist statements (see Latimer)? Does it address undergraduates at a level of knowledge or understanding beyond their abilities (see Con Davis and Schleifer)? Must the teacher supplement the readings with photocopied course packs (now a troublesome area of concern for undergraduate teachers, given copyright laws and conglomerate-owned publishing houses)? Choosing an anthology, teachers often discover, is risky business. The decision-making process involves the teacher's ability to assess student abilities and a given text's difficulty and theoretical "comprehensiveness" as well as his or her professional commitment to modes of knowledge production and transmission.

The casebook, another kind of text currently available, resolves some problems but raises others. The Bedford series Case Studies in Contemporary Criticism, edited by Ross C. Murfin, offers teachers authoritative texts of classic literary works together with critical essays from various schools of contemporary critical theory; edited and written for undergraduates, each casebook introduces students to diverse critical perspectives and provides reception information and biographical and historical contexts (Brontë; Conrad; Hawthorne; Shelley). Another kind of casebook includes a variety of short stories and poems and examples of practical criticism about them from a variety of critical approaches (see Staton). Choosing a casebook rather than or in addition to an anthology of theoretical essays, the teacher adds a literary text or texts to the study of theory, offering students an exemplary cultural document on which to practice the skills of applying critical theory. Despite the clear usefulness of casebooks in the undergraduate classroom, however, they pose problems that also escape theorization. Does the literary text simply provide an "occasion for interpretation," a test case for the application of theory (see Tompkins)? Does the instrumental activity encouraged by casebooks, as Schmitt and Ulin believe, reintroduce the teacher as authoritative leader and the student as submissive imitator? Does the casebook prevent theory from proposing new concepts about nonliterary fields of inquiry in the human sciences, as Finke asks? Whatever choices teachers make about anthologies and casebooks, then, they must discuss these problems with students, who will otherwise join their teacher in unexamined assumptions about the hegemonic status of literary texts and their relation to nonliterary discourse.

Teachers must also choose, finally, whether to include in the theorized course one or more handbooks as required or recommended reading. Here again, philosophical problems and practical considerations structure the teacher's decision-making process. Handbooks may introduce students to the discourse of, for example, feminism or psychoanalysis, each embracing a language and concepts the students might not have encountered elsewhere in English studies. Yet using a handbook may merely satisfy students' needs to be "lectured at" about a topic they find upsetting and defamiliarizing. Handbooks may quantify, taxonomize, and simplify theoretical approaches, listing different positions within a critical school as though they could be easily extracted from a field of knowledge and unproblematically distinguished from one another (see Holland).[1]

Some handbooks themselves present engaged positions in relation to theory. One portrays structuralism as naive, psychoanalysis as enabling a material theory of the human subject, and Marxism as essential to any analysis and therefore not a school of criticism (Eagleton); another represents Anglo-American and French feminism as misguided and announces a materialist feminist account of socially constructed subjectivity as precisely politically correct (Moi). Whether the teacher agrees or disagrees with these writers' positions makes little difference to my assessment here, for students will not have mastered sufficient theoretical content to decipher the handbook writer's position without a good deal of help from the instructor. Adopting a different model, some handbooks provide "coverage" of contemporary critical theories by identifying critical terms as residing within certain discursive practices (e.g., Lentricchia and McLaughlin) or by presenting fields of inquiry and the skills necessary to deploy them (e.g., Belsey; Rimmon-Kenan). In choosing whether to teach a handbook and in selecting one for the theorized English course, teachers must ask how they can situate theoretical discourse without attempting simply to reduce student anxiety about theory. They may choose to adopt as required reading a skills-related handbook, may put on reserve in the library a variety of handbooks to which they might refer during class or in individual conference, or may use study questions or worksheets to introduce students to concepts frequently encountered. Or, going it alone, a teacher may ask students to confront and theorize their own need to be "introduced" to a discourse or critical theory and so teach them about how to tolerate and use their frustration, about curiosity as a necessary part of the process of inquiry, and about the need to know as a form of both power and empowerment.

The teacher of theory might consult, as part of the process of self-educational inquiry, collections of essays about theorized pedagogy. These books address the problems of teaching theory from an institutional and pedagogical perspective and, like this volume, demonstrate the pertinence of theory to curricular development and classroom overhaul. Douglas Atkins and Michael Johnson introduce deconstruction as a broad frame of reference for the teaching of texts; Cary Nelson presents essays about the theory of classroom teaching rather than about practical pedagogies; James Engell and David Perkins focus on pedagogy but offer virtually no new strategies for classroom teaching. In the most sophisticated such collection of essays, Gerald Graff and Reginald Gibbons survey the history of, and crisis in, criticism and suggest that culturally concerned criticisms might best situate contemporary American students within culture, politics, and ideology. These volumes offer useful information on the teaching of theory; they also elucidate current debates on theory and help prepare the teacher to guide students toward an active understanding of theory as a way of thinking about their world. Such an understanding, we argue in this volume, helps students evaluate the choices they make about their lives as literate adults who will continue after college to read, think, and speculate about their situation within and outside their culture and the multicultural world beyond.

Having been assigned or asked—or having chosen—to teach theory, having decided how to frame the course and what materials to use, an English professor may, like Kucich, become "converted" and hence called on to preach to colleagues the advantages of theoretically informed classes. After having encountered, struggled with, and conquered faculty resistance to the teaching of theory, this hypothetical teacher might hope to win the department's assent to a new definition of the English curriculum. Gary Waller's essay in this book speaks to this teacher and this department, for it is not unusual now for faculties of English to redesign the major; to put in place, after committee consideration and faculty debate, a theory-driven curriculum rather than a canons-and-coverage one. After such a decision, Waller insists, teachers must meet to talk about what they know, do not know, and need to learn; they must share ideas or live with the perilous task of designing new courses without peer guidance and support. Reading and study groups, even colleague-taught workshops, can facilitate the often difficult process of retooling from a theoretical perspective. Introductory courses, sophomore surveys from *Beowulf* to Virginia Woolf, and untheorized period courses will be restructured. Film courses may enter the curriculum, since reading narrative across media now seems a task that English studies may rightly undertake. History will enter the curriculum as a theorizable category rather than a Norton anthology container in which to pour cultural and literary artifacts. But the dangers of a theory-driven curriculum, as Waller cautions, are legion. Without departmental conversation, without shared assumptions about the questions raised and skills taught by courses at the introductory, intermediate, and advanced levels, a theorized curriculum may become an intellectual free-for-all in which some faculty members seize the opportunity to teach their theoretical hobbyhorses and others teach theories they do not fully understand. The English major is changing, whether we like it or not, and teachers must struggle to rationalize the changes they initiate or in which they find themselves ensnared.

If my hortative rhetoric strikes my reader as untheorized, I can only, in turn, acknowledge my perspective as desiring. Can teachers of English studies no longer feel that they must perform their lectures, endorse literary

excellence, represent writers as autonomous creative geniuses, and so produce for privileged middle-class or awed working-class students the "great
literary experience"? Given student populations that are less well prepared
scholastically and perhaps more complacent than their predecessors, we
must theorize such categories for and with our students, not allowing
ideologies to masquerade as concepts or letting unexamined assumptions
override or marginalize unpopular understandings of value. Given economic and budgetary constraints on public universities, which are dependent on legislative sympathy and tax-driven funding, and on private
colleges, which worry about tuition increases higher than the size of infla-
tion, we will be called on to justify our educational endeavor as other
than a consumable commodity. Finally, given public skepticism about
the educational process encouraged by political conservatives and the pressure applied at government funding agencies, we must rationalize and
defend our belief that education trains people for participation in a just
society. In view of this necessity, we must also realize that theory, whether
we like it or not, is already with us in the study of literature.

University of Southern Maine

Note

[1] I am indebted in my thinking here to Diana Fuss, *Essentially Speaking*
(34–35).

Works Cited

Adams, Hazard. *Critical Theory since Plato*. New York: Harcourt, 1971.

Atkins, G. Douglas, and Michael L. Johnson. *Writing and Reading Differently:
Deconstruction and the Teaching of Composition and Literature*. Lawrence:
UP of Kansas, 1985.

Belsey, Catherine. *Critical Practice*. New York: Methuen, 1980.

Brontë, Emily. *Wuthering Heights*. Ed. Linda Peterson. Boston: Bedford–St.
Martin's, 1992.

Brooks, Cleanth, and Robert Penn Warren. *Understanding Poetry*. 1938. 4th ed.
New York: Holt, Rinehart, 1976.

Con Davis, Robert, and Laurie Finke. *Literary Criticism and Theory: The Greeks
to the Present*. New York: Longman, 1989.

Con Davis, Robert, and Ronald Schleifer, eds. *Contemporary Literary Criticism:
Literary and Cultural Studies*. 2nd ed. New York: Longman, 1989.

Conrad, Joseph. *Heart of Darkness*. Ed. Ross C. Murfin. Boston: Bedford–St.
Martin's, 1989.

Culler, Jonathan. *On Deconstruction*. Ithaca: Cornell UP, 1982.

de Man, Paul. *The Resistance to Theory*. Minneapolis: U of Minnesota P, 1986.

Eagleton, Terry. *Literary Theory: An Introduction*. Minneapolis: U of Minnesota P, 1983.

Engell, James, and David Perkins. *Teaching Literature: What Is Needed Now*. Cambridge: Harvard UP, 1988.

Freire, Paulo. *Pedagogy of the Oppressed*. Trans. Myra Bergman Ramos. New York: Continuum, 1970.

Fuss, Diana. *Essentially Speaking: Feminism, Nature, and Difference*. New York: Routledge, 1989.

Golding, Alan C. "A History of American Poetry Anthologies." Hallberg 279–308.

Graff, Gerald, and Reginald Gibbons. *Criticism in the University*. Evanston: Northwestern UP, 1985.

Hawthorne, Nathaniel. *The Scarlet Letter*. Ed. Ross C. Murfin. Boston: Bedford–St. Martin's, 1991.

Holland, Norman N. *Holland's Guide to Psychoanalytic Psychology and Literature-and-Psychology*. New York: Oxford UP, 1990.

Kaplan, Charles, and William Anderson, eds. *Criticism: Major Statements*. 3rd ed. New York: St. Martin's, 1991.

Krupat, Arnold. "Native American Literature and the Canon." Hallberg 309–36.

LaCapra, Dominick. "On the Line: Between History and Criticism." *Profession 89*. New York: MLA, 1989. 4–9.

Latimer, Dan, ed. *Contemporary Critical Theory*. New York: Harcourt, 1989.

Leitch, Vincent B. *American Literary Criticism from the Thirties to the Eighties*. New York: Columbia UP, 1988.

Lentricchia, Frank, and Thomas McLaughlin, eds. *Critical Terms for Literary Study*. Chicago: Chicago UP, 1990.

Lodge, David. *Modern Criticism and Theory: A Reader*. New York: Longman, 1988.

Marshall, Donald G. *Contemporary Critical Theory: A Selective Bibliography*. New York: MLA, 1993.

Moi, Toril. *Sexual/Textual Politics: Feminist Literary Theory*. New York: Methuen, 1985.

Nelson, Cary. *Theory in the Classroom*. Urbana: U of Illinois P, 1986.

Richter, David H. *The Critical Tradition: Classic Texts and Contemporary Trends*. Boston: Bedford–St. Martin's, 1989.

Rimmon-Kenan, Shlomith. *Narrative Fiction: Contemporary Poetics*. New York: Methuen, 1983.

Scholes, Robert. "Canonicity and Textuality." *Introduction to Scholarship in Modern Languages and Literatures*. Ed. Joseph Gibaldi. 2nd ed. New York: MLA, 1992. 138–58.

Selden, Raman. *The Theory of Criticism: From Plato to the Present*. New York: Longman, 1988.

Shelley, Mary. *Frankenstein*. Ed. Johanna M. Smith. Boston: Bedford–St. Martin's, 1992.

Staton, Shirley F., ed. *Literary Theories in Praxis*. Philadelphia: U of Pennsylvania P, 1987.

Tompkins, Jane. "The Reader in History: The Changing Shape of Literary Response." *Reader-Response Criticism: From Formalism to Post-structuralism*. Ed. Tompkins. Baltimore: Johns Hopkins UP, 1980. 201–32.

von Hallberg, Robert. *Canons*. Chicago: U of Chicago P, 1984.

Part II
Surveying Theory

Ancients and Moderns: Literary Theory and the History of Criticism

David B. Downing

If, as Paulo Freire has put it, "education is suffering from narration sickness" (3), then the "cure" of theory means that theorists need to examine the consequences of their own pedagogical narratives. The problem, as we now know, is that the institutionalization of theory has often perpetuated the very hierarchies and exclusions it most often critically theorizes. In fact, one noticeable sign of the actual political consequences of publishing "radical theory" is the symbolic capital that accrues to the individuals producing such theory in elite research institutions.[1] Under these conditions, when theory reaches the classroom, it often does so as another body of rhetorically complex and intellectually difficult textual objects to be administered to students by "expert" teachers. In this way, as Heather Murray argues, "the institutionalization of theory has led, against the hopes and labors of many, to a teaching of theory rather than a theorized teaching" (187). Theory, then, is just one more subject to be "covered" according to the "field-coverage" principles that Gerald Graff and others have described.

My purpose in this essay is to describe a course I have taught several times under the title History of Criticism and Theory but that I have also taught under such other generic titles as Literary and Cultural Theory and even as Critical Approaches to Literature. It is intended as a course for upper-division undergraduate English majors (adaptable to the graduate level), and it also addresses the concerns of those teachers in small colleges where the curriculum is not large enough to include courses both on the history of criticism and on theory. My own position is that it is unwise to perpetuate the institutional and cultural separation between history and theory. Accordingly, any course in the former is necessarily engaging the latter, and vice versa.

To my mind, the typical content of any course that attempts to follow traditional models of surveying vast numbers of difficult texts in loosely chronological but culturally decontextualized forms highlights the worst

kind of narration sickness: how can (or why should?) students be asked
to cover 2,500 years of history of criticism, and how can they enter such
difficult discursive narratives as deconstruction, poststructuralism,
Marxism, feminism? In a crude sense, the only answer here is, "You can't,
so give it up." That is, one must critically theorize and discard the very
notion of a survey to cover a fixed body of key and canonical theory
texts, a content that must be presented and narrated by the teacher and
learned by the passively consuming students. But while one can critique
the dominant narrative modes of the authoritative teacher-knower and
the passive student-learner, one cannot simply give up narrative altogether
any more than one can step outside one's culture. We live and breathe
by the stories of our lives from the subject positions we occupy within
the diverse and often conflicting narratives of our cultural and socioeco-
nomic circumstances. It is necessary to confront such differences and
diversity while also constructing courses and curricula that necessarily
force distinct and often exclusive choices and values. In other words, we
can develop a pedagogical praxis that leads us to reorient ourselves critically within the social and institutional narratives we inhabit. Let me turn
now to a more specific description of the course and address these issues
in that context.

To begin with, when I hand out the syllabus on the first day of class,
I explain that the students should view it as a narrative, a text that is
authored and plotted by me as a kind of map of the "history-to-be," which,
over the next fifteen weeks, they will read and interpret—and in a sense
live—much the way they might read a novel. During the last four weeks
of the class, however, they will play a major role in designing the conclusion to the narrative. (I explain this procedure later.) In this way, such
a theorized syllabus operates not as a list of material to be covered but
as an interested narrative, fiction, or story, which, as I explain to the
class, I have designed to dramatize key issues that are important to me
and, I believe, to many others. I challenge students to interpret, resist,
and engage different meanings in the syllabus-text, just as they might in
reading a novel. Although as teachers we cannot eliminate the power
differential and the authority that we possess, we need not mask them,
and we can renegotiate them in ways more egalitarian than misrecognizing
pedagogical violence through benevolent grading or insisting that our
emphasis on the student-centered classroom has solved the problem. (On
feminist agendas in teaching, see Treichler; Bauer.) I suggest, then, that
the various texts we read throughout the semester may, like chapters in
a novel, draw on a number of related and recursive themes and cultural
issues. In short, for instance, it may mean that later in the semester we
will be able to read Wordsworth or Marx in the light of our reading of
Plato at the beginning. This type of syllabus is not like the sequence of
texts, loosely arranged according to chronological order, that one surveys
individually in relatively independent and isolated fashion. Students taking

my course can expect, as they would from a plotted narrative, some suspense and some key crises.

A constant issue in such a "narrativized" syllabus is that my narrative be negotiable through the different roles of the student as audience and reader. And to do that, I need to describe several procedures that facilitate a more dialogical engagement with the class narrative. First, I ask students to appoint a different secretary for each class. That student takes careful notes, freeing everyone else from feeling as if they must write everything down. After class, the secretary then types up the minutes and photocopies them so that they can be distributed to fellow students. At the beginning of each class, the secretary for the previous meeting reads the minutes of the last class, a practice that, among other things, provides a sense of continuity between classes.[2] In addition, every student is asked to textualize the reading experience by bringing to each class a response statement or position paper written on the assigned readings or the issues evolving in class.[3] If the class is small enough, I usually ask students to read or speak about their responses before we begin discussions. This practice ensures that no student's voice is excluded from discussion and critical intervention.

The syllabus itself is clearly divided into three main parts of four or five weeks each. Each part is devoted to one of what I call three "cultural revolutions": the Platonic revolution, inaugurating what we call Western metaphysics; the Romantic revolution; and the contemporary or postmodern revolution. But before we turn to these three "chapters," the first two or three classes are devoted to the present. I begin the course by assigning chapter 2 of Freire's *Pedagogy of the Oppressed* and Terry Eagleton's "What Is Literature?" I also ask the students to write a brief institutional autobiography or narrative account of their experience of English in school and classroom settings. Recalling these earlier experiences often raises feelings of anxiety, pain, and alienation as well as pleasure, and the effort to examine the history of those feelings is itself a first theoretical move. Since students are simultaneously introduced to Freire's "banking model" of education, they can often see many similarities with their own literary "training." Eagleton's historical interrogation of the concept of literature as it arose out of the Romantic revolution foreshadows several major themes with respect to aesthetics, the social function of the artist, and the formation of literary studies as a field. The concept of ideology and how it pertains to the study of literature and the interpretation of culture clearly raises the political issues that are at stake when students invest themselves in literature as English majors.

Having looked at the "crisis in the profession" as a crisis in the stability of the literary object and the value of the banking model of education, we then turn back 2,500 years, my rationale being that the objectifying discursive mode arose in relatively determinable historical contexts and that the students' feelings of alienation and pleasure may have something to do with what happened in ancient Greece. Indeed, my reference to "ancients" in the title of this essay should be read ironically to the extent that such a formative stage of Western culture yielded modes of intellectual and discursive formations that, despite the more extreme claims of post-modern innovation and disruption, are still very much a part of our present historical situation.

We begin with the *Ion* and books 2, 7, and 10 of Plato's *Republic*.[4] The basic question I pose is, Why is Plato so upset at the poet?[5] In other words, to dramatize a key interpretive problem, we try to read the "text itself." But while it is not hard to describe Plato's rationales for resisting poetry as he presents them in the text (the poet is twice-removed and excites emotion), they do not seem to be very smart reasons, and when students try to answer that question, they generally re-create two historically familiar patterns of interpretation: either Plato did not understand poetry or he did not quite mean what he said. The first suggests that Plato is simply wrong; he did not understand poetry, he was uptight about feelings and emotions and the body, and he was such a rigid idealist that we do not need to take his ideas seriously. The second pattern of interpretation is more significant historically since it reflects a wide range of received interpretations that follow what Eric Havelock terms "methods of reduction" (7), basically a whole set of possible ways to demonstrate that Plato did not quite mean what he actually said. By so reducing the unpalatable conclusions to be drawn from Plato's condemnation of the poet, such an interpretation preserves his work and makes it more palatable to contemporary tastes. But students generally realize that these methods do not seem to hold up or satisfy their own sense of adequate explanations. As one student put it, "Plato seems constipated," a view that many students enjoyed hearing, but when asked if it satisfied their own criteria for interpreting the text, they admitted that it did not.

What we often end up with after a week on this problem is a statement of student *need*: a felt need for something more, some other text, some other cultural documents to help us out. Students are aware that in some ways I am playing devil's advocate here, and they occasionally accuse me of unfairly withholding information, and in fact that very act of withholding becomes the topic of inquiry: am I like or unlike teachers who are "open" and "straightforward"? Is this narrative like others that conceal as well as reveal? So my own position of authority, my having the power to withhold information, may seem personal, or even idiosyncratic, but my point is that it is less personal and more social and institutionally sanctioned even though, as Pierre Bourdieu would say, these social distinctions have been perpetuated in "misrecognized" ways (27).

There is often at this point some suspense as to what could help or what I "have in mind" here. But it does not last long, since the following week we read portions of Eric Havelock's *Preface to Plato*, excerpts from Walter Ong's *Orality and Literacy*, and a few pages from my introduction to *Image and Ideology*, in which I present my own argument with respect to this cultural revolution. I have found these sources to be quite accessible to the undergraduate. In fact, the classes following these readings typically include some of the most dramatic moments in the course, since students often experience complete shifts in, or challenges to, their initial readings of Plato. As one student put it, reading Havelock was "like reading a detective story"; it "just blew me away."[6] What gets dramatized is a host of interpretive and political problems revolving around personal and institutionalized forms of cultural literacy. In short, students discover that when they initially read the word *poet* in the *Republic*, they had been using a set of meanings and assumptions that has little to do with what Plato may have been referring to, and without this additional knowledge there is no way they could have read it otherwise. Plato assumes among his contemporaries a view of the poet and of poetry that is wholly unfamiliar to our way of thinking. Following the Romantic revolution, our terms *literature* and *poetry* suggest something original and creative, whereas to members of an oral culture poetry was something memorized, formulaic, full of stereotypes and clichés, the opposite of our conception. Thus, the political consequences of an informed reading of cultural history get dramatized: we reread Plato's attack on poetry as an attack on the oral tradition, blind memorization, and the state (insofar as ancient poetry was dominated by rhetors in the service of the rulers and ruling classes)—a reading not even possible from the "text itself." Students now see that Plato was inaugurating a cultural revolution in the whole way the society organized its knowledge, power, pedagogy, and technology; a revolution that signified a broad-based shift from oral to literate culture.

In small-group work, I generally ask students to examine some of Ong's and Havelock's arguments about the cultural formation of a whole new grammar, syntax, and philosophical rhetoric of abstractions suitable for critical distance, analysis, and critique. Students can see that, with respect to the cultural revolution, Platonic critique had a socially radical orientation, a perspective often lost from the familiar view of the traditional Platonic formism that we have sustained in contemporary cultural receptions of Plato.

We then read the *Phaedrus*, along with a few pages from Derrida's reading of Plato's *pharmakon*. As you can imagine, the difficulty of Derrida's texts draws a wide range of responses, but I argue that Derrida's basic points are not obscure.[7] His observation that "a text is not a text unless it hides from the first comer . . . the law of its composition and the rules of its game" (63) takes on new meaning when students have just had a lesson in how the *Republic* has concealed the laws of its representations of the poet. In general, Derrida leads us to see how the attack on writing in the famous myth of Theuth passage makes sense in a culture shifting from oral to literate modes of communication when the new technology may be valued above the transcendent "truth" of the logos. Now,

Plato's ambivalence about the status of writing mirrors his dialectical insistence on the escape from figurative language while using figures like the allegory of the cave to express such transcendence. The issues of race, class, and gender all enter into the discussion when we encounter an illiterate father-aristocrat who forbids the use of writing by an illegitimate son. And when we examine Derrida's claim that "the origin of logos is *its father*" (77), students can begin to see that the very formation of the discourse of objectivity and reason emerges from the conditions of patriarchy.

Plato's need to separate the body from the soul, reason from emotion, the object from the subject, the knower from the known, the essential form from the imitated content, and so on, introduces the binary way of thinking characterizing what we call Western metaphysics. When we turn to spend a week on Aristotle's consolidation of the formalist rhetoric inaugurated by Plato, we can see fairly dramatically that even the stylistic as well as structural shifts in the portions of the *Rhetoric* and *Poetics* that we read are related to the radical shifts, even in Plato's lifetime, toward a much more literate general public. Consequently, Aristotle's systematic categorizing of the "natural classification of things" proceeds as if the arguments against writing were irrelevant and the supremacy of the dialectic need no longer be questioned. In fact, I choose the passages from books 1–4 of the *Rhetoric* where Aristotle shrewdly assimilates the two modes of rhetoric (the enthymeme and the example) within the dominant modes of dialectic (deduction and induction) and thereby privileges dialectic even in a book titled *Rhetoric*. Aristotle's ability to value highly the poetic/dramatic form of tragedy emerges from a historical context in which he no longer needs to argue against the oral traditions of poetry as a cultural function of the transmission of orthodox views. Instead, he views the poem/drama as a natural object, with formal properties such as plot, melody, spectacle, and character.

In the next five-week segment, on the Romantics (I focus on both Wordsworths [William and Dorothy], Wollstonecraft, Blake, Shelley, Coleridge, along with Marx, Nietzsche, and Darwin), we use our reading of Plato to see how the Romantics tried to reread Plato and Aristotle. The apparent impossibility of "doing justice" to so many complex thinkers in such a short time is reasonably dispelled because my interests are not so much to understand an author or text either in isolation or in totality as to interpret significant cultural revolutions (reduced to narrative chapters, as it were) that influence our own cultural crises. In short, we examine what I call the "failed revolution," wherein the political claims of the creative imagination were depleted by the very separation of the poetic imagination from the political. I typically begin this section with Blake's "The Marriage of Heaven and Hell" as a paradigmatic Romantic text that attempts to invert the Platonic hierarchy: feeling, energy, and emotion provide the avenues to imaginative and aesthetic transcendence while abstract reason (as "Urizen") becomes a fearful and dominating tool of the "devil's party." Sections of Coleridge's *Biographia Literaria* and Shelley's "Defense of Poetry" directly address the Platonic issues and, as the students can now see rather ironically, refer to Plato as the greatest poet. We then examine this inversion in the light of a cultural revolution and discursive formation that could allow Shelley to conceive Plato in such terms only because he did not share our knowledge of the orality and literacy evidence, which has emerged only in the last fifty years. In a sense, then, students can vividly see Shelley arguing that poets are the "unacknowledged legislators" at the very moment when his own discourse is being "legislated" by a discursive formation over which he has little control, in part because the knowledge is literally unavailable to him.

The author I spend the most time on here is William Wordsworth. We read the Preface to the *Lyrical Ballads* and books 9–14 of *The Prelude*, and I use portions of Gayatri Spivak's "Sex and History in *The Prelude*," which I have found can be taught in engaging ways to undergraduates. By reading passages from Dorothy Wordsworth's *Grasmere Journal*, students get a sense of how a text that originated in a woman's narrative enters the public domain only through its incorporation ("plagiarism") by the well-known male author-brother. In the context of the syllabus-narrative, the significance of *The Prelude* is that Wordsworth's personal imaginative conversion is cast as a working through of his experience with the political and cultural significance of the French Revolution. The "Growth of the Poet's Imagination," however, engages psychological, aesthetic, and political domains such that, in Spivak's words, Wordsworth "coped with the experience of the French Revolution by transforming it into an iconic text that he could read and write" and "suggested that poetry was a better cure for the oppression of mankind than political economy or revolution and that his own life had the preordained purpose of teaching mankind this lesson" (46). Students struggle with the difficulty of Spivak's prose, but the basic points are not obscure. Her observations lead students to question further their own liberal beliefs in the "power of literature" when they see that the principle of imaginative opposition becomes the mode of incorporation: that is, the imaginative and idealistic rebellion from the vulgar materialism of the growing industrialization of the West led eventually to the establishment of separate "literate" departments that could safely be incorporated into the structure of the university curriculum without significantly altering or challenging the dominant symbolic and material modes for the production of empirical, scientific, and industrial knowledge. In short, the banking model of disciplinary education has won out.

Spivak draws out Wordsworth's rhetorical question in *The Prelude*: "Our animal wants and the necessities / Which they impose, are these the obstacles?" (12.94–95). Students are now prepared to see that Wordsworth answers this rhetorical question in the negative, in a sense, re-creating the dualistic idealism of Plato, and that Marx answers it affirmatively. Indeed, these discussions lead directly to our reading of passages from *The German Ideology*, "Theses on Feuerbach," and *The Communist Manifesto*. What students now discover is that Marx's basic premises of historical materialism have, in general, provided a model for our collective reading of the cultural revolution in Plato's Greece.[8]

I conclude the section on the Romantics with brief readings from Nietzsche's *Beyond Good and Evil* and with paired readings of John Dewey's "The Influence of Darwin on Philosophy" and Stephen Gould's "Darwin at Sea." As disparate as these readings may seem, they actually play quite well in the context of the course narrative, since Nietzsche's direct attack on foundational philosophies makes perfect sense in the light of our readings of Plato and Marx. The Dewey and Gould pieces on Darwin suggest further revisions of the ahistorical notion of the stability of the generic, "genre," type, and form (as in Platonic forms). Gould's essay, a wonderful account of the muddling of data brought about by Darwin's operating according to creationist rather than evolutionist premises while on board the *Beagle*, suggests the political nature of the scientific discovery of evolution by putting it within the context of the battle for power within the scientific community sustained by the Zoological Society and the Royal Society of Great Britain. I typically begin the last five-week segment, on contemporary issues, with Robert Pirsig's *Zen and the Art of Motorcycle Maintenance*. Students generally enjoy this book, especially since Pirsig's exploration of the narrator's psychological schizophrenia takes on cultural and theoretical force when he plays it out as a battle between classical and Romantic worldviews that we have already explored. The ghostlike doppelgänger of the main character (the narrator) is named Phaedrus (after Plato's *Phaedrus*), and the narrative structure of the book involves a return to the past to recover a self that has been split by Romantic and classic epistemologies. The narrator's return to the personal past leads as well to his exploration of the cultural past of Plato and the Sophists, and this very narrative structure suggests, not incidentally, the structure of our own class narrative, which began with our intellectual inquiry into the culture of ancient Greece. As Pirsig describes our contemporary cultural situation, "The cause of our current social crisis . . . is a genetic defect within the nature of reason itself" (102). But students have now already invested effort in a reading of ancient Greece, so Pirsig's philosophical, emotional, and personal odyssey takes place within a classroom context wherein considerable interest has already been developed with respect to many of these issues.

I devote the last four weeks to issues and consequences of the critical and cultural theory we have been reading in the context of the contemporary moment. Clearly, a pluralistic overview of a variety of "approaches" will not be very satisfying. Since my own role as narrator-author of the first two and a half months of the class has been dominant, my orientation in the last few weeks is toward viewing the students as theorists.[9]

I now ask the students to bear responsibility for negotiating the final chapters of our class narrative. In practice this means that we must spend at least portions of some classes discussing and formulating possible options in the light of student interests and available materials and directions. Since such basic orientations as cultural studies, Marxism, feminism, psychoanalysis, and deconstruction have already been encountered during the first two sections of the course, and since I have suggested from the beginning that students should think about what direction they would like to take in the last few weeks of the course, they generally enter these discussions eager to propose topics and readings. They are in a sense already "in the narrative," so they now need to theorize how they can end the narrative within the arbitrary confines of the institutional requirements for a class. The notion that since students do not know the field they cannot know what texts to select for reading and discussion is exposed by this exercise as an excuse to neglect student interest. My role now becomes more that of a resource than of an author-narrator, since our typical discussions focus on those areas of further pursuit that might engage theoretical considerations arising out of students' own interest in literary and cultural studies. It is my job to supply general suggestions of possible readings, and I do not abandon the expression of my own views: there are two items of my agenda on which I insist. First, whatever area of theoretical or practical investigation we pursue, we must not neglect the issues of race, class, and gender. Second, the proposed topics must be conceived as related to the ongoing course narrative: that is, students must be responsible in their small-group work for relating their specific concerns to the general concerns we have addressed before these final weeks. The one text I assign at the beginning of these last few weeks is Roland Barthes's "The Great Family of Man," a two-page excerpt from his *Mythologies*. The students are now well prepared to recognize how the "universalizing" ideology in the book *The Family of Man* works in contradiction to its claims to represent cultural difference, especially when I show them pictures of how some photographs have been cropped to eliminate less universal contexts of meaning. In other words, they can see how "ancient" Platonism still inhabits our own culture. I bring copies of *The Family of Man* to class, and our brief discussion of this book generally leads us into the topics we want to explore in the final weeks. Again, since students have been able throughout the semester to propose areas of interest and try to set up small groups in advance of the final weeks, this comes as less of a sudden shift than it might appear in this essay. In the end, we must vote as a class to approve the texts each small group has proposed, and my final vote bears the same weight as any student's vote.

In the space alloted here, I cannot describe all the different programs of study that students have negotiated; I can only say that no two courses have ever been the same and that generally the final projects are group projects in which students work with others who share their interest in exploring further a given area of theoretical and practical investigation. This exporation, of course, takes many different shapes; to illustrate, I describe two of the most successful final projects. One class was so taken with Freire's *Pedagogy of the Oppressed* that they wanted to explore his work further. We agreed to read the entire book,[10] and I supplied as well more contemporary articles on and by Freire. The basic issue they wanted to explore was whether Freire's theories could overcome the limitations they had seen in the Romantic revolution, and a more specific issue was to read them in conjunction with recent feminist criticism. So we coupled Freire with readings of such feminist work related to pedagogy and teaching as Paula Treichler's "Teaching Feminist Theory," Dale Bauer's "The Other 'F' Word: The Feminist in the Classroom," and Jane Tompkins's "Pedagogy of the Distressed." We also read several feminist poets, such as Carolyn Forché, Ai, Nikki Giovanni, and Mary Oliver. This combination provided one of the most exciting projects undertaken in my class.

Another class wanted to explore further the work of cultural studies, and their specific focus was on African American literary theory. We read several articles by Henry Louis Gates, Jr., Houston Baker, and Robert Stepto, and we also read the powerful play *Fences*, by August Wilson, an African American playwright from Pittsburgh. We also read poetry by Amiri Baraka, Langston Hughes, and Gwendolyn Brooks. Two members of this class were already interested in several African American writers and so were able to contribute a great deal to our discussions and understanding of these writers. Since the African American literary traditions draw extensively from oral literature, they became a fascinating point of comparison with our earlier study of the shift from oral to literate culture in ancient Greece. We also watched Spike Lee's film *Do the Right Thing*, an event that proved how fruitful the theories we had been reading were to an understanding of contemporary cultural life.

Finally, having given these brief overviews of student cooperation, I should emphasize that some of these debates were highly contentious: depending on the particular makeup of the class, students now have something at stake in making their arguments, which often lead to impassioned moments of anger and frustration as well as the joy and excitement that can come from collaborative work. For the most part, I take the tensions as a sign of health when it means that students can, and indeed want to be, heard rather than suppressed in obeisance to a teacher's obvious position of authority or in deference to another student's ideological opposition. But to conclude on a more polemical and utopian note, I would assert that at its best, theorized teaching can participate in a movement that Paul Bové has recently described:

> Teachers in schools can perhaps help create the space in which something like that fellowship among the living and between the living and the dead can take place in a sort of contrapuntal rhythm of discovery and inspiration. Were this done successfully, despite the massive difficulties we all know,

the School would become not an ideological state apparatus or a device in the disciplinary society, but an academy of poets in fellowship making a new polis. (25–26)

To suggest to students that teaching theory should be anything less is, I believe, to shortchange them in a basic way with respect to their education and their lives as citizens in the multicultural world of late-twentieth-century America. As Donald Morton and Mas'ud Zavarzadeh argue, to make such large claims, we must "understand pedagogy not commonsensically, as classroom practices or instructional methods as such, but as the act of producing and disseminating knowledge in culture, a process of which classroom practices are only one instance" (vii). Viewed in this way, the knowledge that students produce and disseminate within the space of a single class reaches well beyond the classroom walls.

Indiana University of Pennsylvania

Notes

[1] As Watkins describes it, "English has been positioned to function as the crucial intra-educational collection and transferral site to furnish hierarchical certifications of 'merit'" (206).

[2] The elaborate procedure I describe here works best when class is scheduled once or perhaps twice a week. In classes that meet more frequently, this procedure can be modified and shortened so that the minutes are no longer than one page and are specifically aimed at highlighting just the main points of discussion.

[3] I have experimented with a variety of different forms for the response statements. I have used as a model the statement described by Kathleen McCormick, Gary Waller, and Linda Flower in *Reading Texts* (58), but I generally tell students they may modify or respond in any way they wish, whether in the form of a journal or log entry. I encourage them to examine and even emphasize their emotional responses to theoretical texts rather than follow the institutionalized pattern of effacing their feelings in favor of explicating abstract theory. It is also important that these responses not be graded in a conventional way. Students should have the opportunity to textualize their work in the course without worrying that the content of their response will be negatively influenced by the grade. Since grades cannot be eliminated from most courses, I also want to give credit to the effort of the students. As such, what I typically do is grade each response with a check, check plus, or check minus, merely according to effort or length of response. Basically, this system means that those students who really enjoy the personal dimension of these writing assignments can get an average of a check plus at the end of the semester and so raise their grade by a notch (e.g., a B+ would become an A−). Position papers are somewhat more formal written responses in which students articulate their own ideology or beliefs and assumptions that guide their reading of particular texts or discussion issues. (For a good description of what to expect from position papers, see Strickland.)

[4] Initial responses to Plato differ so widely that many students are surprised by the extent of that diversity. For example, one student wrote: "Shocked! This is the first time I have read Plato and I am amazed at what he has to say. I was

prepared for something that has lasted for many centuries. . . . But, what I did not expect was a document of support for the powers of government and control of the masses." Others: "My initial reaction to the text—why all that has been stated is so true! I enjoyed every minute of it." "Well, my response to the *Republic* is that it felt like reading legal briefs for an hour and a half." "I looked forward to reading Plato, but I felt very manipulated by the structure of the dialogue. This feeling surprised me. I found I was becoming antagonistic and hypercritical of the text. Untrusting." "Plato, to me, is very much like watching *Twin Peaks*." Such variety provokes some very interesting class discussions.

⁵ Student responses to the texts I describe in this essay are a more important part of this class than a reader of this essay might suspect. I have had to eliminate most discussion of student reactions in order to meet the space limitations of this essay. I have included a few responses in some of the notes.

⁶ Again, student responses vary considerably. One student who initially felt antagonistic toward Plato now commented: "Overall, this and the Havelock piece have provided the most relaxed read thus far. I enjoyed both texts and felt relatively more inclined to trust them." Another remarked: "Eric Havelock's excerpts were far more intriguing to me because it is apparent from his writing that he has a passion to find out what the hell was wrong with Plato that he was so ticked off at poets and poetry. I could almost see this guy banging away on his typewriter with a frenzied look on his face as he asked questions like, 'Why use mimesis to describe both an act of composition . . . and a performance by an actor who is a mouthpiece or reciter?' " In contrast: "I wasn't far into this reading assignment before [Ong] had elicited a profound negative reaction. Ong dismisses non-oral communication with a rather ambiguous statement. . . . Perhaps my association with the deaf has oversensitized me."

⁷ As often as possible, I warn students about the difficulty of Derrida's texts. Many have, of course, heard his name and are curious, but many are emotionally pained by it: "Right off the bat, this man has lost me, angered and frustrated me, almost to the point of tears, because of his oblique, obfuscating, convoluted style." For others, the warning seems to help: "Because of the warning, I had expected Derrida to be more difficult to read than I found it to be." "I was at first intimidated by Derrida's sophistication. . . . but, in the end, I found the piece to a large degree lucid and relatively enlightening. I found his insights into *Phaedrus*, a work which I had a hard time following much of the time, a great value to me the reader. He provided a context of understanding for which contemporary readers like myself could gain insights."

⁸ This brief précis on Marx, of course, glosses over the complexity of these issues. But, depending on the class interests, we have at times spent some energy on demonstrating the ways in which Marx still gets caught up in the binary logic of material, historical reality versus false consciousness and ideology.

⁹ See Sosnoski's articles "Students as Theorists" and "Why Theory? Rethinking Pedagogy" for important examples of the student as theorist.

¹⁰ Since this class came to this decision early on, because of their enthusiasm for Freire, I was able to order the book in time for its use later in the semester. Colleagues have often asked me how I order or provide texts for this last phase of the course, since I can't possibly know in advance the student selections. Of course, circumstances vary in different institutions, but I have not once found this problem to be disabling. Using library reserve material, photocopying articles with appropriate permission, and ordering books that can be obtained within two weeks open a wide variety of options. Also, several anthologies containing a variety of essays can be ordered in advance as optional texts—see, for example, Atkins and Morrow; Cahalan and Downing; Moran and Penfield; Nelson.

Works Cited

Atkins, G. Douglas, and Laura Morrow, eds. *Contemporary Literary Theory*. Amherst: U of Massachusetts P, 1989.

Bauer, Dale, "The Other 'F' Word: The Feminist in the Classroom." *College English* 52 (1990): 385–96.

Bourdieu, Pierre. *Outline of a Theory of Practice*. Cambridge: Cambridge UP, 1977.

Bové, Paul A. "Theory as Practice; or, How One Studies Literature and Culture." *Works and Days 16* 8.2 (1990): 11–28.

Cahalan, James M., and David B. Downing. *Practicing Theory in Introductory College Literature Courses*. Urbana: NCTE, 1991.

Derrida, Jacques. *Dissemination*. Trans. Barbara Johnson. Chicago: U of Chicago P, 1981.

Dewey, John. "The Influence of Darwin on Philosophy." *The Influence of Darwin on Philosophy*. Bloomington: Indiana UP, 1965. 1–19.

Downing, David B., and Susan Bazargan, eds. *Image and Ideology in Modern/Postmodern Discourse*. Albany: State U of New York P, 1991.

Eagleton, Terry. "What Is Literature?" *Literary Theory: An Introduction*. Minneapolis: U of Minnesota P, 1983. 1–16.

Freire, Paulo. *Pedagogy of the Oppressed*. Trans. Myra Ramos. New York: Continuum, 1970.

Gould, Stephen Jay. "Darwin at Sea." *The McGraw-Hill Reader*. Ed. Gilbert H. Muller. New York: McGraw, 1985. 570–81.

Graff, Gerald. *Professing Literature: An Institutional History*. Chicago: U of Chicago P, 1987.

Havelock, Eric A. *Preface to Plato*. Cambridge: Harvard UP, 1963.

McCormick, Kathleen, Gary Waller, and Linda Flower. *Reading Texts: Reading, Responding, Writing*. Lexington: Heath, 1987.

Moran, Charles, and Elizabeth F. Penfield, eds. *Conversations: Contemporary Critical Theory and the Teaching of Literature*. Urbana: NCTE, 1990.

Morton, Donald, and Mas'ud Zavarzadeh. *Theory/Pedagogy/Politics: Texts for Change*. Urbana: U of Illinois P, 1991.

Murray, Heather. "Charisma and Authority in Literary Study and Theory Study." Morton and Zavarzadeh 187–200.

Nelson, Cary. *Theory in the Classroom*. Urbana: U of Illinois P, 1986.

Ong, Walter. *Orality and Literacy*. New York: Methuen, 1982.

Pirsig, Robert. *Zen and the Art of Motorcycle Maintenance*. New York: Morrow, 1974.

Sosnoski, James J. "Students as Theorists: Collaborative Hyper-textbooks." Cahalan and Downing 271–90.

———. "Why Theory? Rethinking Pedagogy." *Works and Days 16* 8.2 (1990): 29–40.

Spivak, Gayatri Chakravorty. "Sex and History in *The Prelude* (1805): Books Nine to Thirteen." *In Other Worlds: Essays in Cultural Politics*. New York: Methuen, 1987. 46–76.

Strickland, Ronald. "Confrontational Pedagogy and Traditional Literary Studies." *College English* 52 (1990): 291–300.

Tompkins, Jane. "Pedagogy of the Distressed." *College English* 52 (1990): 653–60.

Treichler, Paula A. "Teaching Feminist Theory." Nelson 57–128.

Watkins, Evan. "Intellectual Work and Pedagogical Circulation." Morton and Zavarzadeh 201–21.

Confessions of a Convert: Strategies for Teaching Theory

John Kucich

If I begin with a rather self-indulgent account of my initiation to teaching theory, it is mainly to contextualize some of my discoveries about what works and what doesn't. Secondarily, I want to convey some sense of why I think the common apprehensions about teaching theory to undergraduates are unfounded. But the logic of the story compels me to begin by sympathizing with those apprehensions, simply because when I was first assigned to teach a theory course in my department's honors program, I tried everything I could to get out of it. At the time (back in 1984), no one I knew was doing anything more than smuggling a few quasi-theoretical texts into advanced undergraduate courses.

What I dreaded most about teaching theory to undergraduates was student resistance, which I imagined would be intense. I also deeply suspected my own—or anyone else's—ability to conceptualize a general approach to theory in the context of a survey course. I had certainly never been taught theory in antiseptic isolation, and it was difficult to imagine what undergraduates might use theory for, assuming that they could understand it in the first place. I wasn't sure exactly how I used it myself, since reading theory always provoked more unresolved questions for me than it provided sound methodological tools. Finally, in the light of these reservations, I anticipated contempt from the two or three budding "theory jocks" spawned by some Derrida or de Man essay. In short, I foresaw unhappiness all around.

Though I begged and begged, I was unable to extricate myself from the assignment—and have been forever thankful. It turned out from the very beginning that all these problems were nonissues. I learned a few important lessons by anticipating them, however, although I may not have prepared myself in the manner one might expect. Rather than grope toward a series of ugly compromises, I decided to design a course based solely on my own preoccupations with theory, including all my conflicted feelings. If the course bombed, fine—at least I would never be asked to agonize about theory again.

To begin with, I focused exclusively on contemporary theory. This particular course, which is required of our honors students—many of whom are among the most conservative of our majors—had been taught for years as a survey of literary philosophy from Plato to the Romantics. So I was pretty sure I would confound students by starting with Ferdinand de Saussure. Beyond that, I pulled no punches with the reading list. I included Roland Barthes's *S/Z*; some essays by Jacques Derrida; a chapter from Paul de Man's *Allegories of Reading*; Shoshana Felman's essay on Luce Irigaray, "Women and Madness." If we were going to talk about theory, I decided, we were not going to have sophomoric, uninformed discussions about the nature of life and literature; we were really going to talk theory. I also decided something more important about the course's tone: I planned to teach in a critical, not heroic, spirit and to make no concessions to what I imagined would be my students' Pollyanna-ish hunger for the perfect, redemptive theoretical paradigm.

The first thing I learned about my students, to my surprise, was that they were willing to face the challenges of the reading in order to find out what theory was. Most of them had heard about theory, if only to hear it condemned, and were eager to learn what the fuss was all about. In the past few years, attacks on theory in the mainstream press seem only to have further stimulated that student curiosity. It helps, too, when students discover that most negative characterizations of theory drastically oversimplify the issues. That first term, their persistent curiosity won me over despite myself, and I made efforts to shuffle the syllabus around in more merciful ways—although it turned out that not too many adjustments were necessary. Learning theory is not nearly so difficult as people of my graduate-school generation remember it to be—partly, perhaps, because so many introductory texts are available now, but also (as I discovered that first time around, when I wasn't using introductions) because it helps enormously just to have someone who is willing to explain it in simple language. So the second thing I learned concerned the most useful role for me to play in the classroom. I found that students were slightly disoriented by the reading and needed to have their initial impressions of the material confirmed. But with just a little guidance, they were astonishingly quick to assimilate it. After much experimentation, I fell into a pattern that has since worked well: I usually begin class with a short, absolutely unoriginal outline of the basic ideas in the day's reading assignment, something just detailed enough to circumvent misunderstandings and to bolster my students' self-confidence. This preparation often encourages them to express some very acute responses during the rest of the session, which I run as a discussion.

The third thing I learned right away, and the reason for the emphasis on discussion, is that students are eager to engage theory at the level of evaluation. They really don't want to be told, Here is a theoretical model, and this is how you would apply it to a text. They want to deal with theory theoretically. The first form this response takes may well be an impatience to pass judgment, either on theory as a whole or on a particular theorist. Teachers often mistake this impatience for anti-intellectualism and so try to suppress it, but the underside of that impatience is a laudable desire to understand and to place new ideas. My students have eventually demonstrated an eagerness to be able to trace the genealogies of certain ideas, to evaluate theories comparatively, and to identify and most certainly to modify their own theoretical assumptions. I had expected tremendous frustration to surface when my students fully realized what I had warned them about on the first day of class: that literary theory, unlike music theory or color theory, is an area of problematics, rather than the formula for a straightforward practice. But, instead, they were exhilarated to discover that the models for reading they had been taught—or were learning—occupied a contested conceptual space. This discovery always makes students feel that the stakes of their own education have suddenly been raised. At this stage, the increase in their critical self-awareness, as well as in their enthusiasm for studying literature, is palpable and contagious.

My own discoveries about the qualities of my students' interest taught me a number of other pedagogical lessons. For one, teachers of theory have to perform a complicated balancing act. Contrary to my apprehensions, students' engagement with theory depends largely on their being able to see it as an arena of conflict. I found that I serve them best by presiding over this conflict in a relatively disinterested way. It seems important to them that I be able to grant both the weaknesses and the strengths of any given theoretical model, without playing an advocacy role. At the same time, it would be hypocritical of me to pretend that my approach to theory is neutral, especially since the inevitability of ideological interest must, of course, be one of the recurring themes of the course. At some point in the term, this double bind has to become explicit, either because I feel pressure to clarify my stances or because students themselves begin pointing out that I often seem, on the one hand, to be deconstructing my own teaching and, on the other, to be leaning persistently on certain ideas.

Of course, all English teachers play contradictory roles. But the situation in theory courses is disunifying in a more demanding way: the pressures to make judgments are more urgent and the judgments themselves more uncertain, the possibilities for inconsistency from week to week (or from moment to moment) are more self-evident, and the disjunctions between theoretical alternatives and their consequences are often dramatic. If nothing else, the question What good is all this? keeps being asked, in dozens of different ways that demand spontaneous, straightforward evaluation. One wants to respond out of conviction yet avoid being either reductive or coercive. I refuse, in principle, to acknowledge that problems of "political correctness" apply here as well, but others may find that such anxieties further complicate discussions.

I am not at all sure how successfully any teacher of theory can negotiate these dilemmas. Some of my (lost) students conclude that theory is just relativistic; others simply adopt one or another of my own confessed positions. My best students, however, have eventually come to see theory more pragmatically. That is, they recognize—with my encouragement— that theory and practice cannot, finally, be separated; that one can evaluate a particular theoretical idea only by judging what it does in a particular context; and that theoretical choices depend partly on one's larger intellectual and social ends, not entirely on judging the models against one another abstractly. When I fall into this sermonizing mode during class (and I do sometimes strike the heroic note despite myself), it is usually to make the point that theory should lead one to an interminable but pragmatic self-critique and that such a task is preferable to the complacency of either indifference or dogmatism. Recently, I have weighted the end of my syllabus to include strongly motivated works that nevertheless concede their own theoretical irresolution: works like Peter Stallybrass and Allon White's *The Politics and Poetics of Transgression*; recent feminist work by Joan Scott, Diana Fuss, and Mary Poovey; and Cornel West's work on Marxism and race. Parenthetically, I like to use this very issue, when it surfaces, to show the silliness of arguments that teaching must be either above politics or a propaganda campaign.

Another, related discovery was that students are quick to see the relevance of theory to their own lives. As a rule, once they get past some initial difficulties of comprehension, they do not find theory to be arcane. Students interested in contemporary fiction see the connections almost immediately. Others are sparked by understanding in newly theoretical terms those modernist novels that still seem to galvanize most undergraduates' literary interests. Not only do my students want to talk about the relation between theory and what they are studying (or not studying) in their other English classes, but they also leap at the opportunity to make the kinds of interdisciplinary connections that come so much harder to people who, like me, have suffered through years of graduate training in a single specialization. It turns out that what they are learning in their philosophy of science classes ties directly into poststructuralism, that their anthropology classes are using deconstructive techniques without necessarily so naming them, and that their American studies classes are provoking the same questions inspired by Marxist and feminist theory. Recently, the overlaps between literary theory and other disciplines have snowballed, and students are continually telling me that theory (which they had expected to be completely insular) gives them a stronger grip on the issues in their other courses.

When I began teaching theory (this time at my request) outside the honors program, I found that a sizable percentage of already well informed students came to me from other majors. Above all, what theory shows students in these interdisciplinary contexts is that recent shifts in academic interest involve more than just a change in topics of discussion and that crucial changes in conceptualizing these fields are also at issue. Just as important, students have been quick to see the connections to nonacademic contemporary culture. I used to think I had to preach about the relevance of theory to things outside literature, but when I began to see my students making use of theory in writing reviews of pop music and film for the campus student newspaper, I realized that they were way ahead of me. I believe that one of the most important things we can do for our students is to give them the tools to interpret their own culture, and there can be no doubt that we are living in a culture that revolves as never before around paradigm consciousness.

Naturally, I also quickly learned a number of things about shaping my reading list, and I devote the rest of this essay to explaining some of my strategies with texts since those strategies have been affected by specific pedagogical issues. Recognizing the ways in which my students engaged theory that first term led to the greatest change I have made in the course's format. That is, I realized belatedly that it was a mistake to begin with Saussure. In acknowledging themselves as interpreters, my students want to be able to identify the interpretive models they have grown up with and internalized, not just the models that claim to have dislodged them. I also discovered, inadvertently, that it is much easier to persuade students of the attractions of postmodern theory once they have thought through the limitations of, say, New Criticism. To put this more positively, nothing engages students more quickly than discovering that they all have latent theoretical assumptions, that these assumptions have names and histories and can be grouped together around a few elementary distinctions, and that they themselves may or may not want to think like a Wordsworth or a T. S. Eliot anymore—if that's what it would mean to persist in certain assumptions.

Though I still focus almost exclusively on contemporary theory, I now begin with the Romantics. And while it is a revelation for many students to discover that beliefs about the intimate relation between art and emotion, or between art and self-expression, have a comparatively recent history, I also teach the Romantics as our contemporaries. That is, I teach them as the initiators of the critical ethos of the author that many literature classes still take for granted and as harbingers of the attendant, now familiar problems of cultural marginalization and solipsism (or, conversely, blindness to one's embeddedness in culture), which are readily evident in, say, Wordsworth's Preface to *Lyrical Ballads*. Strange as it may seem, a useful reading selection has turned out to be the first chapter or two of M. H. Abrams's *The Mirror and the Lamp*. Abrams's four-part model of literary paradigms is still an eminently coherent way of categorizing theories, and Abrams articulates the mutual exclusivity of the choices at this level in a way that is eye-opening for students. His alinguistic model is also usefully destabilizable once we do get to Saussure.

Most valuable of all, however, the terms of his outline of the Romantic revolution are still pertinent to my students' ingrained conceptions about literary values, even if its pertinence to the culture of Romanticism itself is in doubt. What is crucial about beginning with Romanticism, at any rate, is that it always produces the kind of alienated self-consciousness I have described, especially when I ask students to report things they've recently heard or read that still sound essentially Romantic or when I ask them about their experiences in creative writing courses.

I now also spend at least a week on modernism. Though students today are often taken aback rather instinctively by the implications of an essay like Eliot's "Tradition and the Individual Talent" or by the judgments in José Ortega y Gasset's still-useful essay "The Dehumanization of Art," they are quick to recognize the affinity between modernist assumptions about art and their own training, especially in the reading of poetry. Joseph Frank's essay on "spatial form" allows them to see how they have been taught to read the "art novel," too, in modernist terms. There is an obvious bridge, of course, between modernism and New Criticism. In addition to the inevitable essays—"The Intentional Fallacy" (Wimsatt and Beardsley) and Cleanth Brooks's essay on Keats—I have found it helpful to teach selections from Brooks and Robert Penn Warren's textbook *Understanding Poetry*. New Criticism is alive and well in high school English classes, and my students are always exhilarated to discover a way of talking about the assumptions they learned there, as well as to discover that close reading was a strange new approach fairly recently.

I find it increasingly important to teach poststructuralist theory, if only because a number of current critical pieties become reductive in the hands of those unfamiliar with complex issues of representation, difference, and symbolic-cultural change. Getting the historical record straight is also important: students have asked me at this point in the term if theorists became interested in linguistic difference as a result of multicultural studies. There are many introductions to Saussure and poststructuralism, of course, and I imagine that almost any of them would convey the essential information. I have found Jane Tompkins's essay effective, as is Peter Dews's chapter on Derrida; alternatively, I have had success with Catherine Belsey's book. I must confess, too, that in discussing poststructuralism we stray farther from the reading than at any other time in the course and that the most effective teaching aids seem to be the "homemade" examples one hears in Philosophy 101. Students simply insist on asking whether dogs have language or whether breathing is culturally mediated, and one had better have ready a wide-ranging set of examples and distinctions. Since most of our students are badly prepared in philosophy, I also find it crucial to point out at the very beginning that philosophical realism has been dead since the Enlightenment and that those who believe they can apprehend the physical world directly are simply not living in the twentieth century. Though this assertion often comes as a shock, getting past issues of presence and absence quickly allows us to focus on Saussure's most important, innovative ideas: those on the structural interdependence of elements within a discursive system and on the dominant epistemological role poststructuralism assigns to culture.

A writing assignment based on poststructuralism may be necessary to goad students to begin struggling with it. But once they catch on, the important feeling of mastery they gain gives them an increased appetite for theory throughout the rest of the course (and they want to talk gleefully about their friends' incomprehension). It is worth bringing their sense of intellectual breakthrough to the surface, asking students to discriminate carefully between the uses and abuses of theory. When, inevitably, the issue of elitism arises with Barthes or Derrida, students are likely to take the easy road to cynicism unless I force them to recognize the good and bad ways in which new ideas can be powerful. Later in the term, I use essays by Barbara Christian, Audre Lorde, or Bell Hooks and Mary Childers to illustrate the potential privileges and dangers of theoretical discourse itself.

I also think it important to spend some time on deconstruction, particularly since the days of decrying deconstruction as excessively formalist have given way to new applications of deconstructive techniques—in feminism, in ethnic studies, and elsewhere. Though some would dispute my choice, I use Jonathan Culler's *On Deconstruction*. For all its problems (including its formalist biases and its arguable appropriations of feminism, both of which often fuel discussion), I think it remains the best introduction for undergraduates. Philosophically, it may be less rigorous than texts by Christopher Norris and Vincent Leitch, but its examples are pithy, and Culler is always lucid.

I have had two principal difficulties introducing political criticism. One is the problem of linking Marx to contemporary materialist thought. The most accessible overviews of Marxist theory—Raymond Williams's book and Terry Eagleton's introductory works—are themselves theoretical interventions, and I find them confusing or inaccurate as introductions. What I sometimes do at this juncture is to fall back on lectures that schematize the basic tenets of classical Marxism and the way in which these have been either modified or displaced by recent materialist criticism, occasionally with the aid of more-detached surveys, like Martin Jay's illuminating essay and chapters from Tony Bennett's book. But the second, more intractable problem is my students' resistance or inability to think in terms of class, which may arise more from their outdated and clichéd images of class identity than from any fundamental innocence about social privilege and power.

What works best for me on both counts, odd as it may seem, is to circumvent orthodox Marxist theory and to begin instead with a work of cultural materialist criticism—John Berger's *Ways of Seeing*, for example. This strategy allows me to get at issues of class indirectly and to generalize the concerns of Marxist, neo-Marxist, and post-Marxist thinking without being pedantic. In terms that make immediate sense to my students, *Ways of Seeing* demonstrates wonderfully how the world of art is saturated with social conflict—the basic point of this section of the course—since Berger bypasses class analysis and theoretical polemic to talk about what students see as more-familiar sources of cultural tension: sexism in the visual arts, for instance, and the friction between high culture and mass culture. For getting both Marx and class in through the back door, the other text that proves enormously useful is Stallybrass and White's *The Politics and Poetics of Transgression*. While students' experience of class may be limited or repressed, this book shows that their experience of "high" and "low" symbolic categories is not.

It makes sense, I think, to start with any text that conceptualizes the dynamics of social and cultural conflict in recognizable contemporary terms. Both the above texts, however, also allow me to trace intersections between political criticism and poststructuralism. In fact, referring to our earlier work in poststructuralism often enables students to generalize about the ideological bases of cultural systems—that is, to turn their understanding of linguistic difference into an understanding of social opposition and to correlate cultural hierarchies with institutional ones. Teaching a few new-historicist essays or introducing Michel Foucault (which I have done, most successfully, by using the early essay "Nietzsche, Genealogy, History") has also allowed me to talk about poststructuralist approaches to history, but it has not enabled discussions of ideology or class in the same ways and has often confirmed whatever tendencies my students have to smooth over inequities between sites of social power. After reading more finger-pointing kinds of cultural analysis, by contrast, students seem receptive to explicitly ideological or class-centered arguments like Terry Eagleton's in "The Rise of English"—an indispensable essay, despite its overblown rhetoric and monolithic generalizations. The ability to historicize the curriculum, as Eagleton does, and to tie curricular changes to the rise of particular social groups within the academy is mind-altering for students, especially in these days of major curricular overhaul.

In teaching feminist criticism, I stage it—at least initially—as a dialogue about competing positions. One advantage of emphasizing options within feminism is that it allows resistant students to see that feminist criticism is a rigorous debate rather than a dogmatic camp. It also allows them to read feminists who critique the potentially exclusionary emphasis on "experience" and on "anger" that many students have come to associate negatively with all feminists. I often begin with the Anglo-American–French controversy, and although the terms of that opposition are now stale and paralyzing, there are always ways to teach it as paralyzing while using it to illuminate long-standing fundamental differences within feminism. I also think it important to qualify many of the critical clichés about Anglo-American feminism that this opposition has generated. So while I frequently begin with Toril Moi's *Sexual/Textual Politics*, I also use essays that help refine the extremist polarization of Moi's account—for example, the first chapter of Sandra Gilbert and Susan Gubar's *The Madwoman in the Attic* and sections from Rita Felski's book *Beyond Feminist Aesthetics*.

To stop at that point, however, would still give a limiting sense of the possibilities for feminism, so I spend some time on other approaches as well. Teaching works that explicitly deconstruct the essentialist-antiessentialist opposition helps; useful examples are Scott's essay and the first and concluding chapters of Fuss's book. But I think it important as well to teach some Marxist feminism (e.g., essays by Nancy Armstrong and Rosalind Coward). An alternative is to use a wide-ranging anthology: two excellent collections are those edited by Teresa de Lauretis and by Marianne Hirsch and Evelyn Keller. Inevitably, what these various readings begin to define for students—and what I try to emphasize as we move through the material—is the relatively large ground of theoretical agreement that manages to unite feminist criticism and that identifies it as a theoretical position rather than simply as a critical bias. This position includes, above all, understanding gender as a fundamental category of interpretive thought that has been systematically mapped—and will continue to be mapped, albeit differently—onto literary analysis. Periodically pointing out the omission of gender from much of political criticism (or, earlier, the omission of politics from the poststructuralist work) helps shore up a general theme I use to unite our discussions of these three areas: the perception that works of art are multiply embedded in various socio-symbolic systems and that these systems often conflict.

The difficulties I have had in teaching ethnic studies are similar to those that crop up with feminism. Though I have used Gates's *"Race,"* *Writing, and Difference* to trace tensions within minority discourse that parallel tensions in feminism—balancing it with essays by Joyce A. Joyce, Barbara Christian, and Norman Harris—I want to avoid freezing students' attention on questions of essentialism. Works by Houston Baker, which argue for a historicization of race as an alternative to double binds about race and identity, and Hazel Carby's *Reconstructing Womanhood* are refreshing escapes into materialism. The excellent collection edited by David Lloyd and Abdul JanMohamed allows the essentialism issue to surface but also includes other approaches.

Students are much more eager—even feverishly so—to bring current events to bear on discussion in the realm of multicultural studies than in other domains of theory, and I find myself spending more time than usual slowing them down and urging them to examine racial issues in the light of what they have learned from other sections of the course. To cite an example, one way to defuse emotional reactions about separatism is to ask students how such moves can be evaluated as specific cultural or discursive strategies—as poststructuralists might see them—rather than in universal or ideal terms. Or, to cite another example, by introducing the issue of class to discussions of race, I can help students see the complexities of theory-versus-antitheory arguments and to reevaluate their snap judgments about "conservative" positions taken by minority intellectuals. I must add, somewhat gratuitously, that in my experience no theoretical topic arouses such acute passions and misunderstandings as does the issue of race, partly because students regularly mistake their own tremendous gaffes for well-meaning remarks. One crucial form of preparation, then, is a readiness to separate intentions from statements in the interest of diplomacy; but a willingness not to let outrageous remarks pass without comment is absolutely necessary as well.

Finally, I should mention that I always teach a literary work, together with a broad range of critical essays on it. The reasons would seem to be obvious: comparing interpretive essays makes the stakes of theoretical reading much more concrete; the assignment gives students a sense of control, knowing that they can identify the presence of deconstructive or New Critical ideas even where they are not explicitly announced; and it's simply a necessary break from theoretical abstraction.

I will no doubt shock many people by saying that I don't regularly teach psychoanalysis, reader-response criticism, gay and lesbian studies, or a host of other approaches, but it must already be clear that my reading list is a good deal heavier than that of the standard English course. Because of the range from literary history to philosophy to politics, I think the areas I do cover give students a good base from which to enter other branches of theory. But the choice one makes about what to cover at this level is probably less important than the simple chance to demonstrate how various kinds of theories can both clash with and illuminate one another. I strongly believe that more-specialized theory courses for undergraduates are necessary to address the omissions of survey courses. But no matter what the abridgments, some form of introductory survey now seems indispensable to me—to introduce students to the existence of theoretical models, to train them how to reflect about the implications of methodology, to give them a variety of tools for interpreting their own intellectual moment, and to alert them to what really motivates the teaching they receive from us. It would be difficult to condense student responses to my course, but the two common changes I sense—changes for which I take no credit, seeing them as a wonderfully inevitable effect of reading theory—are a much more alert sensitivity to the contemporary cultural landscape (both academic and nonacademic) and a greater sense of the urgency of the choices before them as readers and interpreters.

University of Michigan

Works Cited

Abrams, M. H. *The Mirror and the Lamp: Romantic Theory and the Critical Tradition*. New York: Oxford UP, 1953.

Armstrong, Nancy. "The Rise of Feminine Authority in the Novel." *Novel* 15 (1982): 127–45.

Baker, Houston A., Jr. *Blues, Ideology, and Afro-American Literature: A Vernacular Theory*. Chicago: U of Chicago P, 1984.

———. "Generational Shifts and the Recent Criticism of Afro-American Literature." *Black American Literature Forum* (1981): 3–21.

Barthes, Roland. *S/Z*. Trans. Richard Miller. New York: Hill, 1974.

Belsey, Catherine. *Critical Practice*. New York: Methuen, 1980.

Bennett, Tony. *Formalism and Marxism*. New York: Methuen, 1979.

Berger, John. *Ways of Seeing*. Harmondsworth, Eng.: Penguin, 1972.

Brooks, Cleanth. "Keats' Sylvan Historian: History without Footnotes." Kaplan 470–81.

Brooks, Cleanth, and Robert Penn Warren. *Understanding Poetry: An Anthology for College Students*. New York: Henry Holt, 1939.

Carby, Hazel V. *Reconstructing Womanhood: The Emergence of the Afro-American Woman Novelist*. New York: Oxford UP, 1987.

Christian, Barbara. "The Race for Theory." *Feminist Studies* 14 (1988): 67–79.

Coward, Rosalind. "The True Story of How I Became My Own Person." *Female Desires: How They Are Sought, Bought, and Packaged*. New York: Grove, 1985. 173–86.

Culler, Jonathan. *On Deconstruction*. Ithaca: Cornell UP, 1982.

de Lauretis, Teresa, ed. *Feminist Studies, Critical Studies*. Bloomington: Indiana UP, 1986.

de Man, Paul. *Allegories of Reading: Figural Language in Rousseau, Nietzsche, Rilke, and Proust*. New Haven: Yale UP, 1979.

Dews, Peter. "Jacques Derrida: The Transcendental and Difference." *Logics of Disintegration: Post-structuralist Thought and the Claims of Critical Theory*. New York: Verso, 1987. 1–44.

Eagleton, Terry. "The Rise of English." *Literary Theory: An Introduction*. Minneapolis: U of Minnesota P, 1983. 17–53.

Eliot, T. S. "Tradition and the Individual Talent." Kaplan 429–37.

Felman, Shoshana. "Women and Madness: The Critical Phallacy." *Diacritics* 5 (1975): 2–10.

Felski, Rita. *Beyond Feminist Aesthetics: Feminist Literature and Social Change*. Cambridge: Harvard UP, 1989.

Foucault, Michel. "Nietzsche, Genealogy, History." Trans. Donald F. Bouchard and Sherry Simon. *Language, Counter-memory, Practice: Selected Essays and Interviews*. Ithaca: Cornell UP, 1977. 139–64.

Frank, Joseph. "Spatial Form in Modern Literature." *The Widening Gyre: Crisis and Mastery in Modern Literature*. New Brunswick: Rutgers UP, 1963. 3–62.

Fuss, Diana. *Essentially Speaking: Feminism, Nature, and Difference*. New York: Routledge, 1989.

Gates, Henry Louis, Jr., ed. *"Race," Writing, and Difference*. Chicago: U of Chicago P, 1986.

Gilbert, Sandra, and Susan Gubar. *The Madwoman in the Attic: The Woman Writer and the Nineteenth-Century Literary Imagination*. New Haven: Yale UP, 1979.

Harris, Norman. "'Who's Zoomin' Who': The New Black Formalism." *Journal of the Midwest MLA* 20 (1987): 37–45.

Hirsch, Marianne, and Evelyn Fox Keller, eds. *Conflicts in Feminism*. New York: Routledge, 1990.

Hooks, Bell, and Mary Childers. "A Conversation about Race and Class." Hirsch and Keller 60–81.

Jay, Martin. "Fin-de-Siècle Socialism." *Fin-de-Siècle Socialism and Other Essays*. New York: Routledge, 1988. 1–13.

Joyce, Joyce A. "The Black Canon: Reconstructing Black American Literary Criticism." *New Literary History* 18 (1987): 335–44.

———. "'Who the Cap Fit': Unconsciousness and Unconscionableness in the Criticism of Houston A. Baker, Jr., and Henry Louis Gates, Jr." *New Literary History* 18 (1987): 371–84.

Kaplan, Charles, ed. *Criticism: The Major Statements*. New York: St. Martin's, 1986.

Leitch, Vincent. *Deconstructive Criticism: An Advanced Introduction*. New York: Columbia UP, 1983.

Lloyd, David, and Abdul JanMohamed, eds. *The Nature and Context of Minority Discourses*. New York: Oxford UP, 1991.

Lorde, Audre. "The Master's Tools Will Never Dismantle the Master's House." *This Bridge Called My Back: Writings by Radical Women of Color*. Ed. Cherrie Moraga and Gloria Anzaldua. New York: Kitchen Table Women of Color, 1983. 98–101.

Moi, Toril. *Sexual/Textual Politics: Feminist Literary Theory*. New York: Methuen, 1985.

Norris, Christopher. *Deconstruction: Theory and Practice*. New York: Methuen, 1982.

Ortega y Gasset, José. "The Dehumanization of Art." *The Dehumanization of Art and Other Essays on Art, Culture, and Literature*. Princeton: Princeton UP, 1968. 1–52.

Poovey, Mary. "Feminism and Deconstruction." *Feminist Studies* 14 (1988): 51–65.

Scott, Joan W. "Deconstructing Equality-vs.-Difference; or, The Uses of Post-structuralist Theory for Feminism." Hirsch and Keller 134–48.

Stallybrass, Peter, and Allon White. *The Politics and Poetics of Transgression*. London: Methuen, 1986.

Tompkins, Jane. "A Short Course in Post-structuralism." *College English* 50 (1988): 733–47.

West, Cornel. "Marxist Theory and the Specificity of Afro-American Oppression." *Marxism and the Interpretation of Culture*. Ed. Cary Nelson and Lawrence Grossberg. Chicago: U of Illinois P, 1988. 17–34.

Williams, Raymond. *Marxism and Literature*. Oxford: Oxford UP, 1977.

Wimsatt, William, and Monroe Beardsley. "The Intentional Fallacy." *The Verbal Icon: Studies in the Meaning of Poetry*. Lexington: U of Kentucky P, 1954. 3–18.

Wordsworth, William. "Preface to *Lyrical Ballads*." Kaplan 256–75.

The *T* Word: Theory as Trial and Transformation of the Undergraduate Classroom

Susan S. Lanser

In the fall of 1988, during the depths of the presidential campaign, my life as a teacher reached an all-time low. Never had I taught an entire course in literary theory to undergraduates, and never had I faced a class—let alone an honors class—persistently frustrated by the curriculum. By mid-October, when we encountered Chris Weedon's *Feminist Practice and Poststructuralist Theory*, they had dubbed theory the "*T* word"—and there on the syllabus, obstructing the joyful fall into literature, sat several demanding essays, Catherine Belsey's *Critical Practice*, and a hefty chunk of M. M. Bakhtin. The students said they felt overwhelmed, paralyzed, bogged down, and off balance—and so did I. If I'd been asked then, I would have said that a theory course for English undergraduates was a mistake.[1]

But when I read their midterm papers, I realized that these students were producing the most sophisticated critical work I had encountered in an undergraduate course, a judgment the remainder of the semester only intensified. And in the "free space" with which I begin my class sessions—the time when students may raise any subject that concerns them—they had begun to talk about the ways in which critical theory was changing and challenging their encounters outside this class, not only in other courses but in conversations with friends and family. Still, I was surprised when, in the final session, the students proclaimed that literary theory should be taught at every level of the undergraduate curriculum and even in high school.[2] Instead of viewing theory as something opposed to practice or experience, they now considered the experience of theory the most widely practicable study they could undertake.

As these students evaluated both the course and its relation to their English curriculum, I began to see that autumn's trials and December's transformations had common origins. The very intensity of both suggested the deeply traditional, New Critical foundation of the students' literary values despite their education in a department attuned to changing notions of author, reader, and text. For virtually everyone, "great literature" meant literature objectively true and objectively beautiful; the canon was "a sort of spontaneous occurrence" (Maryjoy Argo) gracing these naturally superior texts, and the task of criticism was to "prove aesthetic harmony" or, where none seemed evident, to "decide that the work didn't quite make the grade" (Jean Da Silva).[3] Now the students saw both texts and people as "socially constructed" and had begun, as one of them exulted in global language that was typical, "to think critically about the world" (Charlotte Rabidoux). Most people had more questions than answers, but as Lucy Bailey put it, "The more questions I have, the more fully I am engaged with 'life.'" Similar responses have come from subsequent students in Feminism and Literary Theory at the rather different university where I now teach.

While such responses convince me of the value of literary theory for undergraduates, I am equally convinced that the transformative potential of critical theory is dependent on our strategies for teaching it. Theory taught not as a content to be "mastered" but as an open process of inquiry carries the potential, I believe, for empowering students to read and shape culture. Such students become empowered even to question our own professional and professorial practices, and, as I suggest below, our own resistance to teaching theory to undergraduates is not separable from this possibility.

When I oppose "content" and "mastery" to "process" and "inquiry," I have in mind Paulo Freire's distinction in *Pedagogy of the Oppressed* between "banking" or "narrative education" and "problem-posing education" or education for "critical consciousness" (58, 72, 19). In the former project, successful education involves the reproduction of the teacher's discourse by the student-listeners. "The outstanding characteristic of this narrative education," says Freire, is

> the sonority of words, not their transforming power. "Four times four is sixteen; the capital of Pará is Belém." The student records, memorizes, and repeats these phrases without perceiving what four times four really means or realizing the true significance of "capital" in the affirmation "the capital of Pará is Belém," that is, what Belém means for Pará and what Pará means for Brazil. (57–58)

In such a framework, the successful teacher is of course the master-knower —in a course on theory the one who has read the "important" theorists and can correctly define, distinguish, and evaluate their ideas. No genuine dialogue is possible with this teacher-expert, whose questions are designed to solicit specific answers and who uses "active participation" only to help students learn the theoretical "facts."

Literature education in United States universities has for the past several decades disparaged this banking method: students are no longer, we claim, told how to read texts but are taught the skills by which to propose and support readings of their own. While I suggest later the possibility of a certain self-delusion beneath this liberal policy, I want to argue now that one space within the literary curriculum where banking education may be especially tempting is precisely in the teaching of theory. Because the content of theory is indeed difficult to master, because its mastery carries a certain cachet—or simply for reasons of purity or coverage or preparation for exams—theory is sometimes taught as a body of terms, concepts, and distinctions that the student must "get right," rather than as a less predictable process of thinking that may take a variable and indeterminable course. Ironically, then, banking education returns to literary studies in precisely the framework through which education for critical consciousness seems most eminently possible. A pedagogy of inquiry rather than mastery seems to me especially crucial when the theory in question is not only intellectually but personally difficult and when it implicitly challenges professional and pedagogical practices to which I myself may be tenaciously if unconsciously bound.

Freire calls this second form of education a "problem-posing" mode because it begins "with the conviction that it cannot present its own program but must search for this program dialogically with the people" (118). It does not *use* dialogue; it *is* dialogue—through which each student "wins back" discursive power. Words that once meant nothing to the students they learn not only to speak but, more important, to make speak; they become creators as well as receivers of the theoretical word. Such an education does not function simply "to facilitate the integration of the younger generation into the logic of the present system and bring about conformity to it" but becomes instead " 'the practice of freedom,' the means by which men and women deal critically and creatively with reality and discover how to participate in the transformation of their world" (Shaull 15). Graduate education is often understood to entail just this call to transform the profession if not the world; I am suggesting that undergraduates may also become apprentice theorists engaged in literary and social critique.

But clearly theory must be learned in some sense as content in order for any process to take place; students must understand concepts before they can participate in their application, evaluation, and critique. How, then, can undergraduate students unfamiliar with literary theory move, in the space of a semester, from learning complex and sometimes disturbing new theories to testing and perhaps revising them? And what happens to the students and the department when such a course succeeds? As a way of considering these questions, I want to suggest some specific curricular and pedagogical strategies that recognize theory's trials and may enhance its transformative possibilities. Such practices should be applicable to courses or units focused on theories of various kinds, but I focus my own teaching especially on the structures of power in which literary institutions are embedded and on theories that question universality, canonicity, authorial hegemony, linguistic fixity, coherent subjectivity, and the status of literature itself. I also proceed on the convictions that students learn more from my practices than from my theoretical proclamations, that what I spend educational time on is what I value, and that learning which will "empower students to intervene in the making of history" (Shor 48) must work against the inevitable constraints of the college classroom, an overdetermined site of professorial power (teachers choose the books, form the syllabus, set the assignments, give the grades).

Were it not for the pressure from students and from some colleagues to teach theory only in the interstices of the curriculum, my first suggestion in structuring a theory curriculum for undergraduates would seem obvious: teach theory "up front" for an extended period, even beyond the students' apparent level of tolerance. My courses in theory have always included fiction and poetry, both to give the students an arena for praxis and to deconstruct the opposition between theory and literature. But given both the relative absence of theory from undergraduate education and the challenges theory poses to the naturalized critical positions that pass for common sense, the discourses of critical theory and the very process of thinking theoretically are likely to be deeply unfamiliar to undergraduates. A certain saturation with theory, like immersion in a foreign language, enables students to move past resistance, reach a level of familiarity with theory's languages, and learn to think and read differently. Perhaps one must *let* theory be a trial, then, passing some point of discomfort that will surely vary from student to student and class to class. Despite the ordeal, students will be eager to try out their new understandings, and the strategic use of "primary" literary and social texts helps to make vivid what is at stake in the theoretical inquiry.

In order to create the problem-posing context of which Freire speaks, I teach multiple perspectives, both divergent and complementary, positioned in dialogue. For example, I break up our reading of Virginia Woolf's *A Room of One's Own* with essays by Gloria Anzaldúa, Alice Walker, and Bell Hooks; follow Annette Kolodny's "Dancing through the Minefield" with critiques of that essay which appeared in *Feminist Studies* but are almost never anthologized (Gardiner et al.); juxtapose Audre Lorde's "Poetry Is Not a Luxury" with portions of Julia Kristeva's *Revolution in Poetic Language*; assign Gayatri Spivak's "French Feminism in an International Frame" along with the writings of Hélène Cixous and Luce Irigaray; and teach Barbara Christian's "The Race for Theory" as we read the kind of theory to which she objects. This program does make the reading load trying in two ways: it is relatively heavy, and it gives what one student described as a "slap from a new direction every night." Yet students have agreed that the most powerful aspect of the curriculum is this presentation of diverse and overlapping voices, for in the gaps, repetitions, and discrepancies, most students can negotiate a place from which to stand or at least to understand. Sometimes the most radical writings provide what Victoria Andros called "definition by opposition," and sometimes a reading that creates outrage or confusion at one moment later becomes a touchstone text. This diversity also authorizes differences among the students; as Lisa Hoffman said, since the theorists didn't agree with one another, she certainly could not agree with all of them. Multiplicity does not, then, mean an uncritical pluralism, since the assumptions, implications, and contradictions of various positions are under continual scrutiny.

It took me some time to understand the extent to which, if one does not want to marginalize what has been marginal, one must centralize it instead. In order not to represent theory as a white or academic or privileged-class enterprise and yet to confront the effects of cultural hegemonies, I combine two curricular strategies. On the one hand, I include "marginalized" writers and theories from the start—theories constructed outside the academy by the people Antonio Gramsci might have considered "organic intellectuals": working-class critics, open lesbians, women and men of color—so that for my students these thinkers become normative. At the same time, a specific section of the course focuses explicitly on questions of difference and the position of such writers and texts. This double strategy seems to succeed in making issues of racial, class, and sexual difference powerful sites of transformation for most of the students.

I also combine, in my choices of both theoretical and literary texts, well-known with lesser-known texts strategically arranged. Familiar texts, from a well-loved children's story like "The Giving Tree" to a canonical novel, allow students to see changes in their ways of reading. Juxtaposition is also instructive: in one course, following *Madame Bovary* with Frances Harper's *Iola Leroy* allowed us to raise important questions about aesthetic judgment, narrative strategies, representations of women in nineteenth-century fiction, and the functions of literature; in another, reading *Uncle Tom's Cabin* along with African American slave narratives helped us confront tensions between race and gender politics and differences between antiracism and antislavery. (Given my belief, however, that we represent our values through our practices, a syllabus weighted with canonical texts and "mainstream" writers—including theorists—seems to me inevitably to reproduce that hegemony, no matter how critically we read them.)

To ensure that even this kind of challenging curriculum moves students beyond a banking education, I find it necessary to design a pedagogy that fosters not only understanding but evaluation and revision as well. My classes engage in a three-part project like that proposed by Ira Shor in *Critical Teaching and Everyday Life*. These phases—description, diagnosis, and reconstruction—define different stages for learning literary theory, and I devise for each stage specific pedagogical strategies. While I am separating the three stages for descriptive purposes, they may occur either in separate sequential moments or in a more fluid interrelation, and together they can constitute the shape of an entire course, a course unit, or the learning of a single day's text or idea.

Since one must know something before one can use, evaluate, or question it, *description* constitutes that first stage when the content of various theories gets presented. When I teach these theories, I make clear that they will be subjected to questioning and that the students' reactions to them will matter. Every idea is presented as provisional, and I encourage students to see what I don't see. Because I prefer to use as little classroom time as possible for information processing, I try to give students the tools for learning critical theory themselves. I keep up-front lecturing minimal, prefer accessible to esoteric explanations, and whenever possible provide more than one critical account of a position or concept. To frame the students' individual study, I prepare a reading guide for each week or unit that provides some context for the readings, raises questions, and suggests ways of coping with the material. On the guides and in the classroom I use practical exercises and small-group activities that allow students to test (and become confident with) their grasp of concepts and that show me where they are having difficulties. When possible, these exercises suggest the implications or uses of theories, so that the students may be motivated by perceiving the relevance of what they are being taught.

At this stage it is important that I anticipate and understand various types of resistance to theory and the sources from which they may stem: intimidation by the terminology, discomfort with abstract discourse, distress at the ideological implications of what we are studying. Students may feel foolish and anxious when they're learning literary theory; indeed, the most capable juniors and seniors, used to excelling in their literature classes, may be especially frustrated at having to struggle with wholly unfamiliar material that lies outside their area of accustomed mastery. Add to these difficulties the likelihood that some cherished values are being challenged and the stage is set for the kind of intellectual and emotional overload my students complained of during the fall of 1988.

At those times during the semester when description is the dominant activity, then, students need a considerable degree of support. Although I knew well Thomas Kuhn's *Structure of Scientific Revolutions*, with its warning that intellectual changes are also always changes in belief, and although I had been teaching as a feminist for fifteen years, I was not prepared in 1988 for the degree to which literary theory would challenge my students' visions of themselves, their education, their cultures, their lives; somehow I thought the literary and theoretical would buffer the personal and political. The students themselves were the ones who made me aware of their need for structures of support, asking for extra meetings outside class and urging me to require in a future semester weekly small-group sessions or journals as vehicles for working out the far-reaching and individual implications of the new material. I also learned to offer verbal sympathy about the difficulty of the material and assurances that ideas the students find confusing now are likely to be clearer later on and indeed that for the purposes of my course students need not master everything.

Shor's second phase, *diagnosis*, involves a kind of trial by fire of whatever has been "described," so that our encounter with different ideas becomes not merely a feat of practice but also a test of theory and so that relevance is not taken for granted but open to scrutiny. The teaching of different perspectives positioned in dialogue creates the impetus for such a diagnostic project: we evaluate a theory by applying it and seeing how it has been applied, by imagining alternatives, and by asking what we consequently gain or lose. Instead of taking the position that a particular theory is good for the students, we ask together what the theory is good *for*.

At this point, it seems to me, students need a pedagogical space as free as possible from my control. They need to know that I am not just setting up an exercise but am genuinely committed to the inquiry and open to revising my own views. Since virtually every aspect of a course and a classroom environment operates within a system of (usually unacknowledged) beliefs, most of which are determined by the professor, it is important that at this stage I occupy the smallest role possible. Because institutionalized educational practice encourages me to maintain a large "psychological size" and a virtually perpetual stream of discourse and because in the teaching of theory I may feel an especially strong temptation and even a mandate to centralize classroom authority, I make it a point to create open structures that I cannot control. This pedagogy places on the students a greater intellectual burden, for which my reading guides and supplementary handouts are meant to compensate.

To this end, I build into my theory courses several student-centered pedagogical practices: small groups, student-led discussions, collectively created agendas, and "free space." Free space, a structure I have included in all my courses for more than fifteen years, is simply a time I announce at the beginning of each class during which any subject may be raised: questions or issues based on previous weeks' readings, announcements of relevant coming events, requests that we include a particular topic on our agenda, bibliographical information of general interest, ideas or experiences that seem related to the course. Free space usually occupies but a few minutes of our time; occasionally it has been the basis for extremely important discussions either about course content in the strict sense or about current issues on or off campus to which we can bring our collective analysis.

I use small groups for many different purposes and in different ways: I might open a class by asking groups to spend a few minutes identifying the most troubling or provocative aspects of the day's readings; or, in the middle of a session, I might assign each group a text or question to discuss at some length. I often ask the groups to report back to the class, in effect teaching the rest of us. Sometimes the groups are formed around shared interests. These opportunities for students to meet without my direction often open up new ideas or identify issues of importance that I have overlooked. Needless to say, small groups also engage more actively members who might be reticent in the class as a whole.

In some semesters I have also asked students to sign up in units of two or three to lead a thirty- or forty-minute segment of a class. I insist that the students not lecture; they must create a pedagogy that can involve everyone in active learning, and I encourage them to be innovative in their approach. I also give them pedagogical advice; explaining that new teachers often rush to fill silences, for example, I encourage the leaders to give us time to think about the questions they pose. A more modest version of student-generated discussion occurs when I assign two or three students to bring to class written questions on our readings for the day.

One central strategy through which the students may move from description to diagnosis involves the assignment of short position papers, which students take turns reading aloud on scheduled days throughout the semester. My students usually take this critical and interpretive responsibility very seriously, producing illuminating, often provocative responses, to which other students will refer both in subsequent discussions and in their written work. I have learned that the papers work best when students bring to class copies for everyone, and recently I have begun asking students to respond to the position papers not only in class but by the following week in writing. These letters from individual to individual (with a copy to me) allow for much richer and more rewarding responses, and each student may reproduce excerpts from the various responses and distribute them to the entire class.

These papers thus foster the final phase, *reconstruction*, in which students and teacher are genuinely engaged in a new integrative and creative enterprise. Having come to understand and diagnose various theories, the students begin to advance ideas, revisions, and syntheses of their own. At this point the course itself may come under scrutiny as students ask what is worth knowing and, insofar as the structure of the course permits, decide how we should spend our time. Through the position papers, classroom discussions, and other writing assignments, students are encouraged to take seriously their own and one another's potential to intervene in both academic and nonacademic settings. Some of the writing assignments, for example, give students such options as proposing an alternative syllabus, demonstrating and evaluating the use of critical theory in a setting outside the classroom, and introducing their peers to the benefits and drawbacks of studying literary theory. So that students will take seriously one another's roles as critics and thinkers, each essay (or sometimes a draft) is read not only by me but also by two or three other students; the students often find the comments from one another as useful as mine.

The process of reconstruction requires that students have not only support and freedom but also an authority that demands humility and vulnerability from me, rather than a defense of my turf or a reimposition of dominance. For if I invite students to become critical theorists, it must be not on my terms but on theirs; I must give positive value to the differences likely to follow from their age, their relation to the educational system and to the profession, and the critical-historical moment in which they have grown up. In Freire's words, "The teacher is no longer merely the one-who-teaches, but one who is himself taught in dialogue with the students, who in turn while being taught also teach" (67). When, for example, students critiqued drafts of my essays on feminist criticism of *The Yellow Wallpaper* and on the state of feminist criticism in general, I was inviting them to participate in the profession and to engage the issues facing it. The practices of both the discipline and the academy came up often in our discussions, and in seeing them through my students' eyes, I began to wonder whether the traditional separation between undergraduate classrooms and "the profession," often justified by the assumption that undergraduates wouldn't be interested in our scholarly practices, might be a gesture of self-protection designed to keep students from seeing certain conservative, ambitious, elitist, duplicitous, or insecure sides of us.

This same protective agenda may lie beneath a number of standard arguments against teaching theory to undergraduates. I do not deny that theory and its languages are often difficult, but I wonder whether such an argument deflects from and mystifies more disturbing anxieties. As Lucy Bailey insisted, "None of the theory (even poststructuralism) was too dense to be digested in reasonable amounts." And although most of my theory students have been junior and senior English majors, often honors majors, I know faculty members who have successfully taught literary theory (e.g., by way of Eagleton's *Literary Theory: An Introduction* or Belsey's *Critical Practice*) to the captive audience of a required course. I must agree with William Schroeder, who writes that we "cheat and patronize" our students when we claim they cannot "handle" theory or won't be interested (32). As Victoria Andros told me wryly, theory ought to be particularly welcomed by undergraduates, who "are supposed to be experimenting and finding themselves."

I want, then, to locate a major source of theory's trials in a rationalized resistance to it in the teaching of English in America and to suggest that what may be at stake finally is Humpty-Dumpty's question: Who is to be master? That's all. Our reluctance to teach theory to undergraduates, in other words, may be deeply connected not only to an antitheoretical impulse in American (undergraduate) education generally but also to issues of authority in the undergraduate English classroom and its curriculum. While many of my students hail theory's transformations of their work in other courses, a good number also recount theory's trials in classes to which they now bring different understandings of literature and where they now find themselves resented and estranged. At first their difficulties surprised me, since I considered my department a fairly progressive one, but my students, after all, were learning to read gaps and absences, to stand outside rather than within textually or professorially inscribed reader positions, to question and critique the curriculum—including my own—in ways that I cannot be sure I myself would have welcomed had I not instigated them myself. Indeed, it was painful and a little embarrassing to hear my students identify tendencies within my own classroom practice that were at odds with the theory I'd professed; for example, they believed my course was too focused on literature in its most narrow definition. Clearly, however appealing Freire's call may be in spirit, the pressures of profession and institution, with their more and less subtle forms of surveillance, tend to influence even professors who espouse radical ideas, making us surprisingly invested, as Hooks has argued, in an education not for freedom but for dominance (101).

Theory in the hands of undergraduates, then, may well put the English classroom itself on trial, exposing a conservative agenda beneath the apparently liberal, open-ended, and participatory interpretive pluralism that some students may consider refreshing or comforting when they compare our discipline with other disciplines more obviously devoted to "banking" education. But students exposed to literary theory may press against the limits of that same classroom and find it more ideologically restrictive than they had thought: they learn Terry Eagleton's message that criticism is largely a matter of manipulating a certain discourse, that what one says within that discourse doesn't seem to cause much disturbance, because so many things cannot be said in it (201). Knowledge of theory thus redistributes pedagogical power, on the one hand authorizing the situationally powerless, on the other hand calling the situationally powerful to account. This power could enable undergraduates to shake the foundations of English studies in places where professors, already trained in the ways of the discipline or vulnerable to academic sanctions, might not succeed. Students who study literary theory as undergraduates, lacking our commitment to a career or a discipline, may criticize the foundations of literary studies: Kathy Kizer, for example, decided that its literary language kept feminist criticism conservative and imagined a course that took feminist rather than literary theory as a starting point.

Most students in my undergraduate theory courses agree that if undergraduate education is going to prepare them to be world citizens, readers and shapers of culture, it must engage critical theory across the curriculum. Theory, as Mary Burke stressed, is thus even more important for "people who *don't* go on to graduate school" than for those who do. As for the English classroom, Jean Da Silva, from her double vantage point as graduate student and teaching assistant, concludes that "if we want to foster independent, critical thinking in our students, teaching theory would lessen the mystery of literature and make our students young collaborators." Certainly my students of theory have been among the most powerful influences on my thinking, my teaching, and my scholarship. Such transformations and self-transformations seem to me well worth the trials of teaching theory to undergraduates.

University of Maryland

Notes

[1] I am indebted for my research toward this essay to many students who have studied literary theory in my courses, especially to those in my undergraduate and graduate seminars at Georgetown University during the fall of 1988 who took the time to write down their ideas about teaching theory to undergraduates. Some of their names appear in this essay.

[2] For a brilliant discussion about both the need for a pedagogy consonant with postmodern theory and the teaching of theory in secondary schools—a discussion with profound value for college teaching as well—see Delia.

[3] Throughout this essay I cite individual written responses by my fall 1988 graduate and undergraduate students in feminist literary theory at Georgetown University.

Works Cited

Anzaldúa, Gloria. "Speaking in Tongues: A Letter to Third World Women Writers." *This Bridge Called My Back: Writings by Radical Women of Color*. Ed. Cherríe Moraga and Gloria Anzaldúa. Watertown: Persephone, 1981. 165–73.

Bakhtin, M. M. *The Dialogic Imagination*. Trans. Caryl Emerson and Michael Holquist. Austin: U of Texas P, 1981.

Belsey, Catherine. *Critical Practice*. London: Methuen, 1980.

Christian, Barbara. "The Race for Theory." *Cultural Critique* 6 (Spring 1987): 51–64.

Delia, Mary Alice. "Killer English: Postmodern Theory and the High School Classroom." Diss. University of Maryland, 1991.

Eagleton, Terry. *Literary Theory: An Introduction*. Minneapolis: U of Minnesota P, 1983.

Freire, Paulo. *Pedagogy of the Oppressed*. Trans. Myra Bergman Ramos. New York: Continuum, 1970.

Gardiner, Judith Kegan, Elly Bulkin, Rena Grasso Patterson, and Annette Kolodny. "An Interchange on Feminist Criticism: On 'Dancing through the Minefield.'" *Feminist Studies* 8 (Fall 1982): 629–75.

Hooks, Bell. *Talking Back: Thinking Feminist, Thinking Black*. Boston: South End, 1989.

Kolodny, Annette. "Dancing through the Minefield: Some Observations on the Theory, Practice, and Politics of a Feminist Literary Criticism." *Feminist Studies* 6 (Spring 1980): 1–25.

Kristeva, Julia. *Revolution in Poetic Language*. Trans. Margaret Waller. New York: Columbia UP, 1984.

Kuhn, S. Thomas. *The Structure of Scientific Revolutions*. Chicago: U of Chicago P, 1970.

Lanser, Susan S. "Feminist Criticism, *The Yellow Wallpaper*, and the Politics of Color in America." *Feminist Studies* 15 (Fall 1989): 415–42.

———. "Feminist Literary Criticism: How Feminist? How Literary? How Critical?" *NWSA* [Natl. Women's Study Assn.] *Journal* 3 (Winter 1991): 3–19.

Lorde, Audre. "Poetry Is Not a Luxury." *Sister/Outsider*. Freedom: Crossing, 1984. 36–39.

Schroeder, William R. "A Teachable Theory of Interpretation." *Theory in the Classroom*. Ed. Cary Nelson. Urbana: U of Illinois P, 1986. 9–44.

Shor, Ira. *Critical Teaching and Everyday Life*. Boston: South End, 1980.

Shaull, Richard. Foreword. Freire 9–15.

Spivak, Gayatri Chakravorty. "French Feminism in an International Frame." *In Other Worlds: Essays in Cultural Politics*. London: Routledge, 1988. 134–53.

Walker, Alice. *In Search of Our Mothers' Gardens: Womanist Prose*. New York: Harcourt, 1973.

Weedon, Chris. *Feminist Practice and Poststructuralist Theory*. London: Blackwell, 1987.

Everything You Always Wanted to Know about English: Critical Theory in the Multipurpose Course

Lynette Felber

While the profession is busily defending its emphasis on cultural diversity and parrying attacks on deconstruction, feminism, and other recent critical approaches, many of our beginning English majors remain oblivious to the conflict. They often echo the questions their predecessors asked their own professors, the New Critics, fifty years ago: "What did the author intend this story to mean?" and "How can I find the hidden meanings in the work?" Those students who have been exposed to current controversies are often confused: "Where can I get a copy of *The Canon*?" I am sometimes asked. Designed to initiate English majors into major critical issues, approaches, and resources, Practical Criticism is a required sophomore-level course at New Mexico State University. We cover critical theory from Aristotle to the present, research methodology (using the library, MLA documentation, and bibliography), and, according to the catalog description, emphasize writing about literature—all in fifteen weeks. The course is one of two required skills classes for the major; the other is expository writing. This catchall might be titled, from the students' point of view, Everything You Always Wanted (and Didn't Want) to Know about English. Teaching critical theory to undergraduates is a challenge because the material is difficult for the uninitiated—or the uninterested. The additional challenge for the instructor in a multipurpose course such as the one I teach is to organize such a hodgepodge and to move students from understanding various critical approaches to writing their own theoretically sophisticated literary criticism.

When I ask students to fill out information cards on the first day of class and to tell me what they expect to learn in the course, I usually receive two basic responses. About half of the students write, "I don't know what to expect"; the other half write, "To improve my writing" or "To improve my grades in English classes." Given the course title, Practical Criticism, I am not surprised at the confusion. The title evokes different associations for professor and students. To me it suggests I. A. Richards and F. R. Leavis, protocols and close reading, a focus on the New Critics; students assume that they will finally be initiated into the "practical" skills that will improve their grades in literature. A broadly conceived introduction to English studies, this course was instituted as a requirement for our majors in the spring of 1987, at which time department faculty members recognized the need to introduce students to the theory that was informing their own research and teaching of literature and to prepare majors bound for graduate programs. We hoped that such a course would help students in our advanced literature courses conceptualize an approach for a long, thoroughly researched paper and would identify appropriate critical problems for discussion in all their essays. With hindsight, the class seems overambitious. It was proposed on the heels of curriculum reform to deemphasize period courses and attract more majors—which we have been extraordinarily successful at doing. At the time, however, although we had several objectives in mind, we did not think we could require *two* classes addressing those objectives.

As it has been taught since 1987, the course is both a content course in criticism and a skills class in research and writing, although some faculty members have emphasized writing about criticism, others writing about literature. My goal is to teach students "how to do things with texts." In an attempt to impose order on this diverse array of materials, I divide the course into two unequal parts. The first part, which occupies one third of the semester (five weeks), I describe on the syllabus as Text-Reader-Writer: Issues and Assumptions in Literary Criticism and Research. We begin with an exploration of some basic questions: What is literature? What is criticism? This discussion of issues in canon and criticism will move us from the assumptions behind the course to reading classic texts in literary criticism such as Aristotle's *Poetics*, Pierre Corneille's "Of the Three Unities of Action, Time and Place," and Charles-Augustin Sainte-Beuve's "What Is a Classic?" During this period we also complete our research unit, visiting the library, studying MLA documentation, and compiling an annotated bibliography; in addition, we read and discuss our first core text, Shakespeare's *The Taming of the Shrew*.

The second part of the course is entitled Contemporary Literary Criticism. During these last ten weeks, we spend an average of one and one-half weeks on each of six critical approaches: formalism, psychoanalysis, reader response, feminism, deconstruction, and new historicism. Each unit begins with an introductory lecture in which I present the major critical assumptions and methodology of the given approach. To link the contemporary portion of the course with the earlier one on assumptions and classical criticism, I define each approach with reference to its conception of text-reader-writer, which I dub the holy trinity; students find that this construct provides a means to compare the various approaches. We read essays that define and exemplify each mode of thought; then, on the last day of each unit, a group of students gives an oral presentation in which they interpret a short literary text using the approach we've been studying. Although this organization seems relatively complex, on the class evaluations at the end of the semester students generally comment favorably on the integration of materials. Miraculously, by the end of the semester students can approach literature from different critical perspectives, and most are excited about having acquired this skill.

Some problems we encounter along the way, however, are students' resistance, the difficulty of theoretical readings, the sheer amount of work to be completed, and students' lack of confidence in their ability to approach literature theoretically. Overcoming students' resistance is the major challenge, as is typical in a required course. Because some students resent being required to take such a class—especially those who would rather take creative writing, contemporary literature, or even a "useful" writing course—I work especially hard in Practical Criticism to be intellectually and personally engaging. (Any conscientious instructor will, of course, try to be a good host in class, but there's a difference between teaching criticism and conducting an elective Dickens seminar where the readings sell the class. I make a special effort to project an animated and witty persona.) Every period is divided into two or more activities (lecture, discussion, group work) so that the pace is always lively and brisk. One student resentfully told me, "I'm afraid to skip because you make sure something happens in every class, and everything is connected."

From the first day of class I encourage students to challenge me, one another, and especially the critics we are reading. At the beginning of the unit on contemporary critical theory, I give an overview of the approaches we will cover. This introduction establishes a context for the evolution of theory and helps me exploit students' expectations—that formalists are rigid and restrictive, that reader-response criticism is easy and untheoretical (a potential free-for-all), and that deconstruction is delightfully irreverent. These expectations are nevertheless refined and generally rejected throughout the rest of the semester. Students find that reader response can be more complex than "whatever I think." When we study formalism, students feel superior and scoff at formalists' petty taboos and fallacies, but when we get to deconstruction, they find themselves reacting as formalists. They often panic and ask, "What's the point of destroying a coherent, unified interpretation?" or "If the text dismantles itself, what's the point of reading it? What's the point of criticism?" Throughout the semester my primary goal is to engage students as critics and in this way break down their resistance.

One of my students' main complaints about this course is that the readings are hard, boring, and dry. After all, they became English majors because they like to read fiction and poetry, texts that entertain, at least to some degree. Theory is by nature abstract, and students aren't familiar with the texts Aristotle or Corneille use as concrete examples and illustrations

to support their generalizations. Although "Apology for Poetry" is enlivened by humor, most students don't really appreciate Sir Philip Sidney's
simultaneous self-glorification and tongue-in-cheek self-deprecation. Early
critics elicit the most complaints about "dryness," but contemporaries are
not immune to the charge. (One morning students greeted me with a
chorus of "Jauss is boring" [that's Hans Robert Jauss] as I walked into
my 8:30 class. The same student who led the chorus raised his hand to
demand, near the end of the semester, if there were a Cliff's Notes on
contemporary criticism.)

My solution to this problem is to try to find the most accessible readings possible. Our major text is Robert Con Davis and Laurie Finke's
Literary Criticism and Theory. For further examples of contemporary
critical approaches, we read the essays in Ross Murfin's *Heart of Darkness:
A Case Study in Contemporary Criticism*. We use Joseph Gibaldi and
Walter Achtert's *MLA Handbook for Writers of Research Papers* for the
bibliography component of the class. Two core literary texts, *The Taming
of the Shrew* and *Heart of Darkness*, provide exemplars for our discussions of theory and are the basis of the first writing assignment. Even
with a number of textbooks, I need additional short literary works (poems
and short stories), so I use reserve readings as well.

My strategy for the first week of class is to introduce students to
criticism and to convince them—before we get to Aristotle—that it need
not be boring. The first essay I assign is Susan Leonardi's "Recipes for
Reading: Summer Pasta, Lobster à la Riseholme, and Key Lime Pie," a
clever, chatty, and unusual essay that uses *The Joy of Cooking*, E. F.
Benson's *Mapp and Lucia*, and Nora Ephron's *Heartburn* to discuss the
recipe as a feminine genre that elicits certain kinds of response from
readers. Although female students are often more receptive to this essay
than males are, it demonstrates to all students that criticism can take as
its object texts as diverse as cookbooks and comic novels. Although Leonardi's subject is not traditional, her essay admirably exemplifies conventions of literary criticism, and in our discussion of this essay we talk
about her organization and strategy as a critic. Moreover, the critical
stance of this essay anticipates two contemporary approaches we will
study in the second part of the class: feminism and reader-response criticism. With this essay, I hope to shock students and broaden their expectations about what constitutes literary criticism. Following this assignment, students often bring me gifts of food (like homemade chutney relish)
or share recipes and old cookbooks; the essay thus also functions as an
icebreaker, creating rapport at the beginning of a course previously perceived as dry and difficult.

I am careful to include readings that introduce concepts students are
sure to encounter in future literature classes. Since Practical Criticism
covers readings from Aristotle to the present, I must be selective; the course
provides an overview rather than a survey of criticism. Aristotle's *Poetics*

introduces the concept of mimesis; his dramatic criticism and Corneille's discussion of the unities provide principles students will encounter in Shakespeare and other dramatic texts. We read Longinus and Edmund Burke on the sublime, crucial to studying the Romantic period. I choose classical texts that have obvious links with our readings in the contemporary portion of the class. When we study reader-response criticism, for example, I point back to Aristotle's concept of catharsis as a type of reader response. The first segment of the course establishes the background and skills for the second half, in which I introduce students to contemporary criticism and they begin to apply research skills.

Another major challenge I face in this multipurpose course is to motivate students to complete a great deal of reading and writing, along with some research. Our students are hardworking and highly motivated, but typically, in addition to carrying a full load of classes, they hold part- or even full-time jobs, and many are parents (often single). The first semester I taught Practical Criticism, I discovered a group of students gathered in the hallway after my introductory class, griping about the five-page syllabus. In subsequent semesters I lightened the reading load somewhat, but the most important change I made was to divide the syllabus into two parts (Readings; Course Procedures and Policies), which I then distributed at different points in the first session. At the same time, I must ensure that students get sufficient practice in articulating for themselves the discourses we are studying. Comprehensive testing on all the assignments would take valuable class time and would result in a mass exodus moments after I distribute the syllabus on the first day of class. My major strategy for simultaneously testing students and developing writing skills is the periodic assignment of a one-page response to a well-defined question about the readings. In another kind of short-response assignment, I ask students to read an excerpt from a recently published critical essay, identify the approach, and analyze its critical assumptions and methodology. During the semester I usually assign fifteen responses; since these are informal assignments, I do not expect students to submit their most polished writing (although some do), and I comment sparingly, if at all. Although these assignments are not popular with the weaker students, most of the others prepare their responses carefully, leading to discussions that are detailed and probing.

When I construct the three formal graded assignments, I try to integrate several objectives into each. For the research component of the class, students complete a select annotated bibliography on some narrow topic; I ask for only ten various sources of certain required kinds (e.g., journal articles, book-length studies, a biography). The models I provide as examples, however, include *substantial* annotations; in this way students are introduced to detailed modes of research and documentation. Furthermore, the bibliography functions as a major writing assignment, since the annotations turn out to be minireviews of the sources. My strategy for their first formal essay is also multipurpose. I ask students to find a critical essay on one of our core texts, *The Taming of the Shrew* or *Heart of Darkness*, and to refute at least part of the critic's argument. The purpose of the assignment is to give them practice locating criticism in the library (students are never content with the first essay they find), evaluating an argument, using the MLA's parenthetical documentation to cite the critic and the major text, and compiling a Works Cited page, however brief. Most important, students must construct an argument in response to a critic, thus learning a basic discourse of literary criticism, what Olivia Frey, borrowing from Janice Moulton, has recently (and disparagingly) termed the "adversarial method" (510). While I agree with Frey's critique and discuss it when I assign this paper, I still feel it is necessary to prepare students to argue in this major discourse of the profession.

Perhaps the greatest challenge in teaching such a course is to develop students' confidence in their ability to formulate critical responses to texts; internalizing the new vocabulary and approaches, however, takes some time and practice. Even when students demonstrate in writing that they understand an approach, some remain timid about exploring these ideas orally in class. My principal solution to this problem is collaborative learning, a technique drawn from composition classes. Throughout the semester I use student peer groups to facilitate sophisticated critical responses. Collaboration encourages students to explore their ideas in a small, supportive community and has the advantage of producing more sophistication in their readings than any student might achieve alone. As Kenneth Bruffee writes in characterizing the advantages of collaboration, "Pooling the resources that a group of peers brings with them to the task may make accessible the normal discourse of the new community they together hope to enter" (644). Feeling the safety of numbers, students in groups are willing to advance arguments that they would hesitate to articulate individually.

I introduce collaborative work early in the semester, and we move from the completion of group activities to true collaborative learning—from working together on a task with a correct answer to what Harvey Wiener has described as "a task that demands consensual learning" (55). Since our freshman composition classes use collaborative techniques extensively and effectively, most students are already familiar with them. I can therefore spend more time on defining tasks than on training students to work cooperatively. During our research unit, for example, I ask students to work in groups of three to compile a short bibliography in class. After I have briefly introduced bibliography form and students have read the relevant sections in the *MLA Handbook*, I bring to class ten "artifacts": journals, microfilm, anthologies, even a program from the MLA convention. To each I affix an adhesive note, telling students what part of the source to document (e.g., a story in an anthology); students find the model for citing these various sources in their handbook and write a bibliographic entry for each. My role in this project is to serve as a resource, answering questions about sources and the handbook: "Why did you give us two journal articles?" (one uses continuous, the other separate pagination); "Is this thing [Gertrude Stein's *Three Lives*] an anthology or a novel?" (good question). Although it takes more time for students to work collaboratively on this assignment than it would if they worked individually, the advantage is that they learn more in negotiating with one another the correct entries; there is less guessing about proper form. At the end of class we transcribe the Works Cited page onto the blackboard, the references in alphabetical order, and discuss any discrepancies between the various groups' entries. This project is, I realize, merely a group endeavor in problem solving, but it prepares students for increasingly challenging collaborative work later in the term.

I use collaboration most extensively in our study of contemporary criticism. During our unit on reader-response theory, I use an overhead projector to reveal a poem—Sylvia Plath's "The Arrival of the Bee Box," a sort of riddle poem—stanza by stanza, without giving its title. Students write down their individual responses until we reach a point when I feel they should begin to form an interpretation. At that point we share our reactions. This exercise illustrates the individuality of response as well as Hans Robert Jauss's "horizon of expectation" and Stanley Fish's "interpretive community," concepts we've covered in lecture and in the readings. Individually, students surmise that the box is a coffin, a television, a wood box. Collectively, because as a class we've all recently completed *Heart of Darkness*, the line "With the swarmy feeling of African hands" (line 13) makes us think of Conrad's depiction of Africans, and many students speculate that the box is filled with slaves.

In a truer kind of collaboration, students work in groups to construct an interpretation of a literary text. The groups present their interpretation during the last class of each contemporary criticism unit, using whatever approach (e.g., feminism, psychoanalysis) we have just studied. I choose the texts myself, to ensure the approach will work: the formalist group prepares a reading of two Donne poems, another group presents a psychoanalytic reading of Kafka's "The Judgment," another gives a feminist reading of Plath's "Daddy," and so forth. Students are required to meet outside class to discuss their text and devise the interpretation. In this way, we do not use up valuable class time, and I am not tempted to "suggest" a reading to the group. The public nature of the presentation encourages them to do their best work, and I ask the class to comment on and critique each group's presentation: What principles of formalist, feminist, or reader-response criticism did the group illustrate? What other readings might we devise using the same approach? Although I have tried to ensure students' success in matching texts with approaches, there is no correct reading. From a psychoanalytical perspective, for example, "The Judgment" may just as well yield an illustration of the Jungian shadow in Georg's relationship with his mysterious friend in Russia as it may an

Oedipal reading of the father-son relationship—or any other of a multitude of readings. Students who would be individually unwilling to utter the word *phallus* and who are horrified when we read an excerpt from Marie Bonaparte's *The Life and Works of Edgar Allan Poe: A Psycho-analytic Interpretation* are delighted to tell the class about their collective discovery of the various phallic symbols associated with Georg Bendemann's father in "The Judgment." By this point in the semester, students are truly collaborating; they can now "reach consensus by their own authority . . . distinguish[ing] collaborative learning from mere work in groups" (Wiener 54).

By this time I am reassured that the course can work. When I first designed this assignment, I feared that students, even collaboratively, would not be able to produce any kind of coherent reading of a text, but almost every student succeeds. Moreover, students are often surprisingly creative. One group not only offered a viable feminist reading of Plath's "Daddy" but also dramatized their presentation as a dialogue: One (male) student posed as a "phallic critic" (as defined by Mary Ellmann), attacking Plath for her petty feminine imagery and mad housewife persona while a second (female) student defended Plath. A third group member analyzed her colleagues' feminist and antifeminist assumptions and articulated their group interpretation of the poem. The rest of the class was initially shocked and then delighted with this seemingly impromptu performance. One male student dared to agree with the phallic critic and engaged the class in further debate.

The final assignment in the course—the compilation of critical editions that imitate one of our textbooks, Murfin's *Heart of Darkness* casebook—exploits collaborative techniques and students' mastery of various critical approaches. I distribute a list of literary texts that I feel are open to multiple critical approaches and ask each group to pick one. Although the list varies from semester to semester, it always includes short texts from various genres such as Samuel Beckett's *Krapp's Last Tape*, Christina Rossetti's "Goblin Market," Alexander Pope's *The Rape of the Lock*, William Faulkner's "A Rose for Emily," and Nathaniel Hawthorne's "The Birthmark." Within the groups, I require that each student produce an essay which approaches the text using a critical perspective different from those of his cohorts. I give students one full class period to organize their group, and I provide contact time in subsequent classes if necessary, but they must also meet outside of class. While I supply an agenda for the in-class meeting (among other tasks, they must produce a written proposal), I do not intervene in groups except to answer questions about the assignment. Students have learned to trust their understanding of critical approaches and to use their colleagues as sounding boards, so they rarely turn to me for guidance or suggestions. Each student writes an individual essay, but by working together they challenge one another's readings of the text, and as a group they experience the diversity and complementarity of various approaches to one text.

The editions they produce testify to the success of collaborative efforts and demonstrate that they have mastered—albeit at an introductory level— various approaches. On the last day of class, each group presents its edition and describes the content of individual essays and the relations between the various approaches of their shared text. The enthusiasm in the air that day reassures me that critical theory can be taught effectively at the sophomore level and that students' initial reservations about the study of criticism can be overcome. I am often astounded at the originality and persuasiveness of their readings. One student, for example, wrote a reader-response essay on "A Rose for Emily" in which she found evidence that Emily's cousins killed Homer Barron, eliciting gasps from the class as we followed her detective work. Another such moment occurred when a student presented her feminist reading of *The Metamorphosis*, demonstrating that Grete, a seemingly minor character, triumphs over her brother Gregor's incestuous desire to stifle her and control the entire family.

These critical feats are all the more impressive as I recall the first day of class, when many students discovered that there was such a thing as literary criticism, when many students had yet to learn how to articulate any sort of argument about a text. Although this assignment is due during the last, busy week of the semester, students go out of their way to produce visually stunning editions, handsomely bound, illustrated with their own original artwork, printed in attractive computer fonts. Students often comment favorably on the critical editions in their course evaluations, claiming that they came away from the class with something tangible. As in composition classes, "publication" is an incentive to producing high-quality writing.

In Practical Criticism I work very hard to overcome undergraduates' reservations about a required skills and theory course by fostering excitement about the material and a sense of community within the class. Frankly, now that our enrollments are swelling, I would like to see my department reform the curriculum so that this course would have fewer objectives and would be able to meet them more fully. I have therefore proposed adapting our current required expository writing class to create a special section for English majors. This class would incorporate the research and intensive-writing components of Practical Criticism into a course in writing about literature; the companion course would then be revised to cover "only" critical theory from Aristotle to the present. Despite my reservations about a theory class that is a department catchall—as I suspect it is at many small and medium-size institutions like my own, critical theory having been added only recently to the curriculum—my experiences in teaching Practical Criticism have been positive. Students respond favorably to a well-organized course, even if the organization seems artificial to the instructor, who is painfully aware of what the course fails to cover. An informal workshop format and the use of collaborative techniques make the course particularly enjoyable for students, who often exclaim at the end of the semester, "I don't know why I dreaded this course!" Successful in their endeavor, students see themselves as initiates and feel a sense of authority as a result of their entrance into "a community of knowledgeable peers" (Bruffee 642). As one student wrote on his class evaluation, "Now I'm part of the intelligentsia."

(Since this essay was written, the English department at New Mexico State University has approved the curriculum reform I proposed. We now require two companion courses: one teaches research and writing about literature, the other is exclusively devoted to critical theory.)

New Mexico State University

Note

I would like to thank the editors, William E. Cain and Dianne Sadoff, as well as my colleagues Christopher Burnham and Reed Way Dasenbrock at New Mexico State University, for their intelligent readings and helpful suggestions regarding earlier drafts of this essay.

Works Cited

Aristotle. Selection from the *Poetics*. Trans. Jean T. Oesterle. Con Davis and Finke 60–83.

Bonaparte, Marie. Selection from *The Life and Works of Edgar Allan Poe: A Psycho-analytic Interpretation*. Trans. John Rodker. *The Purloined Poe: Lacan, Derrida, and Psychoanalytic Reading*. Ed. John P. Muller and William J. Richardson. Baltimore: Johns Hopkins UP, 1988. 101–32.

Bruffee, Kenneth. "Collaborative Learning and the 'Conversation of Mankind.'" *College English* 46 (1984): 635–52.

Burke, Edmund. Selection from *A Philosophical Enquiry into the Origin of Our Ideas of the Sublime and Beautiful*. Con Davis and Finke 370–81.

Con Davis, Robert, and Laurie Finke, eds. *Literary Criticism and Theory: The Greeks to the Present*. New York: Longman, 1989.

Corneille, Pierre. Selection from "Of the Three Unities of Action, Time, and Place." Trans. Donald Schier. Con Davis and Finke 239–49.

Ellmann, Mary. "Phallic Criticism." Ch. 2 of *Thinking about Women*. Con Davis and Finke 678–90.

Fish, Stanley E. "Interpreting the *Variorum*." Con Davis and Finke 757–74.

Frey, Olivia. "Beyond Literary Darwinism: Women's Voices and Critical Discourse." *College English* 52 (1990): 507–26.

Gibaldi, Joseph, and Walter S. Achtert. *MLA Handbook for Writers of Research Papers*. 3rd ed. New York: MLA, 1988.

Jauss, Hans Robert. Selection from *Literary History as a Challenge to Literary Theory*. Trans. Timothy Bahti. Richter 1198–218.

Leonardi, Susan J. "Recipes for Reading: Summer Pasta, Lobster à la Riseholme, and Key Lime Pie." *PMLA* 104 (1989): 340–47.

Longinus. Selection from *On the Sublime*. Trans. A. O. Prickard. Con Davis and Finke 104–14.

Murfin, Ross, ed. *Joseph Conrad's* Heart of Darkness: *A Case Study in Contemporary Criticism*. New York: St. Martin's, 1989.

Plath, Sylvia. "The Arrival of the Bee Box." *Ariel*. 1961. New York: Harper, 1965. 59–60.

Richter, David, ed. *The Critical Tradition: Classic Texts and Contemporary Trends*. New York: St. Martin's, 1989.

Sainte-Beuve, Charles-Augustin. "What Is a Classic?" Trans. A. J. Butler. Richter 1292–99.

Sidney, Philip. "Apology for Poetry." Con Davis and Finke 198–228.

Wiener, Harvey. "Collaborative Learning in the Classroom: A Guide to Evaluation." *College English* 48 (1986): 52–61.

Doxography versus Inquiry:
Two Ways of Teaching Theory

Donald G. Marshall

Open an anthology of contemporary critical theory or one of the surveys intended for use as a textbook and you will likely find that the contents are sorted into a series of pigeonholes. The list differs a bit from book to book, but most of the rubrics are familiar: formalism, structuralism, poststructuralism and deconstruction, Marxism, feminism, new historicism, psychoanalysis, African American criticism. Several recently published series of volumes provide anthologies of essays, reprinted or specially commissioned, to illustrate various approaches to a single prominent work.[1] Because market viability depends on their meshing with ordinary pedagogic practices, textbooks testify to the workaday opinions and working practices of academics. This *doxa* deserves to be drawn into the orbit of a reflective self-consciousness about how theory should be taught.

It is only reasonable to begin by acknowledging that both teachers and students find it useful and attractive to deploy a taxonomy of theoretical schools or approaches—a method of organizing the field that the history of philosophy terms *doxography*. Such a method provides an obvious way to structure a syllabus so that it appears comprehensive or at least selectively representative of the actual variety of current work in theory. Teachers have a manageable, definable task: to bring out the central doctrines of each school, to find readings that clearly exemplify them, and to show how they have been or might be applied to literary works. Essays and examination topics will follow the same lines, leading to a well-integrated course. Students have something definite to study, and their mastery can be fairly measured and graded. They are gratified to find that they have learned to use the technical language of theory knowledgeably and that they can name and defend the approach they prefer and apply it consciously in their own analyses of literary works.

Moreover, there are intellectual justifications for the doxographic approach that go beyond the merely practical. It is true that in literary theory, as in all our experience, taxonomies simplify and set up artificially sharp borders. But that is exactly what taxonomies are supposed to do. Without some scheme of abstracted differentia, we would be baffled and rendered mute by the "buzzing, booming confusion" of phenomena, to borrow William James's apt phrase. Undoubtedly, taxonomies can generate intellectual pseudophenomena, such as questions on whether a particular work "truly" fits this or that category or efforts to define "transitional" or "mixed" cases, whose ambiguous status is simply an artifact of the taxonomy. But no methodological procedure is guilty of the abuses its foolish application will produce.

While structuring a theory course as an array of schools thus seems commonsensical, doing so distorts students' understanding of the role theory ought to play in the study of literature and indeed distorts their understanding of theory itself. The harm becomes apparent if we ask what kind of reading this approach nurtures in students. They learn to look for explicit general propositions that can be extracted and articulated into a system. What students draw in this way from a single essay or excerpt they will generalize further by treating it as exemplary of a school. Whether the basic tenets of the school are presented to them before or after they examine a particular reading, they will be orientated toward seeing what illustrates the school rather than what may be specific to the reading. To ensure success in the enterprise, teachers tend to choose readings that clearly and unambiguously exemplify the given school. Consequently, once the school is defined by some process of inductive generalization that is legitimate in itself, that generalization is applied retroactively to suppress any evidence that might undo it. Since writings by serious theorists are traversed by multiple and complex lines of thought, teachers are strongly tempted to make things easier for students by assigning not actual theorists but textbook summaries, even when the teacher recognizes that such summaries are simplified and crude.[2] A student ends up "learning" deconstruction without actually reading any more of Derrida than a few phrases and quotations in a summary. Typically, when taught in this fashion, each school's main ideas will appear to have been formulated by a few founding figures; work by other members of the school will be positioned in relation to the founders under rubrics like elaboration and variation that shade off into marginal, distorted, revisionist, or "eclectic" versions. In short, one is inevitably drawn into identifying canonical texts and formulating an orthodoxy. The reading style is dogmatic—and I use the term in its strict sense, including its pejorative connotations.

The risk is serious that a doxographic course will break apart into a string of noncommunicating monads. The risk is not much alleviated by the obvious ways of staging relations between the schools presented. Setting different systems into polemic opposition, for example, requires the postulation of common issues or problems as the point of contact, and teachers will be tempted to add drama by letting a later school trump an earlier. The obvious danger is that a system will be forced to address questions it didn't pose and to answer in terms set by another line of thought. Teachers may also be tempted to arrange schools in an evolutionary or genealogical scheme. The kind of history that results will almost certainly be too neatly logical, as though the unresolved problems in one theory cause a better or deeper theory to emerge. Moreover, the level of abstraction at which this kind of exercise is conducted invites supporting or criticizing general views in literary theory on the basis of equally general views from other fields, particularly philosophy and politics. For example, formalism may be criticized because it allegedly aestheticizes literature and severs it from political and economic realities. A student would need unusual independence of mind to break through these abstractions and ask, for instance, Are all or only some literary works "political" and in what sense? Instead of concretizing and testing generalities from their own discipline, teachers and students of literature may thus prematurely link them to generalities from other fields without being well versed in the concrete details of those fields. Once inquiry is set in motion toward abstract and general systems, inertia will tend to carry the mind farther in the same direction. If the teacher guards against triumphalist endorsement of a single school, students may be left with an unresolved pluralism. They may suppose that literary study provides no internal grounds for choosing among critical schools or principles and that such choice merely expresses temperamental inclinations or metaphysical, political, or other external convictions.

It remains necessary for the teacher and student to find the way back from their doxographic excursions to commentary on particular works of literature. Ordinarily, the teacher chooses some highly problematic work, to which students must apply various theoretical approaches. The terms reveal the dominance of an unexamined scientific model, where theory is applied to regulate practice, conceived as the methodical construction of an object that belongs to a preconceived project.[3] But unlike science, here theory dominates the object, which has no power to reject an approach as irrelevant or distorting. Each approach is seen as valid within its own terms. One can show its limitations only by setting it against alternative theories. The acknowledged one-sidedness of each approach is repaired simply by a process of mutual supplementation. The realm of practice is thus reconceived as the field of theory's application, not as its ground and touchstone. One takes up or sets aside various theories at will, and the possibility of achieving new insights or "results" depends on the elaboration of the theoretical instrument, on a mixing of existing approaches, or on the invention of a new theory, rather than on any attentiveness to the literary work itself.

The resulting reconception of practice has been a major source of tension in the profession. The doxographic approach almost inevitably leads to a denigration of critics who, however learned, intelligent, or sophisticated they may be, neither state nor defend explicitly the theoretical perspectives that inform their criticism. When teachers and students "problematize" or "bring into question" a critic's unstated presupposition, their analysis takes on an air of triumph, even when the presupposition has merely been formulated and in no way shown to be illegitimate or unreasonable. Critics who express irritation at such a proceeding may be told that every practitioner must inevitably have a "theory." This claim will not bear much scrutiny.[4] Those who make it actually have something different in mind—namely, that the critic thus challenged must adopt one of the already worked-out theories, preferably that of the theorist who asserts the claim.

In professional and curricular terms, the outcome is that theory becomes one more specialty among others, but one with a peculiar power to force the diversity of practice into channels defined doxographically.[5] Every research university wants to have a theorist—even, if the budget allows, a theorist of each defined school. The university adds a required course in theory to the curriculum, providing students with the grid through which they are to understand the rest of their literary studies. Having made a theoretical commitment, they may concentrate on the literary works that let them deploy it most fully. Other works will be fitted to a procrustean bed, and in extreme cases the very notion that one may be distorting a work will be warded off with the claim that all facts are theory-laden and one theory is as valid as another.

In what I have said so far, I make no pretense of neutral or dispassionate description. The doxographic approach to teaching theory seems to me a fundamental mistake. I believe my view is consistent with that of Paul de Man, who speaks of theory as itself the resistance to theory—meaning, I take it, resistance to the doxographic reduction of theory and to the scientific model of its application. But I do not wish to be merely negative. I will try to sketch an alternative, fully conceding that what I want to propose is elusive and difficult for teachers and students alike. I only hope that its difficulties are of a practical rather than theoretical kind.

The place to begin, I believe, is with Aristotle's insight that philosophy starts from wonder. In literary study, as we read works of literature, we must ask what we wonder about that instigates critical thinking. In literary theory, we must ask what we wonder about in critical thinking that instigates the reflective turn to which theory must remain faithful. In almost any curriculum, this moment is somewhat artificially induced. The fatal weakness of schooling, as Rousseau noted (57), is the impulse to hurry things along, to tell the students what they should be wondering about instead of waiting until experience impels their inquiry. Nevertheless, we must keep in sight what that instigating moment is like. Doing so requires that we pass beyond the foreseeable benefits at which our practical projects aim. For instance, students can't expect to be given a set of tools or notions that will guarantee success in their other literature courses. Fidelity to the instigating moment of wonder demands susceptibility to what we call

intellectual interest. And, above all, it requires the assumption of an intellectual responsibility. However vague or idealistic the prescription may
sound, teachers must exert whatever capacity they can muster to attract
students to their own vocation as intellectuals—namely, to be thinkers
who know their own minds. Without this reflective vocation and commitment, all that can be achieved is the most superficial form of thinking.

Fortunately, most students bring a great deal of trust and goodwill
to meeting a teacher's assignment. Moreover, the capacity to observe and
appreciate this vocation in others is far more widespread than the capacity
to assume it oneself. Many students are considering a career as teachers.
For these and other reasons, students can welcome the opportunity to
see what such a vocation would involve before choosing to commit themselves to it. They will be asked to become, in a sense, anthropologists
or ethnographers, observing what actual critics say and making themselves into the reflective self-consciousness of those critics. It is not the
function of such a reflective self-consciousness to regulate or supersede
the thinking on which it reflects. Its task is to locate the instigating questions or moments of wonder to which particular critics respond and to
discern what is at stake for those critics in their responses. The experience
of working through a number of critics' texts in this way gives substance
to the basic questions of literary theory, which arise when particular critics
seek a mediation between their work and the social or institutional reality
of literary study.

Some examples may help clarify these general remarks. Cleanth
Brooks's "Irony as a Principle of Structure" is a well-known and frequently
reprinted specimen of New Criticism. In the course of class discussions
and a number of short written assignments, I work with students to identify some strategies of reading or analysis that can help them reflect on
what Brooks says explicitly. Following are examples of such strategies:

1. List the critic's key terms. Which terms does the critic define, and how?
   Are these definitions different from the ordinary meanings of the terms?
   What do the differences suggest about the author's way of thinking?
   Some terms may be defined implicitly—for instance, by the kinds of
   examples grouped under them. Try to make these definitions explicit.
   If some terms are left undefined, does that omission suggest anything
   about the critic's thinking?
2. What are the critic's main concerns? What problems or questions is
   the critic aware of posing, and how does he or she hope to answer
   them in the essay? Why are those particular problems important to
   the critic (the answer may be explicit or implicit)?
3. What is the critic's method? Is an explicit methodology laid out for
   answering the questions posed? What method is implicit in the actual
   answering of those questions? What moves does the critic make in arguing the answers?

4. How does the critic deal with specific literary works? What interpretive points are made, and what issues constitute the focus? What does the interpretation overlook? You must distinguish here between what you believe a critic could say if it were not irrelevant to a specific argument or topic and what you think the critic can't see because of his or her particular way of thinking. How does the critic's way of dealing with an actual example relate to the presuppositions, topics, and method of the essay?

Brooks's title leads a reader to ask about the relation between irony and structure. Brooks claims that *ironical* is our customary term for "the *obvious* warping of a statement by the context" (800). He goes on eventually to generalize this definition until irony is simply every "acknowledgement of the pressures of context" (805) on any statement. The question for the reflective reader is, What work is Brooks trying to accomplish by doing so? He repeatedly concedes that the term *irony* may not be quite the right one and that he himself overuses or even abuses it (801). But he insists that it points to something elusive but important in "poetry of every period and even in simple lyrical poetry" (805). That *irony* is evidently being used and extended metaphorically draws our attention to a whole series of metaphors in the essay: a kite's tail resists but also steadies its flight; in a bouquet, blossoms are merely juxtaposed, but in a blooming plant, the blossom is organically related to the plant's other parts (799); a poem is "like a little drama," with no wasted motion or superfluous parts (800); a poem is like an arch, in which the drag of gravity is converted into the thrust and counterthrust that "become the means of stability" (802); the properly loaded and balanced kite rises, balancing tension along the kite string against "the thrust of the wind" (807). It is clear enough that Brooks is treating *irony* "ironically" by defining it within the whole context of the essay. He is constantly aware of working *against* his reader's established views. This awareness is evident not only in his extending the meaning of *irony* but also in his series of examples. He presents as test cases Shakespeare's song "Who is Silvia?" (*Two Gentlemen of Verona* 4.2.40) and two of Wordsworth's "Lucy" poems. His conclusion in each case is highly qualified. In Shakespeare we "get something very close to irony" (802); in Wordsworth, perhaps we ought not to call "A slumber did my spirit seal" ironical: "I am trying to account for my temptation to call such a poem ironical—not to justify my yielding to the temptation—least of all to insist that others so transgress" (804).

We must ask, then, What is at stake in Brooks's essay? The answer radiates from our asking how we can "justify" particular lines in a poem and ultimately a whole poem (801). By following the clue of a series of oppositions, a reader gains a particular insight into the motive and the bounds of Brooks's project. These oppositions include meaning/theme; concrete/abstract; particular/universal; part/whole; imaginative insight/

abstract creed; participation in experience/belief; justification/proof, validated truth; indirect/direct statement; metaphor (contextual)/mathematical formula (contextless); connotation/denotation; rhetoric/philosophy. The logical register of this vocabulary is evident, even though Brooks's point is the inadequacy of these very terms. Brooks distinguishes what may serve to "validate" a statement in a poem from the methods of sociologists, physical scientists, metaphysicians (801); and from the belief that belongs to "abstract creed[s]" (806), whether religious or political (806). The poet must rehabilitate language "so that it can convey meanings once more with force and with exactitude" to "a public corrupted by Hollywood and the Book of the Month Club" (805). A reader intent on constructing the platform of New Criticism will gladly extract the concept of irony. But what is at stake for Brooks is more tellingly revealed in an apparent self-contradiction, for his postulated ideal is not irony but "invulnerability to irony," defined as "the stability of a context in which the internal pressures balance and mutually support each other" (802). What Brooks asks of a good poem and finds in it is "an insight, rooted in and growing out of concrete experience, many-sided, three-dimensional" (806).

What I am saying will hardly be new to those who have read and taught this essay many times over many years. My point is to illustrate the kind of reading students should be asked to do. Instead of following a reductive and dogmatic approach, a course in critical theory should be consistent with and nurture precisely the kind of attentive reading students are asked to bring to literary works. Instead of simply paying attention to explicit propositions and constructing a logical, systematic framework of doctrines, students should attend to a theorist's tone, hesitations, self-characterizations, metaphors, and rhetorical interactions with the reader. They should attempt to uncover the problems or experiences that puzzled and instigated the theorist's inquiry, to see how the theorist formulated his or her guiding questions, and to trace the movement of the theorist's mind along a given line of thought.

The same kind of reading can be brought to a variety of theorists and theoretical writings: to E. D. Hirsch's "Objective Interpretation," with its anxiety to lead criticism out of subjectivism and relativism and make it a corporate and progressive discipline; to Geoffrey Hartman's "Beyond Formalism," as it wrestles to come to terms with "history," not excluding the figure of revolution; to Paul de Man's "The Rhetoric of Temporality," as it rethinks irony in relation to subjectivity and hence to an experience of temporality that is authentic just insofar as it yields a radically negative instability; or to Marjorie Levinson's reading of Wordsworth's "Tintern Abbey," as it tries to demystify the poem's aesthetic strategies for suppressing its historical situation. The aim will be not to construct and contrast a series of systems but to put the readings into a dialogue with one another (a dialogue sometimes explicit in the readings themselves) at a specific level: the varying work got out of terms like *irony* and *history*;

the varying investments in stability and the consensual as opposed to the unstable and politically oppositional. But the inevitable tendency to consolidate schools should be resisted as often as possible (if not always successfully). All the critical readings I have named discuss at greater or lesser length some poems by Wordsworth, especially the "Lucy" poems. Students will be encouraged to see these not as "applications" of theories producing incommensurable results but as examples of how thoughtful critics take up their rich experience of literary works into a self-conscious engagement with the far-reaching issues that arise in the course of literary study. This kind of theory course aims to cultivate reflective thinking whose profit, such as it is, lies in clarifying experience, not mastering, still less reconstructing, it.

As I remarked earlier, a prudent teacher will not expect students to be comfortable with or grateful for such a course. If the application of theory means anything in this context, it means bringing home thinking to oneself—never a comfortable process. But the course will be successful insofar as it has kept students exposed to the risk of thinking and not sheltered them against it in a doxographic structure.[6]

University of Illinois, Chicago

Notes

[1] See the anthologies by Con Davis; Con Davis and Schleifer; Lambropoulos and Miller; Latimer; Lodge; and Richter. See the surveys by Atkins and Morrow; Birch; Eagleton; Jefferson and Robey; Natoli; and Selden. For illustrations of various approaches applied to texts, see the books edited by Staton and by Murfin (a volume in a series from St. Martin's Press).

[2] Eagleton's survey, for example, is often a core text in theory courses though it is plainly reductive and tendentious. Those characteristics would not render the book illegitimate if students read it as proposing theses they should test critically. But it is quite another matter when such a book stands as the sole source of information about the theories and theorists it surveys.

[3] Here I follow Gadamer, "What Is Practice? The Conditions of Social Reason" (69–87); see also his "Hermeneutics as Practical Philosophy" (88–112) and "Hermeneutics as a Theoretical and Practical Task" (113–38).

[4] Throughout his later work, Wittgenstein labors to free philosophy from the seductive notions, as old as Plato, that behind everything we say and do lie presuppositions and precommitments and that intellectual ethics obligate us to pull them together into a consistent scheme on which we must then act deliberately.

[5] In recent years, theory has become the lingua franca of the profession, which means not just that all academics find themselves more or less compelled to speak in its terms but that theory has become the substance of professional literary study as a social practice. I would argue that previously this role was played by a shared narrative of British and American literary history. The shortcomings of that narrative are doubtless legion, but my point is just to underscore that

theory is not the only candidate for this important job. In fact, we may be asking it to perform a function for which it is ill suited and thus falling into the delusions of foundationalism against which Rorty has eloquently warned.

⁶ Sosnoski's essay appeared after my own was completed, but I believe my argument agrees with his, and I gladly acknowledge his priority. Sosnoski writes, "I no longer use textbooks based on the 'schools and movements' principle of selection. They undermine my teaching. Students all too readily construe a theory as a method and bulldoze texts into plots on which they can assemble critical prefabrications. . . . So I no longer teach Derrida as Derrida or Barbara Johnson as an exemplary deconstructive critic. Instead, I try to show when centering or decentering texts is a perspicacious reading strategy depending on difficulties our work presents to us." He concludes succinctly, "Theory works more efficaciously as an activity, as a verb" (28).

Works Cited

Atkins, G. Douglas, and Laura Morrow, eds. *Contemporary Literary Theory.* Amherst: U of Massachusetts P, 1989.

Birch, David. *Language, Literature and Critical Practice: Ways of Analysing Text.* London: Routledge, 1989.

Brooks, Cleanth. "Irony as a Principle of Structure." Richter 799–807.

Con Davis, Robert, ed. *Contemporary Literary Criticism: Modernism through Post-structuralism.* 2nd ed. London: Longman, 1989.

Con Davis, Robert, and Ronald Schleifer, eds. *Contemporary Literary Criticism: Literary and Cultural Studies.* 2nd ed. London: Longman, 1989.

de Man, Paul. "The Resistance to Theory." *The Resistance to Theory.* Minneapolis: U of Minnesota P, 1986. 3–20.

———. "The Rhetoric of Temporality." *Blindness and Insight: Essays in the Rhetoric of Contemporary Criticism.* 2nd ed. Minneapolis: U of Minnesota P, 1983. 187–228.

Eagleton, Terry. *Literary Theory: An Introduction.* Minneapolis: U of Minnesota P, 1983.

Gadamer, Hans-Georg. *Reason in the Age of Science.* Trans. Frederick G. Lawrence. Cambridge: MIT P, 1981.

Hartman, Geoffrey. "Beyond Formalism." *Beyond Formalism: Literary Essays 1958–1970.* New Haven: Yale UP, 1970. 42–57.

Hirsch, E. D., Jr. "Objective Interpretation." *Validity in Interpretation.* New Haven: Yale UP, 1967. 209–44.

Jefferson, Ann, and David Robey, eds. *Modern Literary Theory: A Comparative Introduction.* 2nd ed. London: Batsford, 1986.

Lambropoulos, Vassilis, and David Neal Miller, eds. *Twentieth Century Literary Theory: An Introductory Anthology.* Albany: State U of New York P, 1987.

Latimer, Dan, ed. *Contemporary Critical Theory.* San Diego: Harcourt, 1988.

Levinson, Marjorie. "Insight and Oversight: Reading 'Tintern Abbey.'" *Wordsworth's Great Period Poems: Four Essays.* Cambridge: Cambridge UP, 1986. 14–57.

Lodge, David, ed. *Modern Criticism and Theory.* London: Longman, 1988.

Murfin, Ross C., ed. *Joseph Conrad's* Heart of Darkness: *A Case Study in Contemporary Criticism.* New York: St. Martin's, 1989.

Natoli, Joseph, ed. *Tracing Literary Theory*. Urbana: U of Illinois P, 1987.

Richter, David H., ed. *The Critical Tradition: Classic Texts and Contemporary Trends*. New York: St. Martin's, 1989.

Rorty, Richard. *Philosophy and the Mirror of Nature*. Princeton: Princeton UP, 1979.

Rousseau, Jean-Jacques. *Emile*. Trans. Barbara Foxley. 1911. Introd. P. D. Jimack. London: Dent-Everyman's, 1974.

Selden, Raman. *Practicing Theory and Reading Literature: An Introduction*. Lexington: UP of Kentucky, 1989.

———. *A Reader's Guide to Contemporary Literary Theory*. Lexington: UP of Kentucky, 1985.

Sosnoski, James J. "Requiem for a Noun." *ADE Bulletin* 104 (1993): 26–28.

Staton, Shirley F., ed. *Literary Theories in Praxis*. Philadelphia: U of Pennsylvania P, 1987.

Wittgenstein, Ludwig. *Philosophical Investigations*. Trans. G. E. M. Anscombe. Oxford: Blackwell, 1974.

Polylogue: Some (Mainly Pleasurable) Observations on the Carnegie Mellon Literary and Cultural Studies Curriculum, 1983–89

Gary Waller

I

Established in 1983, and retaining much of its original intent and structure for the next six years, the Carnegie Mellon English department's theory-centered undergraduate curriculum has received considerable attention. It was commented on in the *Chronicle of Higher Education* (4 Mar. 1988) and discussed at conferences including those of the ADE and NCTE. It gave rise to two textbooks that have attracted a great deal of interest (for instance, substantial reviews and articles in *College English*, *Genre*, and the *MMLA Bulletin*); its principles influenced the recommendations on the English major at the 1987 English Coalition; and in 1988 an outside committee evaluating the department said the core courses of the curriculum should become a model for those taught at other universities and colleges. This essay, however, focuses less on its details, which have been described elsewhere (Waller, "Working"; Waller, McCormick, and Fowler), than on issues and questions that could apply to other situations and to the general issue of teaching theory to undergraduates. After briefly describing the core courses in the curriculum, I address some of the wider theoretical and pedagogical issues that these courses attempt to address. Adapting a phrase of Freud's, I want to stress enthusiastically the "pleasures" we encountered in introducing theory into the undergraduate curriculum, while acknowledging that there are also potential "unpleasures" that deserve to be given some mention.

At Carnegie Mellon in 1983–84, we instituted a group of literary and cultural studies courses that were required of all undergraduate English majors—those majoring in creative, technical, and professional writing as well as literature (or what soon became literary and cultural studies). What we termed the English core consisted of four theoretically centered courses. First, we developed a new freshman course, Reading Texts. This course was taught primarily by graduate students, who prepared, intellectually and pedagogically, by taking a required graduate seminar entitled Theories of Reading and by participating in a weekly teaching seminar on the connections of pedagogy to theory. Second, we instituted a required core of three sophomore courses: Discursive Practices, Discourse and Historical Change, and Reading Twentieth-Century Culture. The freshman course, which replaced a traditional introduction to literature, responded to issues in current theory in a number of ways. First of all, the notion of "text" was extended to include texts outside the traditional literary canon, including essays, films, television programs, and advertising. Second, and more significant, we organized the course around the theoretical issue of reading as a culturally produced activity. Reading, after all, is not a natural process but a culturally produced practice; its assumptions vary according to different reading formations and to readers' (very diverse) immediate purposes. We therefore made the issue of interpretation, of "reading texts," the central theoretical focus of the course. As a further principle of organization, we built the course around three concepts: *language* (which incorporated some attention to cultural semiotics and the interplay of cultural production and discourse), *history* (which considered questions of historical difference and appropriation), and *culture* (which focused on cultural diversity and theories of culture).

These three concepts in turn became the organizing principles for the three required sophomore courses. We designed these courses not to present students with accounts of contemporary theory—and certainly not to encourage them to take up any kind of party line on theoretical or political issues—but, rather, through the study of carefully selected theoretical readings (including but not exclusively literary texts), to help them discuss and write about some of the most important debates raised by contemporary theory. Thus feminist, materialist, semiotic, new historicist, and deconstructive approaches to texts were not to be privileged, but the power and interest of such approaches, and others, even in a relatively simplified form, were to be made part of the dialogues—or, since there were many voices, "polylogues"—in which we invited students to participate, encouraging them to bring their own reactions and views. We intended to maintain a careful balance between the slight overlapping among the three courses, so as to ensure continuity and reinforcement, and the necessary and even appropriate contradictions of approach and material. We also tried to ensure that literary material would be well represented, even if it was distributed across the courses in what, by traditional standards, would be an unfamiliar way. We hoped that if we were successful in our rethinking of the curriculum, the number of English majors might well increase; at the same time, since many might want to go on to graduate school, most of us were concerned that they should not suffer from their unusual preparation for the Graduate Record Examinations. Early planning meetings of the faculty were, therefore, replete with pie diagrams and discussions of shared (and differing) concepts, approaches, and texts. It was an exciting project; it was certainly full of pleasures.

Language, history, and culture are not in themselves theories. Nor are they theoretical approaches. We did not want to structure our curriculum around a history or taxonomy of critical theories. Rather, language, history, and culture provided opportunities for theorizing; they were presented to students as sites of interest, sometimes of intense struggle, that have generated diverse and often contradictory critical practices in past as well as recent theory. In many ways the fundamental principle of our curriculum was close to Gerald Graff's often repeated suggestion that a curriculum should foreground the conflicts within the discipline. We hoped, however, that the conflicts would not entail agonistic struggles, with triumphantly "correct" and defeated "incorrect" positions, but would instead produce a shared awareness that such debates were intensely interesting, complex, and important, not just for academic studies but for our understanding of and actions in the broader society.

Instituting such a structured curriculum opened up various organizational and intellectual problems and challenges that, more than these brief details of the program's structure, may be of interest to others wrestling with the place of theory in the undergraduate experience. Such matters include—in addition to determining the appropriate levels at which to teach theory to freshmen and majors—whether theory is an autonomous discipline, replacing "literature," and whether it can even be "applied" to literary or other "nontheoretical" texts; whether (as some of our detractors maintained) giving theoretical issues such a high priority degenerates into a kind of pseudo- or shadow philosophy; and whether raising questions of race, gender, and class (as most of us did) predetermines a certain range of answers. Other considerations are how to stop the conflicts from deteriorating into simply another kind of antagonistic (and some would say "masculinist") struggle for hegemony among theoretical factions, how to determine the place of "classics" in theoretically oriented courses, and how to address the much overlooked issue of pedagogy. I touch on some of these matters in the following remarks.

II

Given the current ferment over the theory and practice of English, there is clearly no one correct way of teaching theory. In addition to the highly laudatory general aim of extending the canon of texts studied in English courses to include more diverse positions of gender, race, or class, there are, as Kathleen McCormick has argued, three ways in which theory is being brought into the undergraduate curriculum ("Always"). The first is by substituting the study of theoretical texts for literary texts, thus constituting something like a new canon and transforming the study of English from the study of one body of texts to the study of another. There are some gains in this approach: for example, students discuss important writings outside the belletrist canon and subject them to careful analysis. But while the content of courses may change, the underlying assumptions about pedagogy and learning may be untouched, too easily producing the silly attitude that "all texts are equal except 'literary' texts, which are *less* equal than others," the overforceful iconoclasm of which position has not helped the acceptance of theory and theorizing of the curriculum. Plays, poems, novels, and other fictional discourses have for too long been the focus of power and pleasure (both concepts that require close attention) to allow the new puritans to deny them places in the curriculum and replace, rather than complement, the study of Wordsworth's lyrics, say, with Terry Eagleton or Paul de Man on Kant, or *King Lear* with All-Star Wrestling.

The second approach is to add a course or two in theory to an existing traditional, canonical curriculum. This gradualist strategy—what I once termed the park-bench approach (6)—is probably the most widespread. It can have effective long-term effects and will not disrupt a department as severely as do revolutionary approaches; but without actually staging within the structure and rationale of the curriculum the type of debates that theoretical courses should raise about the rest of the curriculum, the approach may result in only piecemeal and incoherent changes. It is likely to produce students who are puzzled, intellectually schizophrenic, and cynical: in X's class, we are neoformalists, in Y's we are neo-Marxists. The park-bench approach tends to produce departments with a token theorist or two, and the opportunity for polylogue may never develop.

The third approach, which is closest to what we did at Carnegie Mellon in the 1980s, is to develop some theoretically structured courses like those I have described and to make them the intellectual focus of the curriculum. Our core courses were not only required of students but also constructed to make them rewarding for faculty members to design and teach. As the key courses in our curriculum, they privileged the issues they raised, thus encouraging those issues to permeate other courses and make a difference to the whole curriculum. For the first few years of the program, all teachers of the core courses shared their syllabi, meeting regularly to discuss issues and pedagogy (and in doing so, of course, demonstrating how a theoretical issue like intertextuality operates in the most apparently mundane material practices!). I cannot stress too strongly my belief that such interchanges are an essential part of successfully introducing theory and theorizing into the curriculum. Teamwork and commitment are crucial—not to a party line but to the importance of the issues being enacted and to the right of all participants, faculty members, and students alike, to enter into the polylogue.

In a sense, to say that we were teaching theory to our students is a slight misnomer. There were, indeed, courses in which theoretical texts were the main focus, and the three core courses all included theoretical essays. But our main goal was to integrate not so much theory as the practice of *theorizing* into the curriculum as a whole. A theorizing curriculum, which is how ours at that time could best be characterized, is not only one in which students may study a variety of literary and other cultural texts, including theoretical texts (and, indeed, why not Eagleton or de Man on Kant?) but, above all, one in which students are encouraged explicitly to raise theoretical issues and integrate them into all areas of study. It is also one in which they are encouraged to scrutinize their own, developing positions. Although they may not necessarily, or easily, be able to articulate or analyze those positions, students do in fact bring to their reading experiences a complex repertoire of assumptions, beliefs, and expectations about theoretical issues—including, among others, the relation of "fiction" to "reality"; the nature of the canon; the relevance of issues of gender, class, and race; and the shifting authority of authors and readers. One of the discoveries we made in our curricular development was that, simply, we have no choice of whether or not to have theory in the classroom. We needed, we believed, not only to introduce our students to the diversity of textual experiences available in English studies but also to provide as many as possible of the connections, the multiple and interactive perspectives, of the approaches we all bring to those textual experiences. Students are, like all discursive subjects, "always already theorists": theory "is always there—in (and among) us and in our students. We only have a choice of whether or not we and our students will be self-conscious (that is to say, theoretical) about the theories that guide our perceptions" (McCormick, "Always" 112). Every position a student or teacher adopts is theoretically inscribed and, we insisted, should be taken seriously in the classroom: students should be encouraged to enter into the debates, discovering, refining, and revising their own positions on the various issues that arose.

A number of people—including some of our colleagues—criticized the goals of our curriculum, claiming we had settled for a liberal pluralism (we were, in the space of a few months, attacked by members of both the ultra-Right, for betraying Western civilization, and the ultra-Left, for maintaining bourgeois liberalism under a gloss of poststructuralism). Polylogue is not simply a valorization of relativism, any more than in the classroom it is a simplistic recommendation of a pedagogy based on discussion. It is, rather, the encouragement and empowering of a multiplicity of positions, combined with the willingness to examine and critique the assumptions underlying those positions. A healthy curriculum, however the particular details within it may change, should be built not just on the recognition of pluralism, but also on carefully structured ways of making that pluralism work intellectually and educationally. If we can find creative ways of bringing together the variety of theories, methodologies, and conceptions of what "English" is—not just to facilitate administration but also, as Graff argues, actually to stage or teach the conflicts—then we may do much more than merely make our curriculum appear innovative: we may prepare students for an informed entry into a genuinely participatory democracy. I believe that such an educational goal acknowledges that college gives students an opportunity not simply to "bank" knowledge and methods but to develop some perspectives on, some meta-awareness about, them—and also to act on that awareness.

Such a goal has undeniable practical consequences. The paradigmatic shift the language disciplines are undergoing is educational as well as theoretical. Departments need to find not only curricular structures but classroom practices that will help students stage the contradictions in which our society and history have placed us and which the texts of our culture, including those we valorize as literature, articulate. As administrators and teachers, we all need to ask ourselves, How creatively are we using the overlappings and conflicts in the education of our students? How well, for instance, are we involving our students in the debates on that group of key words—*gender, race, ethnicity, class*? These key words are, of course, the focus of major challenges to our future as a society, and they are not easy challenges to meet. To these words, I would add another, which our curriculum attempted to enact, and that is *agency*—a word embracing those areas of action, choice, knowledge, and commitment we struggle to claim for ourselves on the basis of understanding something of how we are constructed by our societies and our histories. In my view, the major goal of a curriculum built on polylogue is to enable students to become agents in this sense—aware of how they are constructed, in their different histories, by society, culture, ethnicity, gender; by scientific or religious paradigms of thought and material practices. In doing so, they can become aware of the possibilities of choice and action and the principles by which they articulate those choices and actions.

There are, clearly, signs that many departments are starting to face such matters and, in different ways, to move away from the traditional unwillingness (or inability) to stage the issues raised by theory within the curriculum and classroom. The English Coalition of 1987 provided a blueprint for the kind of integrative and outreaching curriculum that addresses itself to all departments of English at the college and university level. I recommend to readers both the coalition's official report (Lloyd-Jones and Lunsford) and Peter Elbow's thoughtful meditation on the coalition, *What Is English?*

III

I turn now directly to the classroom. As the coalition report, in fact, pointed out, one of the most intriguing challenges that we face in teaching theory, or theorizing, to undergraduates—and that every department and individual teacher involved in or contemplating such a development needs to face—concerns pedagogy. When a course places such emphasis on theoretical self-awareness as our core courses demand, teachers may be afraid to lose the still-seductive illusion of their residual objective authority. This fear, as we found in our curriculum, can affect those who have politically progressive positions as well as those with conservative views. As Paulo Freire notes ironically, regardless of how progressive an educator's intent may be, the "banking system" of education "may simply make the students the depositories and the teacher a depositor, issuing communiqués and making deposits that the students patiently memorize, and repeat" (58). Nowhere is such a temptation more evident than in the teaching of theory. Students may easily be encouraged just to master theoretical texts rather than, as would be preferable, to interrogate the texts and to locate themselves in relation to the multiple positions polylogue can open up. Students need to know that neither their own positions nor those of a teacher should be immune from scrutiny. As teachers, we need to acknowledge the "situatedness" of all reading and to do so genuinely; otherwise we will discourage critical debate or may find ourselves unknowingly or cynically rewarding a student for adopting a teacher's overtly asserted position as authoritative. To situate all theoretical positions, including the teacher's, is to enable students to realize that they have a stake in the positions they adopt—and, not least, in the confidence with which they assert themselves in classroom discussions and term papers. Traditionally, pedagogy has been accorded little status as an object of inquiry, but there are signs that this situation is changing, and the retheorizing of the discipline can only benefit from such a development.

I want to mention now the important question of the appropriate level in a department's curriculum at which theoretical material should be used. My suggestion is that at the freshman level theoretical essays should be discussed alongside literary and media texts, but sparingly, and only after intense preparation by the instructor. Teachers need to be aware and make clear to their students what issues might be at stake and should encourage self-conscious and detailed discussion of them, but they should not rush directly to a sophisticated level of theoretical discussion. Textbooks such as *Reading Texts* (McCormick and Waller) and *Textual Power* (Scholes) can be of great help in alerting relatively inexperienced teachers to some of the relevant theoretical issues. At Florida State University, for instance, in the summer before graduate teachers start teaching the freshman course, they are introduced to how theoretical issues may arise in the classroom by studying *Reading Texts*. Our own Theories of Reading course sometimes included a critique of *Reading Texts*, *Textual Power* and other innovative texts that are trickling onto the market so that graduate instructors can discover ways they might convey complicated theoretical issues to their freshman students.

If at the freshman level some caution ought to be exercised over the introduction of theoretical essays, at the sophomore or junior levels, in my view, they can certainly be introduced, discussed, and read along with other literary and cultural texts—not to establish an orthodox "line" on a text or theoretical issue but to open discussion, allowing students both to deepen and to problematize their own developing perspectives. In my section of Discourse and Historical Change, along with a selection of literary and related texts from past periods, I used such essays as Tony Bennett's "Texts in History" and Raymond Williams's "Dominant, Residual, and Emergent" and extracts from as broad a spectrum of theorists as T. S. Eliot to Louis Althusser. On occasion, I will also use Williams's *Key Words* and one of the course assignments will be for students to construct the history of a key word not found in Williams. (That exercise has been very successful.)

Courses devoted primarily or exclusively to particular theories, theoretical movements, or theorists are in my view certainly appropriate for juniors and seniors, as are of course those in which students read literary or media texts in conjunction with theoretical texts and issues. I thus structured a recent course on the sixteenth-century lyric around the issue of the interconnections of gender, reading, and writing. We read poems by the canonical male Petrarchists along with popular-song lyrics and lyrics by (until recently) neglected women poets, along with essays on gender and language by Sigmund Freud, Julia Kristeva, Laura Mulvey, Roland Barthes, and others. We also had a three-week segment on Klaus Theweleit's *Male Fantasies*, a psychocultural study of the *Freikorps*, the German Fascist mercenaries of the 1920s, in which we asked questions both about particular insights Theweleit offers into gender construction and about his methodology. All the students contributed to a collective project that we titled "The Book of Stuff," a collection of theoretical and historical writings that they all could use for their readings and research papers. The result was, I think, a successful combination of reading, theorizing, and multiple pleasures.

Two detailed examples illustrate how both theorizing and polylogue operate in the classroom. In 1988 I taught a section of Discourse and Historical Change. As noted above, I used a number of theoretical essays to raise questions about reading historically remote texts, dividing the course into two units, each of which took about six weeks: first, a representation of gender in a selection of Renaissance poetry and drama and, second, the development of a sense of American "identity" in a selection of writings from the Puritans to Hawthorne. At the end of the semester, we were studying *The Scarlet Letter*. As late-twentieth-century readers, we were reading Hawthorne's reading of the Puritans, who were in turn reading the inscrutable ways of the Almighty. In addition, we were reading —and, not incidentally, reading as educated and therefore distinctly privileged men or women within a society gradually becoming more sensitive to gender construction—a nineteenth-century male's reading of the struggles of being a woman in the seventeenth century. These multiple perspectives provided the basis of a final theoretical paper on reading texts in "their" time and in "ours." But we (a word that takes on a less certain tone in a theorizing context) gave the perspectival aspect of reading historically a further dimension: we were reading a white male's reading of the ways in which a white woman was being constructed within the distinctive ideological pressures of European American history.

What gave our study an interest in the interrelations not only of reading and gender but of reading and race and class was that alongside *The Scarlet Letter* we read extracts from Frederick Douglass's autobiography. One of my African American students raised the question of where she fitted in in the unfolding drama of the historical construction of the American subject that our study of Hawthorne had raised. She had felt silenced and marginalized by the Puritans we read, and now, in reading Douglass, we had come to a text through which she could enter the critical discourse. Her repertoire at last intersected with that of a text she was required to study. It was not that she now had a way of ignoring or not reading *The Scarlet Letter* on the grounds that it was canonical or merely literature; on the contrary, Douglass's writing added another perspective to her paper on Hawthorne and helped her to take part in a particularly powerful polylogue—one that incorporated her history and personal repertoire as a twentieth-century African American woman. She wrote a superb, passionate, well-documented paper on how she was positioned in this debate as she tried to construct a history of herself as a multiple subject of different educational, ethnic, and gendered discourses; she displayed both her knowledge of the subject—literature, questions of taste and relevance, the relations between a canonical and a marginal work—and her sense of herself as a subject. She became, in her paper, a theorizer—of the canon, of traditional literary criticism, and of English. Theorizing became a way for her to understand not only herself as a historical being but also the broader culture as itself constructed in history.

My second classroom example comes from our freshman course. It contained a research paper unit in which students focused on a literary or cultural studies topic—for instance, a current issue in the news, a major myth or dominant metaphor in literature or the broader culture—and were introduced to a critique of the commonplace and seemingly neutral apparatus of the research paper itself. Students read at least six essays that took varying viewpoints on their topics. Instead of simply summarizing the essays, or sorting out which were more or less biased or objective and coming up with their own viewpoints, students were asked to situate these various "expert" opinions, as well as their own, within the contradictions of the contemporary cultural formation.

This assignment produced some fascinating cultural (not merely cognitive) dissonances. Even after they had been able culturally to situate their opinions in earlier, more informal papers or discussion, most students tended to fall back into a residual objectivism when asked to write a re-search paper. It was in wrestling with this problem, in short by theorizing, that they learned a great deal about an important theoretical problem, the ideological nature of language and the institutionally sanctioned ap-paratuses in which the problems are articulated. Even when they realized that the critical language they had been taught to privilege—primarily as an objectivist lexicon derived from formalism—was itself a product of a particular ideological history—and one, moreover, that might impede polylogic thinking—they nonetheless found themselves drawn back into it because it seemed more "natural," presumably because their schooling had taught them that it was rewarded. But by being self-conscious about their own assumptions, they also started to discover that the other widely valorized mode of writing—"expressive" articulation of "subjective" opinion, which likewise seemed natural to them—was equally the product of major cultural and ideological assumptions. Their educational assumptions were revealed as a contradictory mixture: somehow they were supposed to be at once objective and universal yet subjective and personal. Alan Sinfield comments ironically on such a contradiction, which he locates in the British equivalent of the American research paper, the national examination: "the projection of local conditions on to the eternal . . . [and] the con-struction of individual subjectivity as a given which is undetermined and unconstituted and hence a ground of meaning and coherence" (Sinfield 138, 140). Growing up in a culture that values meritocracy, competition, and the ethic of success (which, admittedly, are not entirely unrelated to the concept of agency), these students understandably found it difficult to see themselves as constructed by what they resisted as deterministic and alien historical or cultural forces. (As one of my students once re-marked, "The Russians [perhaps now the Iraqis?] have ideology; we Americans have democracy.") Becoming conscious of the contradictory discourses that they were writing, or that were writing them, was helping to make them aware of the possibility of agency within their reading and writing practices. For many, such a discovery was confusing or threaten-ing; for others, highly liberating.

These two scenarios from two levels of our curriculum may convey something of our practices during the years in which our program was taking shape. So that the evident pleasures of theorizing the undergraduate curriculum do not turn into unpleasures, my examples are meant to rein-force a necessary warning: that the theories and theorizings of the teachers cannot remain immune from the scrutiny that we wish our students to undergo in relation to their reading and writing experiences. Theory has currently acquired such prestige in the discipline that there are all-too-evident signs it will engender an all-too-familiar elitism and a lack of con-cern for curriculum, classroom practices, and the students themselves. But given the prevalence of both committed and rigorous theoretical thinkers and, more particularly, enthusiastic and flexible teachers, the pleasures of teaching theorizing to undergraduates in an atmosphere of generosity will, I believe, far outweigh the unpleasures.

University of Hartford

Works Cited

Bennett, Tony. "Texts in History." *Journal of the Midwest Modern Language Association* 18.1 (1985): 1–18.

Elbow, Peter. *What Is English?* New York: MLA; Urbana: NCTE, 1990.

Freire, Paulo. *Pedagogy of the Oppressed.* New York: Continuum, 1989.

Graff, Gerald. *Professing Literature.* Chicago: U of Chicago P, 1987.

Lloyd-Jones, Richard, and Andrea Lunsford, eds. *The English Coalition Report: Democracy through Language.* Urbana: NCTE, 1989.

McCormick, Kathleen. "Always Already Theorists: Literary Theory in the Undergraduate Curriculum." *Pedagogy Is Politics: Literary Theory and the Teaching of Literature.* Ed. Maria Regina Kecht. Urbana: U of Illinois P, 1992. 111–31.

———. "Using Cultural Theory to Critique and Reconceptualize the Research Paper." *Cultural Studies in the English Classroom.* Ed. James Berlin and Michael Vivion. Portsmouth: Boynton/Cook, 1983. 111–27.

McCormick, Kathleen, and Gary Waller. *Reading Texts.* Lexington: Heath, 1987.

Scholes, Robert. *Textual Power.* New Haven: Yale UP, 1985.

Sinfield, Alan. "Give an Account of Shakespeare and Education. . . ." *Political Shakespeare.* Ed. Jonathan Dollimore and Alan Sinfield. Manchester: Manchester UP, 1985. 134–57.

Theweleit, Klaus. *Male Fantasies.* Vol. 1. *Women, Floods, Bodies, History.* Trans. Stephen Conway. Vol. 2. *Male Bodies: Psychoanalyzing the White Terror.* Trans. Erica Carter and Chris Turner. Minneapolis: U of Minnesota P, 1988, 1989.

Waller, Gary. "Working within the Paradigm Shift: Poststructuralism and the College Curriculum." *ADE Bulletin* 81 (1985): 6–12.

Waller, Gary, Kathleen McCormick, and Lois Fowler, eds. *The Lexington Introduction to Literature.* Lexington: Heath, 1986.

Williams, Raymond. "Dominant, Residual, and Emergent." *Marxism and Literature.* London: Oxford UP, 1977. 121–27.

———. *Key Words.* London: Oxford UP, 1976.

Part III
Focusing

Accounting for Theory
in the Undergraduate Classroom

Diana Fuss

Recent discussions of the place of theory in the humanities classroom have sought to explain the "interjection" of theory into the scene of teaching as, variously, a long-overdue critical intervention, a suspect incursion of politics into the academy, a dangerous transgression or contamination of disciplinary boundaries, and an inevitable by-product of institutional and historical change. Wherever one stands on the question of what role theory should play in our classrooms and in our curricula, in this debate theory is frequently assumed to be a relative newcomer to the pedagogical scene—a practice at the very least in need of explanation and, for many of its practitioners, in continual need of defense. But this pedagogical and resolutely theoretical debate on the question "Why theory?" conceals a potentially more interesting and pressing question, a question of historical and political interest perhaps first and foremost: When, exactly, did the space of the classroom come to be seen as an inappropriate site for theory? If we understand the classroom in its most functionalist sense as that social space culturally assigned to the production of knowledge, and if we see theory, also in one of its most rudimentary connotations, as that process capable of transforming thought itself, then the assumed disharmony between the institutional stage of knowledge production and its actual performance seems curious, not to say baffling. Currently, the problem of "theory in the classroom" is posed in such a way as, first, to assume that it is a problem and, second, to obfuscate the long-standing historical and structural dependency between the two.

But of course theory in its present formulation no longer stands in for, metonymically, all of what has conventionally come under the sign of "knowledge"; instead, theory has come to be understood as "the *practice* of interrogating the production of knowledge" (Rooney 16). Put another way, theory is concerned less with the dispassionate transmission of knowledge than with the ideological and institutional conditions of its performance, with, as one theoretician puts it, its conditions of "imposability"—"the conditions under which arguments, categories, and values impose and maintain a certain authority" (Weber 19). The classroom, too, has undergone a critical reevaluation. Formerly considered by an Enlightenment culture as a neutral storehouse of information, dedicated to the cultural preservation and generational dispatch of knowledge, the classroom (and the academy at large) is viewed by most post-Althusserians as a social institution designed to reproduce the interests, values, and politics of the dominant social classes.[1] Far from postulating the space of the classroom as a nonpartisan and uncontaminated ground, educational reformers now generally recognize it as always and inevitably "implicated in relations of power, social practices, and the privileging of forms of knowledge that support a specific vision of past, present, and future" (Giroux and McLaren 153). Theory, in its conceptual shift from that which is "known" to that which asks how we know—a shift, in other words, from the epistemic to the technic, from passive object to active subject, or even from theory to practice—emerges to challenge the very foundation and operational logic of the Enlightenment classroom.

Given that contemporary theory *in* the classroom cannot help changing our theory *of* the classroom, how do we account for theory in today's classroom? What contributions has theory made to pedagogy? How has the teaching of theory changed our theories of teaching? Is the theory classroom different, in any philosophical or structural way, from other (supposedly nontheoretical) classrooms? In this essay I attempt to get at these questions by investigating the centrality of temporality in epistemological work and by exploring the thresholds of speed involved in the teaching and learning of theory. My own underlying theoretical premise is that all acts have particular temporalities—including the act of theorizing. The purpose of this reflection on theory and epistemology is to identify some of these modes of temporalization produced in the sphere of theoretical activity and to examine their implications for contemporary pedagogy. The examples in the first section come from my teaching psychoanalytic theory, in both a lesbian and gay studies course and a feminist studies classroom, although I feel it is crucial to point out that my own experiences teaching theory to undergraduates are by no means representative and that sharing them poses all the dangers attendant on a universalizing presentation of self as exemplar. Nor are any of the tentative conclusions I have come to on the teaching of theory necessarily thematically bound to the fields of lesbian, gay, or feminist theory or to the teaching of psychoanalysis. Instead, I offer these examples to localize an otherwise distended discussion of theory and to suggest that while it may be necessary to speak of this practice called theory in more general terms (as I do in the essay's second section) in order to delimit the boundaries of its operational fields, it nonetheless becomes particularly important in the space of the classroom to ask not only "Why theory?" but also "Which theory?"

Resistance, History, and Obsolescence

"Today we're living through a speed-up of time which no longer corresponds to biological time," Luce Irigaray has reflected ("Language" 32). Cultural time and biological time appear weirdly out of sync as the techno-scientific race for more information and more efficient ways of acquiring it revolutionizes our entire lived relation to knowledge, history, and socio-political change. Jacques Derrida's "No Apocalypse, Not Now," an energetic and *timely* analysis of the new thresholds of speed and motion produced in the nuclear age, indirectly excavates the new terrain of what we might call (with all its inevitable technological as well as familial connotations) the nuclear classroom: "the 'nuclear age' makes for a certain type of colloquium, with its particular technology of information, diffusion and storage, its rhythm of speech, its demonstration procedures,and thus its armaments, its modes of persuasion or intimidation" (21). In the nuclear classroom, invention itself is perpetually reinvented; what gets reworked and repositioned are the continually shifting relations "between knowing and acting, . . . between the invention that finds what was already there and the one that produces new mechanisms or new spaces" (23).

Theory, in this respect, is very much of its time. To the degree that theory always engages questions of invention, change, and movement, theory is itself a temporal lever, a gearshift with accelerating speeds of operation. Theory's internal dynamism accounts for both the excitement and the anxiety students and practitioners of theory inevitably experience as they grapple with the new epistemological questions posed by ever more complicated modes of invention and levels of inquiry. "The worst thing about theory these days," Jonathan Culler observes, "is that it is endless"—suggesting that one possible source of the contemporary resistance to theory is the fear of always being "upstaged" by newer and more sophisticated theories (1569). Though theory itself may routinely put the notion of mastery, of total and complete knowledge, under suspicion, students of theory (by which I mean to include teachers as well) nevertheless continue to express particular frustration over the time it takes to learn, to teach, or to "master" these new acts of reading. Perhaps the most common form such resistance takes among students is the complaint that the theory they are being asked to perform (and sometimes theory in toto) is just the latest intellectual novelty, which will surely be eclipsed by yet another modernization before they have had time to learn how to "apply" the first one. Students worry that, like the latest military weapons system, the newest theory will be obsolete long before it becomes operational; according to this view, investing in theory constitutes a waste of time, an inefficient expenditure of energy and intellect.

In my recent experience teaching psychoanalysis in a Princeton undergraduate Introduction to Feminist Theory class, these initial points of resistance to studying theory paradoxically provoked the most interesting and

impassioned classroom debates and almost immediately catapulted the
class into a more performative mode. Student responses to their introduction to psychoanalysis ran the gamut from fear, frustration, and demoni-
zation to seduction, fetishization, and idealization. Especially striking,
however, was how the commotion triggered by several fevered statements
of antitheoreticism inspired the class's most theoretical discussions. The
students, all English majors with little if any previous training in psychoanalysis, and the most racially mixed and economically diverse class I
have taught at Princeton, were quick to point out that psychoanalysis
is largely a middle-class discourse of sexual difference that speaks only
inadequately to questions of racial difference and not at all to questions
of class difference. The students' resistance to psychoanalysis, far from
representing a naive rejection of "abstract theory" in favor of "real-world
politics," was grounded in a sophisticated theory of its own that gradually
emerged to focus and energize our discussions: a theory of how identities
(racial, ethnic, economic, sexual, national) are conferred relationally, produced across and within differences by means of a complicated network
of social and cultural identifications. The resistance to psychoanalysis
became the jumping-off point for an ongoing collective class project to
adapt, rework, and redeploy the fundamental psychoanalytic concepts
of desire, fantasy, memory, and repression to read specifically the phenomenon of class and ethnic identifications. This section of the course,
which initially triggered the most ardent denouncements of theory as exces-
sive and apolitical, also provoked the most exciting and consistently interesting theoretical work from the class. The "theory versus politics" debate,
which eventually became the "theory *as* politics" debate (a subject of lively
contention throughout the psychoanalysis section of the course), finally
moved the class along from the familiar place of talking about theory
to the riskier point of actually doing it.[2]

The incipient theoreticism of such resistances to theory finds its most
eloquent and influential articulation in Paul de Man's by now famous
pronouncement that "nothing can overcome the resistance to theory since
theory *is* itself this resistance" (19). Sometimes a second level of resistance operates in the theory classroom—the teacher's resistance to the students' resistance, which, if not also incorporated into the logic of the
de Manian paradox, may block rather than facilitate the learning process.
Let me offer another example, from a gay and lesbian studies course I
recently taught at Rutgers University, the State University of New Jersey.
The students—mostly white, mostly women, predominantly middle- and
working-class, all concentrating in women's studies—were drawn to the
course out of a shared commitment to combat homophobia and hetero-
sexism wherever they may do their work, including (and especially) in
the practices of medicine, psychiatry, and the law, which historically have
collaborated to pathologize and to criminalize "homosexuals." The resistance to psychoanalysis was thus the very motivation that brought the

students to my class, while my own pedagogical objective was to investigate the potential *uses* of psychoanalysis and how it might be deployed in the service of an antihomophobic politics.

My resistance to the students' resistance to psychoanalysis initially took the form of persistent and tireless efforts to explicate Freud, to "save" his work before it was prematurely jettisoned, for I assumed that the students' resistance could eventually be overcome if only they took the time to *read* Freud. But no such magical transformation occurred. The students did, over time, become more intrigued by the problems posed by psychoanalysis, and a few even appeared partially swayed by my arsenal of arguments on psychoanalysis's disruptive potential: its tendency to denaturalize and deessentialize all sexual identities, its ability to make visible the ideology of invisibility on which normative heterosexualities are based, its capacity to map new modes of identification and generate new forms of desire. But not until we collectively decided to adopt resistance itself as a theoretical strategy did we gain firm entry into the Freudian corpus and achieve some measure of understanding of our own complicated transferences onto the text (and indeed onto one another). In short, the breakthrough came when we began to read Freud against Freud, when we began to unpack, through close textual readings and intertextual crosscuttings, the theory's own structural contradictions and internal resistances. For me to recognize the ways in which pedagogical counterresistance (not unlike psychoanalytic countertransference) may conceal rather than exploit the intrinsic value of resistance for the teaching of theory was a first step toward beginning to restructure the theory classroom through rather than around student resistance.

The resistance to theory often tells us more about theory's importance, usefulness, and potential effectiveness than anything inherent in theory itself. Theory as resistance carries its own obsolescence within it, changing and mutating under historical and cultural pressure. That theory is not permanent or stationary, that it is not immune to historical process, that it is not outside the changing temporal order (that it can and does transform our very experience of temporality)—all these qualities represent a state of affairs to be welcomed rather than bemoaned. Theory's interminability and its extraordinary capacity to retheorize and reorganize the grounds and the terms of its own production account for its critical utility and staying power. The renewal of theory works precisely through its temporal exhaustion and, one might say, through its "nuclear" capabilities of fusion, recombination, and regeneration.

The idea that theory may be simply too much "of its time"—a fad or fashion subject to every new technological invention or intellectual innovation—is, in my mind, less an objection to theory than a recommendation for it. The notion that objects of knowledge do not change over time while the theories that seek to "explain" them come and go with the winds of historical change simply disguises the way in which theory *effects* historical change by perpetually inventing and reinventing its objects. For example, psychoanalysis, one of the dominant narratives of sexual difference in Western modernity, is itself largely responsible for inventing, consolidating, and reproducing in the first place the categories of its own analysis ("homosexual," "heterosexual," "bisexual"). The history of psychoanalysis reveals a striking adaptability to and influence on the changing cultural politics of sexual identifications, and any theoretical investigations of these differences cannot help taking into account the historical role the psychoanalytic institution has played in the production of sexual identity formations as well as the shaping influence its notions of trauma, memory, and repression have had on our modern theories of history. Theory, in other words, locates itself within history, not outside it, and it is exactly this spatial locality that accounts for theory's contemporary relevance, its historical importance, and its changing relation to pedagogy. Moreover, I take the production, interrogation, and reinvention of these critical objects to be the very labor of the theory classroom.

While every new theorization is an act of acceleration, a process of increasing the rate and output of knowledge production, the time it takes to learn these theories and to engage in different kinds of theoretical labor is simultaneously prolonged and intensified. As theories themselves proliferate at an impressive rate, the experience of learning how to think theoretically produces more of a braking effect or a reduction in speed. What distinguishes the theory class from other classes I have taught is this temporal slowdown—a decelerated rhythm that noticeably controls the rate of intellectual exchange while encouraging from all the participants a markedly different quality of attention. Derrida's description in "*Geschlecht* II" of "the slow rhythm of a seminar engaged in a difficult reading" (161) comes perhaps closest to describing my own experience over the years, as both student and teacher, in the theory classroom. The activity of theorizing, far from encouraging facile or trendy judgments (common criticism leveled against both psychoanalysis and deconstruction), by its very difficulty promotes meticulous, careful, and detailed readings. Since most theoretical investigations take the form of rigorous interpretations, in-depth etymological explorations, or precise linguistic analyses (all exercises in which readers pay careful attention to questions of language and its structuration or to problems of address and enunciation), theoretical readings are generally exhaustive ones.

The time, patience, and effort involved in any apprenticeship in theory necessarily affects the design, methodology, and pacing of the classroom. By assigning fewer readings and shorter texts than in other courses (or by allotting more time for lengthy, intricate pieces), we can more easily accommodate these new critical methodologies. In my classes I find it useful to introduce the same text or set of texts at recurrent intervals for renewed consideration, analysis, and group discussion. In my feminist theory class, Luce Irigaray's *This Sex Which Is Not One* emerged as the book that haunted us throughout the course; in my gay and lesbian studies seminar, Freud's "A Case of Paranoia Running Counter to the Psychoanalytic Theory of the Disease" and "The Psychogenesis of a Case of Homosexuality in a Woman" were two grounding essays that the students themselves repeatedly called back for rereading and debate. In a psychoanalysis classroom, one perhaps need look no further than the principle of "repetition and return" to authorize the practice of such periodic re-readings, but I have experimented with this déjà-vu format in several other theory classes as well because the strategy, perhaps more than any other, seems to demand allowance for what Jacques Lacan identifies in his seminar on the temporal dimension of analysis as the "time-for-understanding" ("Concept" 285).

In the analytic encounter, the time-for-understanding directly acknowledges the role resistance plays in the learning process, reconfiguring and deploying temporality as a support rather than a harness in the analysand's striving toward critical self-understanding. So, too, in that other famous quarter of transferential action, the theater of teaching, where timing and patience are critical to the success of the pedagogic endeavor and necessary for any real change to take place. I have come to realize that often students are making the most progress when they only appear to have stalled or become obsessed with a particularly difficult theoretical problem or an especially dense textual passage. As Margaret Whitford comments on her experiences teaching the work of the psychoanalyst, linguist, and philosopher Luce Irigaray, "far from being an impediment, the effort of understanding needed to read her may be part of the cost of change" (5).

The actual practice of teaching theory to undergraduates has forced me to acknowledge the importance of what one might call leisure time in the act of theorizing, and it has taught me to adapt my teaching strategy by keeping the reading load to a minimum and creating, wherever possible, "open spaces" the students themselves can fill with suggestions for new approaches to reading the most stubborn texts. Instead of leading to inefficient use of class time, these periodic reconsiderations, like the retrospective act of analysis itself, offer the promise of forward progress *through* backward motion, through the hard epistemological work of recollection, rethinking, and reenvisioning.

Accounting for Theory

Epistemology itself has changed over time. Contemporary theory, which insists on the time of theory as the nonsimultaneity of perception and understanding, powerfully calls into question earlier theories of knowing based on the idea of temporal immediacy—of knowledge purchased in an instant. The subtlety of this shift from one epistemology to the other may find its most historically significant formulation in Freud's theorization of sexual difference as originating for the young girl in the sight of the male organ, which is experienced as "a momentous discovery": "She makes her judgement and her decision in a flash. She has seen it and knows that she is without it and wants to have it." For the young boy, however, knowledge of sexual difference comes *after* the visual perception of a girl's genitalia: "he sees nothing or disavows what he has seen"; it is only later, under the threat of castration, that the boy "recollects or repeats" the scene and so comes to a conscious awareness of sexual difference ("Some Psychical Consequences" 252).[3] Freud's epistemology of sexual difference is itself highly sexualized, overdetermined by a whole range of cultural and philosophical assumptions about gender, knowledge, temporality, and the relation among them. The girl's knowledge is immediate, intuitive, calculated in the moment of a camera's flash; the boy's knowledge is delayed, constructed, achieved in the time of a mind's recollection and retrospection. Only the boy is capable of theorizing, in the strictest sense, because only the boy can achieve the proper distance between seeing and knowing. Only the boy, in other words, is capable of fetishism, and in this respect fetishism is structurally indispensable to the Freudian notion of theorization.

Feminist theorists have been quick to challenge the precarious, asymmetrical grounds of Freud's theory of sexual difference, particularly as it relates to the subject of fetishism and the perversions.[4] I need not rehearse here the ways in which psychoanalysis, by resubmitting women to the order of intuition and immediacy, bolsters the very epistemological order it ostensibly claims to subvert. I do want to hold onto Freud's more radical association of theory with fetishism, however, and to stress the importance of reading the theoretical in a temporal register. In Freud's alternative (and privileged) epistemology, theory is achieved not in the instance of a single take or in a flash of recognition but in the time of the double take, the time of the fetish.

Invoking the idea of a double take to describe the work of theory appropriately conveys the intellectual drama of the act itself: the sense of curiosity, shock, or (more benignly) what Barbara Johnson calls "the surprise of otherness" (15), the surprise of discovery that happens at the very moment we are confronted with our ignorance, with (in Freud's rendition of the problem) what we have seen but chosen to disavow. Where theory does its work is in the temporal oscillation between knowledge and ignorance, belief and doubt, certainty and uncertainty, immediacy and interminability, seeing and knowing. This critical suspension is encoded etymologically in the Greek term *theoria*, which may signify the act of looking at, contemplating, and viewing an object or (alternatively) the object itself, the sight or spectacle. Theory opens up this gap between seeing and what is seen, producing the critical distance necessary to read and to intervene in the complicated dynamics between discourses of knowledge production and the objects they themselves have produced for "discovery."

Any such tampering with the organization of knowledge, and with the symbolic laws by which its objects of study are posited and secured, is bound to be viewed or experienced as a troubling exercise. And theory is indeed "troubling" in the sense that every theoretical act is an act of interference that bothers and unsettles previously taken-for-granted norms and assumptions. More than a disturbance, theory operates within its institutional confines as something of a pest—a vexing and nagging presence that continually calls one to account. How do we account for theory in the classroom? Perhaps precisely as a practice of accountability, a ceaseless calling to action that takes the form of a communal reckoning. Accounting, from the Latin *computare*—"to reckon together" or "to calculate"—insists on theory's status *as* a practice, specifically as a particular kind of labor that entails the precision work of measuring, considering, weighing, estimating, deliberating, evaluating. In the most economical sense, theory takes stock, scrutinizes the store of information before it and renders a calculation of its usages, settlements, and yields, always taking into consideration whose interest this knowledge serves and who stands to profit. Theory is itself an "interested" enterprise, working to expose the politicality at the heart of every epistemological act, including its own.

It seems critical at this point to acknowledge theory's own changing and various investitures, for when theory claims neutrality for itself, it ceases to function in the ways I have described, no longer cognizant of the Other—the Other whose very postulation makes any question of neutrality and disinterestedness an impossibility, a fantasy, or a ruse. Theory as a practice of accountability also operates, axiomatically, as a mode of responsibility, especially in the pedagogical encounter in which each party is always answerable to the Other, responsible for the Other, bound in a contractual relation of interaction and exchange with the Other. Simply put, there can be no knowledge without the Other. "If the unconscious has taught us anything, it is firstly this, that somewhere, in the Other, it knows," Lacan tells his students in a seminar on the determinative role of discursive knowledge in the formation of social ties ("Love Letter" 158). As if in confirmation of Lacan's social epistemology, one of his own students, Moustafa Safouan, from his position *as* student, interprets the teacher's enigmatic words to mean that knowledge "is somewhere other than in the subject, in another place: the place of the Other where the question mark comes to an end" (132). The location of the Other ("where the question mark comes to an end") in the structural foundations of discourse no doubt explains why, for Lacanians, all knowledge is structurally paranoiac. The subject can know only through an identification with the Other (with "the subject presumed to know"), putting its own claims to mastery and complete knowledge into perpetual abeyance. In terms of the teaching of theory, this notion implies simply that all knowledge is inherently *social*, that identification is involved in every epistemological execution, and that theory, as a process fully implicated in this mimetic relation to the Other, is itself a cultural practice wholly accountable for its own procedures and effects.

It is perhaps for this reason that theory classes are famous for their self-reflexiveness. To retain its political edge, every theoretical innovation must reflect critically on its philosophical presuppositions. Theory's proclivity for continually repositioning and reformulating its objects inevitably produces a certain deceleration effect, but at the same time it is precisely this vigilant and sometimes laborious taking stock that permits any important theoretical advances to take place. The slower the process, the more rapid and potentially startling the gains. The theory classroom is often the most dramatic site of these competing temporal orders, producing in students the confusing impression that they are bogged down and out of breath at the same time. If pedagogy is going to keep up with the new revolutions in epistemology, it may have to learn how to slow down, or at least how to manage more inventively a new age, a nuclear age, in which going slow and going fast are no longer necessarily competing ways of reaching the same destination.

Princeton University

Notes

[1] Louis Althusser, in fact, views the educational system not just as one of many such "ideological state apparatuses" but also as the dominant site of class struggle in capitalist social formations. See Althusser, especially 147–53.

[2] I am reminded here of Shoshana Felman's astute observation on the subject of psychoanalytic learning that "to learn something *from* psychoanalysis is a very different thing than to learn something *about* it" (74), later explaining that, rather than "teach Freud," we teach "the condition that makes it possible to learn Freud" (81). This assertion confirms my own sense that the only effective way to learn from (and about) theory is to practice it. See Felman's chapter "Psychoanalysis and Education: Teaching Terminable and Interminable" in Felman (69–97).

[3] Mary Ann Doane's reading of the motif of distance and proximity in psychoanalysis, film criticism, and feminist theory, based in part on the passage from Freud cited here, first alerted me to the central place accorded to temporality in theories of epistemology. For an excellent reading of fetishism and problems of spectatorship, see both of Doane's essays on masquerade.

[4] Discussions of the role of fantasy and desire in the production of sexual identity have suggested that women, too, are capable of fetishism. See, for example, Schor; Silverman.

Works Cited

Althusser, Louis. *Lenin and Philosophy and Other Essays*. Trans. Ben Brewster. New York: Monthly Review, 1971.

Culler, Jonathan. "Resisting Theory." *Cardoza Law Review* 11.5–6 (1990): 1565–83.

de Man, Paul. *The Resistance to Theory*. Minneapolis: U of Minnesota P, 1986.

Derrida, Jacques. *"Geschlecht* II: Heidegger's Hand." *Deconstruction and Philosophy: The Texts of Jacques Derrida*. Ed. John Sallis. Chicago: U of Chicago P, 1987. 161–96.

———. "No Apocalypse, Not Now." Trans. Catherine Porter and Philip Lewis. *Diacritics* 14.2 (1984): 20–31.

Doane, Mary Ann. "Film and the Masquerade: Theorising the Female Spectator." *Screen* 23.3–4 (1982): 74–87.

———. "Masquerade Reconsidered: Further Thoughts on the Female Spectator." *Discourse* 11.1 (1988–89): 42–54.

Felman, Shoshana. *Jacques Lacan and the Adventure of Insight: Psychoanalysis in Contemporary Culture*. Cambridge: Harvard UP, 1987.

Freud, Sigmund. "A Case of Paranoia Running Counter to the Psychoanalytic Theory of the Disease." 1915. *Standard Edition* 14: 261–72.

———. "The Psychogenesis of a Case of Homosexuality in a Woman." 1920. *Standard Edition* 18: 145–72.

———. "Some Psychical Consequences of the Anatomical Distinction between the Sexes." 1925. *Standard Edition* 19: 241–58.

———. *The Standard Edition of the Complete Psychological Works of Sigmund Freud*. 24 vols. London: Hogarth, 1953–74.

Giroux, Henry, and Peter L. McLaren. "Radical Pedagogy as Cultural Politics: Beyond the Discourse of Critique and Anti-utopianism." *Theory/Pedagogy/Politics: Texts for Change*. Ed. Donald Morton and Mas'ud Zavarzadeh. Urbana: U of Illinois P, 1991. 152–86.

Irigaray, Luce. "Language, Persephone, and Sacrifice." Interview cond. and trans. Heather Jon Maroney. *Border/lines* 4 (1985–86): 30–32.

———. *This Sex Which Is Not One*. Trans. Catherine Porter with Carolyn Burke. Ithaca: Cornell UP, 1985.

Johnson, Barbara. "Nothing Fails like Success." *A World of Difference*. Baltimore: Johns Hopkins UP, 1987. 11–16.

Lacan, Jacques. "The Concept of Analysis." *Seminar I: Freud's Papers on Technique*. Ed. Jacques-Alain Miller. Trans. John Forrester. New York: Norton, 1988. 273–87.

———. "A Love Letter." Mitchell and Rose 149–61.

Mitchell, Juliet, and Jacqueline Rose, eds. *Feminine Sexuality: Jacques Lacan and the École Freudienne*. Trans. Jacqueline Rose. New York: Norton, 1982.

Rooney, Ellen. "Discipline and Vanish: Feminism, the Resistance to Theory, and the Politics of Cultural Studies." *Differences* 2.3 (1990): 14–28.

Safouan, Moustafa. "Feminine Sexuality in Psychoanalytic Doctrine." Mitchell and Rose 123–36.

Schor, Naomi. "Female Fetishism: The Case of George Sand." *The Female Body in Western Culture: Contemporary Perspectives*. Ed. Susan Rubin Suleiman. Cambridge: Harvard UP, 1986. 363–72.

Silverman, Kaja. *The Acoustic Mirror: The Female Voice in Psychoanalysis and Cinema*. Bloomington: Indiana UP, 1988.

Weber, Samuel. *Institution and Interpretation*. Minneapolis: U of Minnesota P, 1987.

Whitford, Margaret. *Luce Irigaray: Philosophy in the Feminine*. New York: Routledge, 1991.

Teaching Realism as Theory

Sandra A. Grayson

My course Problems in Literary Theory: Realism was conceived neither as a genre course with readings in theory nor as a survey of theories of realism. Instead, I hoped to employ realist fictions and literary theory to problematize students' notions of realism, representation, and the real. And, equally important in a course for undergraduates, I wanted the students to trade the unconscious assumptions that structured their critical judgments for conscious choices; I wanted them to become aware of their own reading practices.

I knew that many students would find the course difficult because it would demand that they reconsider their ways of understanding both literature and the world. But I assumed that if the logic of the course were made plain to them, if they tested every theoretical argument by applying it to their reading of novels, and if each student participated in discussing each reading, then the course would succeed. On the syllabus, I therefore asked what realism is and whether realistic representation is possible, and I reminded my students throughout the semester that they should be asking those questions and constantly revising their answers as they read. I created a detailed course outline, moving from traditional discussions of realism to poststructuralist attacks on representation. In class, we compared theoretical positions as we proceeded and periodically reviewed the ground we had covered.

My own reading of recent theory had taught me no truths, but it had made me aware of the problems inherent in the notion of representation, especially of the difficulties and contradictions in the realist enterprise of describing the world as it is. Therefore I knew as the course began that I could not assume the heroic and impossible role of the realist novelist, supplying the authoritative perspective that would make sense of a confusing body of information. Instead, I hoped that by the end of the semester each student would begin to develop an *individual* reasoned perspective on realism and the larger issue of representation. My pedagogical method reflected this intellectual goal. As the students should become theorists themselves, they should take primary responsibility for what happened in the classroom. Thus, I would neither lecture in class nor ask a series of questions that would lead students to predetermined conclusions. Instead, students would primarily talk with one another, raising questions, arguing, trying to correct one another's errors. As they grappled with representation, they would also learn to represent themselves. While I would help them to understand the readings, the conclusions they drew would be their own. Some students would probably end up as defenders of a realist poetic, others would reject the notion of representation, and still others would find their places between these positions.

To create the course I envisioned, I emphasized from the beginning that classes would be conversations among students. To make each day's assignment manageable, we read the novels in parts. To prepare students to speak in class in a reasoned and knowledgeable way, I required that each one bring a detailed written response to each day's reading (these responses would contribute to their grades). I also required that all students participate in the conversation and enforced this rule by asking those who had remained silent for most of the hour to comment on what they had heard that day. These requirements provided strong incentives for students to read carefully and thoughtfully.

Typically, classes began with the students' questions. When I spoke, it was usually to keep their conversation focused and serious. If students spoke in broad generalizations, I might ask them to become more specific; fairly often, I requested evidence for their positions; and at times I would push them to see the assumptions and implications buried in their arguments. But I proposed solutions to problems only when the discussion was truly foundering—and then I tried to mention more than one possible solution, leaving students with the responsibility to choose. Finally, since I was not determining the direction or pace of the discussion, I took detailed notes in each class. In the last few minutes of the hour, I would use these notes to summarize the day's arguments, point out agreements and disagreements, and remind the students of issues that had been raised and left unresolved.

This method of teaching is labor-intensive (after every class, I read and commented on twenty-two responses). It also demands great patience (to remain silent was sometimes a struggle). But the discussions in my class achieved results that a lecture or even a teacher-dominated discussion could not. I found that if I consistently required students to begin classes with their questions and to listen to their classmates respectfully, their conversations would be productive, serious, and lively. Students were at times genuinely puzzled by the theoretical readings, but they arrived eager to pose their questions. They wanted answers and learned to trust that the discussion would provide some and point the way toward others. Students came to see the class as a cooperative intellectual effort. Because they understood that we were raising genuinely open questions, with many possible answers, they knew their opinions counted, and they took seriously their responsibility to read thoughtfully and to contribute to discussions.

What follows is a narrative of the course's progress. It sounds more seamless than it was, because, like any realist writer, I want to create a coherent account, and I have lessons to teach. I thus emphasize the students' growth in sophistication and understanding, and I describe the theoretical and critical readings that led to that result. Although I do indicate disagreements among the students and suggest how I would teach the course differently next time, thirteen weeks of student-centered discussions included many more false starts, blind alleys, and backslidings than I have space to describe. The students did not all progress at the same pace, nor did they end the course in the same place. They did, however, all finish in a different place from the one where they began.

In the first class, I asked the students to define realism. They illustrated their ideas with examples from films as well as novels, mainly focusing on plot and character: in a realistic work events should be plausible; characters' motives and actions should be understandable. No supernatural beings, and little wish fulfillment, would be allowed. A few students commented on modes of narration; the class decided that omniscient narrators are probably not realistic. Their implicit definition of realism at this point was correspondence to reality as they conceived of it.

Then we began reading *Robinson Crusoe*, and we talked about whether, how, and why the novel seemed realistic. I wanted the class to develop a naive working definition of realism, which we would test in later readings and qualify or abandon before the course ended. I expected that any issues the students raised would be relevant to our consideration of realism and, finally, representation since I could follow almost any comment with the same question: Does that make the novel realistic? What I did not expect was the tenacity with which many of the students pursued that question themselves. Our early discussions of *Robinson Crusoe* concentrated on issues of plot and character. The students commented at length on the implausibility of the novel's events. But most of them felt that the character-narrator himself seemed real, compensating for any failures in the plot; they believed that they knew Crusoe, and they liked talking about his foibles and eccentricities.

In the second class on the novel, to move students beyond speaking of Crusoe as if he were real, I asked them to name the qualities that make him *seem* real. Students then discussed him as an ordinary middle-class character with middle-class concerns: money, success, order, the need to plan. They devoted much time to discussing whether Crusoe develops over time, and they never came to an agreement; nor could they decide whether growth in a character is necessary to realism. But they did all view Crusoe as an exemplary capitalist, amassing possessions and money, delaying gratification, teaching readers how to succeed. When I asked whether they saw a contradiction between presenting a story as individual and real, on the one hand, and representative and morally exemplary, on the other, the students answered in terms of the novel before them and finally said no; this character-narrator *would* find lessons in events. Similarly, he would believe God was actively involved in his life, so his providential explanations in no way diminished the novel's realism.

Character is familiar and comfortable ground for undergraduate English majors. To make sure they covered other ground as well, I asked them at one point to evaluate the novel's opening in terms of how it defines some important realities of its world. They readily focused on Crusoe's foregrounding of money, property, class, family, and parent-child relations. As we went on to read of Crusoe's life on the island, some students continued that line of analysis. They saw Crusoe importing with him the European idea that human beings should dominate their environment, and creating a world to conform to his preconceptions. His worldview thus precedes and creates his world.

The students also discussed some formal issues. As we finished reading the novel, for example, one student commented that *Crusoe*'s ending seems unrealistic because it trails off inconclusively. Most of the others seemed puzzled about how to evaluate the ending, so I asked whether closure is real or a literary convention. At this point, we began to consider the role of convention in realist representation.

While reading *Crusoe* raised many more issues than it resolved, it clearly led students to begin formulating their own definitions of realism. While not all of them concurred, most postulated a close correspondence between literature and life. They expected "ordinary" characters and "possible" events. Formal features of realist fiction would include mundane details and a matter-of-fact narratorial tone.

Armed with ideas and questions, the students were ready to begin to consider others' views. Our critical readings began with Ian Watt's historically based genre definition of realism and, to complicate Watt's view, Wayne Booth's discussion of "realisms." The students found these readings clear and immediately useful. Watt's chapter prompted further reflections on *Robinson Crusoe* as a middle-class text. Booth's arguments led, as we turned to *Adam Bede*, to questions about whether George Eliot's realism differed significantly from Daniel Defoe's. Together, these readings helped students to become less naive and more critical as readers—to think of realism as a complex *literary* issue, to begin to separate their judgments of realism from their sense of what is real.

Reading the first chapters of *Adam Bede*, the students concentrated their attention on the strong presence of the narrator, who guides readers in understanding the novel's characters and events while presenting a particular interpretation of the world. In the second class on the novel, the students discussed chapter 17, in which the narrator self-consciously defends the novel's realism. When I asked how this passage defines realism, students concluded after much discussion that Eliot conceives of realism in terms of subject matter. Remembering Booth, who argues that realism can be an end or a means for a writer, some students also saw that realism served a moral purpose for Eliot.

As we continued to discuss the novel, the students devoted much time to the characters and their motives: how does Arthur Donnithorne feel about Hetty Sorrel, and why does Adam love Hetty? This discussion became complicated, though, by our reading of Leo Bersani's "Realism and the Fear of Desire." This was the most challenging text we tackled early in the semester, and students grappled throughout the course with Bersani's argument that realistic fiction reassures readers by presenting character as unified and comprehensibly motivated and the world as intelligible, ruled by laws of cause and effect. Since the students shared the assumptions that Bersani attributes to realism, it was difficult for them to understand those assumptions *as* assumptions. At first they emphasized instead Bersani's distinction between characters who are governed by desire and characters who suppress desire. *Adam Bede* provides a clear illustration of the dangers of desire, the ways in which desire can disrupt social order and threaten a character's coherence. The class began to understand Hetty's fate in Bersani's terms: the novel maintains its realism by punishing her indulgence in desire.

We next read several nineteenth-century writers on realism: Charles Dickens, George Gissing, George Henry Lewes, and George Moir. These writers surprised the students by acknowledging (like *Adam Bede*'s narrator) that all writing is subjective, that novels necessarily reflect and construct a particular view of reality. The essays provided a useful introduction to Dickens's *Great Expectations*, a novel in which reality is decidedly strange. Here I wanted the students to abandon the notions of an unproblematic objective reality and an unproblematic realism, as they saw the differences between Dickens's realism and the realisms of Defoe and Eliot. But I also hoped that the sophistication of the nineteenth-century critics might influence the students to question the notion of representation.

Great Expectations, of course, follows the pattern of the standard realist novel: a story in which the protagonist must abandon his illusions and learn to live in the real world. In this novel, however, the real world is at least as improbable as the main character's wildest fantasy. I wondered what the class would do with a novel that seems so often to parody its own basic premise.

The students focused first, as usual, on issues of character and argued, as they had when reading *Robinson Crusoe*, that the hero was so real that readers could almost ignore improbabilities in the action. But they also applied their readings in theory to Pip and his self-indulgent dreams. Some understood the first-person narration in terms suggested by Bersani: they argued that the novel would lose pattern and intelligibility if we became caught up in Pip's desires and that therefore Dickens chose an adult narrator whose viewpoint distances the character Pip from the reader and so puts the character's desires in perspective. The students moved easily from discussing desire to noting other standard features of the realist novel, especially the central role played by class and money. But they noticed antirealist elements of the novel as well—the plot, with its egregious coincidences, and such obvious symbols as Satis House and Miss Havisham's wedding cake. Symbols are everywhere, the students agreed. And why, they asked, don't the characters have the ordinary names that Watt identifies as a feature of realist fiction?

Finally we discussed the novel's two endings. Most students chose Dickens's first, unpublished ending as more realistic, because it so clearly requires Pip to renounce his early dreams. Others, though, defended the openness and indeterminacy of the published ending. As that day's class ended, I asked the students to think again about the problem of closure that had come up at the end of *Robinson Crusoe*: is the traditional realist ending, in its closure, inevitably unreal?

Following *Great Expectations*, we read several essays designed to challenge the idea that a novel could represent an objective reality. Among these, Walter Pater's "Conclusion" to *The Renaissance* was the most powerfully persuasive. The class readily incorporated Pater into its (by now firmly held) notion of realisms: Pater redefines realism by locating knowable reality in subjective experience. Some students asked whether a novel can represent the inner experience that for Pater is the only reality. Others, having learned to question their initial faith that they could directly measure the realism of novels against their own notions of what is real, asked how one could judge the success of such an attempt. And should one try? Can we read novels in terms of representation? Or is the point of reading simply to experience a series of sensations?

We next read *To the Lighthouse*. The class saw Virginia Woolf as Pater's intellectual ally, foregrounding mental process, describing an internal reality. They defined this internal focus as "her realism." In addition, several students contrasted Woolf with Defoe; unlike him, they argued, she believes that human life is shaped predominantly by personal relationships. One student posed this question: If each novelist is a realist in his or her own way, are any qualities common to all realist texts? The class debated this issue, using as evidence the four novels they had read. Many students, endorsing Bersani, maintained that realistic psychology is essential for an effect of realism; we must feel we understand the central character as we would a living person. Most students also agreed that we must find the world of the novel intelligible. One student shifted the focus of the questioning, asking whether different novels would seem realistic to different readers. Do readers have their own realisms? Several students argued that *To the Lighthouse* was the most realistic novel the class had read; they agreed with Woolf's portrayal of experience as fragmented and

constantly changing. For others, however, the novel seemed unnatural
and contrived; they were conscious throughout of the narrator, who describes characters and events in a way shaped by her particular beliefs
and interests. For the best students, realism had by this point become
thoroughly problematized.

To move the discussion toward a consideration of representation as
a problem, I asked whether authors and readers can be realists without
having ideas about art as well as about reality—notions not only about
what aspects of life it is important to represent but also about how to
represent them. The class responded by discussing the opposed views of
reality that Mr. and Mrs. Ramsey hold; the novels these characters might
write would be vastly different. But a few students also mentioned Lily
Briscoe's struggles with her painting, and I suggested that the class think
about the implications of her problems for novel writing as well.

The class next read selections from E. H. Gombrich's *Art and Illusion*
(12–25, 87–90), in which Gombrich argues that seeing is a complex mental
process and that representation depends on formulas. Most students
had become lost in Gombrich's text, largely because they could not immediately see how his comments on visual art related to literature. They
meandered: "Is he saying primitive art is good?" asked one student, while
another proposed, "It's important how people feel about what they see."
A few students addressed the issue of realism: "What we know affects
what we see," one commented, and another agreed: "He's saying we
see what we learn to see." We had reached a crucial point in the course,
when students should be thinking not only about literary realism but
also about the larger question of representation. So I raised two questions. First, I asked what Gombrich means by the statement "all art is
'conceptual'" (87). Students argued that he means the real is subjective,
that everyone has a different conception and therefore perception of
the world. "Then what does he mean," I asked, "by the statement 'art is
born of art'?" (24). When only one student attempted a response, I spoke
for a few minutes on period styles in realist painting, making the point
that vision is not simply individual. I also distributed a cartoon, reproduced in Gombrich's book, showing a life-drawing class in ancient
Egypt, in which the students are learning to paint in the proper flat style.
The students explained the joke: the Egyptians didn't paint what they
saw; they painted an idea. But I had to prod further—"An idea about
what?"—before they could clearly explain that it was an idea not just about
the nature of reality but also about the proper way to represent reality.
At this point a student remembered Lily Briscoe's struggle to find the right
way to convey her vision.

To translate these ideas from the realm of visual art to that of literature, I reminded the students of their disappointment with the lack of
closure at the end of *Robinson Crusoe* and asked them to think about how
one novel shapes their expectations of another. As the class ended, I asked
them to remember Gombrich's crucial statements: "All art is conceptual"

and "Art is born of art." One student tried to summarize what everyone had learned: "There are no clear windows on reality." The students had far to go before they could come to terms with representation, but this attempt was a start.

We moved from this reading to a set of more-difficult essays: I attempted to use the brief discussions of semiotics, structuralism, and deconstruction in M. H. Abrams's *Glossary of Literary Terms* to introduce poststructuralist attacks on representation. For discussion of this reading, I had allotted only one class, which was far too little time. Students confessed their confusion, and I agreed to explain the readings as they listened and asked questions. Most of the class could not really comprehend, with such brief explanations from Abrams and me, why one might think of language as a system of differences rather than as referential. But our previous reading allowed them to understand why a "signified" is an idea, not a material object; and they understood also how one would come to view what is culturally conditioned as natural, inevitable, and therefore real. Novels would thus strike us as realistic if they reflected our culture's ways of understanding the world and followed certain rules of representation. Literature could not in any simple way be real.

We followed this reading with J. Hillis Miller's deconstruction of the realism of Dickens's *Sketches by Boz* and tried in this class to apply the lessons of the previous one. Students focused most closely on Miller's claim that society in Dickens's text depends on conventions and fictions. Some rewriting of Miller went on; students saw Dickens as employing a realist strategy, exposing society's fictions in order to replace lies with truth. I withheld comment for much of the class but finally challenged this reading by reminding them of some bizarre coincidences in the plot of *Great Expectations*. I asked if Dickens expected readers to consider his plot truer than his characters' fictions or if we should apply to this novel Miller's definition of literature: language that calls attention to its own fictionality? Should we apply this definition to all the novels we had read? Without committing themselves to Miller's approach, students found examples of blatantly improbable elements in each novel, beginning with Crusoe's great luck in being so well provisioned on his island. A few students went further, embracing Miller's definition of liberation (telling lies while asserting that they are lies) and applying it to Dickens and the other novelists whose work we had read. They enjoyed this dethronement of realism as a value. Other students, however, protested this radical new standard. A few, who felt the course had gone too far in challenging their comfortable ways of reading, attempted to return to an atheoretical innocence; they defended judging a novel's reality according to their own sense of the real. Still others historicized the issue, arguing that Miller's values were not those of the eighteenth- and nineteenth-century novelists, who were trying to represent the world accurately even if they knew they could not succeed. In this class, Miller won few converts, but most of the students grappled seriously with the issues he raises.

We completed our week of poststructuralist readings with Shoshana Felman's "Women and Madness: The Critical Phallacy," omitting most of her difficult introductory section. Many students became at least somewhat lost in Felman's language, but they were interested in her summary of Balzac's "Adieu" and in her indictment of the story's misogynist critics. When they were having trouble posing a question, I began with this indictment, asking what it had to do with realism. In response, a student read Felman's statement that for Balzac's critics "what happens to men is more important, and/or more 'real,' than what happens to women" (6). The class understood this statement in terms of their debate on *To the Lighthouse*: critics, like authors, bring to their work conceptions of reality and hence realism. I asked if, according to Felman, they bring to their work other ideas as well. A few students commented tentatively on how realist texts construct women.

No one, however, could develop this point. Instead, several students spoke about the difficulty of reading Felman's essay. I asked them to be specific, to point out sentences and paragraphs they found unclear. We labored together over several passages dense with nominalizations, and after half an hour two important points had emerged. First, the class understood Felman's claim that cultures naturalize their own assumptions, making the world explicable. Second, they could follow her argument that the realist enterprise, which must banish or tame the inexplicable, insists that women be definable; women who do not conform to patriarchal expectations are thus labeled "mad."

As the hour was ending, the students worked out their own understanding of the essay by referring to characters and narrators who make the world explicable by taming or banishing the "other." Some students spoke of Crusoe's work to adapt the island to his mode of life and to convert Friday into a Christian and a servant. Others remembered how women are dealt with in *Adam Bede*: Bartle Massey claims to understand females (canine and human) in terms of a few traits; Adam cannot believe Hetty is pregnant, because this fact violates his idea of her.

We next read John Fowles's *The French Lieutenant's Woman*, and "Women and Madness" became a richly suggestive text. The students, all of whom had struggled and some of whom had given up while reading poststructuralist attacks on representation, became interested in the way Fowles plays with the notion of Sarah's madness, while he also plays with and challenges many conventions of realism.

In our first discussion about *The French Lieutenant's Woman*, students found many reasons for and against classifying it as realistic. They noted that the novel takes place in a particular setting at a particular time and that the central character seems fairly ordinary. But they also commented on the novel's many allusions to other texts; a few pointed out that the narrator creates his Victorian world by modeling it on fictions. For example, he repeatedly compares his protagonist's servant with Sam Weller of Dickens's *Pickwick Papers*. A few students probed the implications of this fact: is Fowles suggesting, one asked, that texts reflect only other texts?

Throughout our discussion of the novel, the students invoked Felman. From the beginning, they asked what it meant to label Sarah mad and to attribute her madness to sexual passion. In a later class, one student argued that Sarah must be called mad because she is threateningly other—a text that Victorian men cannot read. Sarah is punished, perhaps, less for indulging desire than for introducing an unfamiliar text into her world.

In the second class on Fowles's novel, we tried to deal with the narrator's comments, in Chapter 13, on the novel's fictionality. Students were troubled by the contradiction of an author's saying that a novel is "all imagination" (80) while maintaining that his characters have freedom. To generalize the discussion, I asked if these contradictions are inherent in realism; yes, the students answered, but some objected to Fowles's highlighting the contradictions. Why, one student asked, is Fowles's direct address to the reader more disturbing than Eliot's in *Adam Bede*? Another argued that Fowles was making his novel other, thus forcing readers to question their normal ways of understanding fiction.

As we ended our discussion of this novel, students pondered Fowles's alternative endings, asking why he included both in the novel. They employed Bersani to differentiate between the two: in one the hero suffers for pursuing his desire; in the other he is rewarded with Sarah, the object of his desire. Inevitably, they compared these endings with those of *Great Expectations*. The class clearly saw that Fowles violates a convention of realism by giving readers a choice. Some students complained that he is as authoritative as any nineteenth-century writer, and far too didactic: "Why keep teaching us about our conventional expectations?" But the most sophisticated students argued that the novel presents reality as something constructed, not given. One pointed out that Charles writes a novel about Sarah in his head only to learn that he has been a character in the fiction she creates. Another argued that the narrator, in warning readers to question the authority of novels and narrators, exemplifies Miller's definition of literature as antirealistic, antirepresentational: language that foregrounds its own fictionality.

As the course ended, I asked the students to discuss the notion of representation: could a fiction represent a world, a truth, external to itself? The class was strongly divided. I had chosen the course's focus on realism as a means to ponder representation, because I'd correctly surmised that realism is the intellectual territory in which most students live. Some of them remained there even at the end. Others embraced the notion of fictional worlds with fictional referents, language leading us not toward the world but toward language. Still others stood somewhere in the middle, defending the power of novelists, even as they worked within cultural constructions of reality, nevertheless to challenge those constructions with their own visions of the real. That the students felt free to disagree, finally, and that they could defend their positions was a measure of the course's success. But they also reached consensus on some issues. As they engaged in an important theoretical debate, they all understood—sooner or later—that no fiction can be a clear window on the world, that novels mediate reality through individual visions, cultural codes, and formulas of representation. Perhaps more important, for this is what finally was at stake in the course, the students learned—from reading theory, from debating one another—that their own critical judgments were informed by theoretical assumptions and that those assumptions could be challenged. The course thus succeeded in problematizing reading for all the students, while for the best students it problematized representation and reality as well.

Saint Mary's College of California

Works Cited

Abrams, M. H. *A Glossary of Literary Terms*. 5th ed. New York: Holt, Rinehart, 1988.

Bersani, Leo. "Realism and the Fear of Desire." *A Future for Astyanax: Character and Desire in Literature*. Boston: Little, 1976. 51–88.

Booth, Wayne C. "On Discriminating among Realisms." *The Rhetoric of Fiction*. Chicago: U of Chicago P, 1961. 53–60.

[Dickens, Charles.] "The Sensational Williams." Platz-Waury 68–71.

[Dickens, Charles?] "The Spirit of Fiction." *All the Year Round* 27 July 1867: 118–20.

Felman, Shoshana. "Women and Madness: The Critical Phallacy." *Diacritics* 5 (1975): 2–10.

Gissing, George. "The Place of Realism in Fiction." Platz-Waury 115–18.

Gombrich, E. H. *Art and Illusion: A Study in the Psychology of Pictorial Representation*. 2nd ed. Princeton: Princeton UP, 1961.

Lewes, George Henry. "Realism in Art: Recent German Fiction." 1858. Platz-Waury 58.

Miller, J. Hillis. "The Fiction of Realism: *Sketches by Boz, Oliver Twist,* and Cruikshank's Illustrations." *Dickens Centennial Essays*. Ed. Ada Nisbet and Blake Nevius. Berkeley: U of California P, 1971. 95–126.

Moir, George. "Modern Novel and Romance." Platz-Waury 34–38.

Pater, Walter. "Conclusion." *The Renaissance*. New York: Random, n.d. 194–99.

Platz-Waury, Elke, ed. *Nineteenth Century*. Vol. 3 of *English Theories of the Novel*. Tübingen: Niemeyer, 1972.

Watt, Ian. "Realism and the Novel Form." *The Rise of the Novel*. Berkeley: U of California P, 1957. 9–34.

Giving Voice to Feminist Criticism:
A Conversation

Beverly Lyon Clark, Heather I. Braun, Susan Dearing,
Kerry-Beth Garvey, Karen M. Gennari, Becky Hemperly,
and Michelle Henneberry

One of my more overused jokes is that I'm allergic to poetry. Yet now
I'm wondering what would have happened if the poetic bill of fare in
high school had included Emily Dickinson or even Sylvia Plath. Even
now, when I think of poetry, I think of T. S. Eliot. And my hands shake.
Why, why, why do high schools do this to students? My idea of poetry
in high school was that it was something some really weird and egotistical
men wrote. (Sidney Coutts)

    I spent four years at Brown without ever speaking in class. It took
me years as an adult to learn how to speak up. (Susan Dearing)

    As I read over my notes, I realize that the contradictions presented
in this Harlequin romance are a direct reflection of the contradictions
I find in myself. (Heather Braun)

    The above comments come from students who have taken Feminist
Criticism, an upper-level English course with a typical enrollment of twelve
or thirteen white middle-class undergraduate women of traditional college
age (sometimes there are older students, on rare occasions a black, so
far no men). Some of the students are interested primarily in literature,
some primarily in theory, some primarily in feminism; a substantial
minority are social science majors. The course attempts to build bridges
between the concrete and the abstract, between the experiential and the
theoretical, between literature and theory—at the same time calling each
pairing into question.

    One aim of this essay is to interrupt the monolithic voice of the aca-
demic essay by creating a dialogue that echoes the dialogue of the classroom, a textual analogue for student-centered teaching. For students' perspectives are as important as mine (Bev Clark)—more important, in fact,
if teachers truly want to gain insight into teaching. I may still be the one

who assumes greatest authority in both class and essay, yet I try to de-mystify my authority as well. Or, rather, not I but we—we demystify it. Those whose names appear at the top of this essay have queried and edited one another's writing (we quote, with permission, the work of other students as well), though I am primarily responsible for the passages in roman type. The others have been "students" in the course, though one, Susan Dearing, is also a faculty member. Most passages in italics derive from classwork, usually journals; some are responses to drafts of this essay. Overall, we attempt a mode of writing that relies less on the logic of reason than on the logic of association, that is less hierarchical and more evocative than the norm.

In some ways you want the essay to be hard to read—you want to unsettle your readers, derail them/us so that they/we will pay more attention to the terrain we are covering together. (Susan Dearing)

Much of what we attempt to say is not spelled out but, rather, is in the spaces between the roman and italicized passages. We realize that we are making special demands on the reader. The teacher does not securely frame each "student" passage, subordinating it to an overriding thesis. Instead, we try to let each individual speak for herself. Often passages are in dialogue with one another. Often we disagree. And thus in the intervening spaces readers can listen for affect, for dissonances and harmonies, and can chart their own ways.

To ease the reader into our conversation, however, I provide a couple of maps (just as, the first day of class, I attempt to chart strands of feminist criticism on the blackboard; while this framework does oversimplify, it also reassures apprehensive students). First, a map of substantive issues addressed in the essay: we start with theoretical issues (such as how students find theory difficult), then turn to strategies (for writing, for dis-cussion—in general, for building trust), then return to theoretical issues (connecting the personal and the theoretical, valorizing diversity). Second, a map of the substantive issues I cover. In the most recent version of the course, I framed the assignments for each week or two with overarch-ing questions: Do women read differently? Have women been silenced? What is feminist criticism? Do women write differently? Do women favor different genres? Do women have a different tradition? Should women redefine the canon? How does gender intersect with class? How does gender intersect with race and sexual orientation?

Yet though it is important at times to be utilitarian, to provide maps, I feel that, as in the class itself, the process of getting to wherever we're going is more important than any final answers. We attempt to attend to the individual, to validate difference, in an essay and a course that alternately essentialize and dismantle.

I remember when you would ask everyone or specific women to dis-cuss what they thought or felt about the theories we had learned that week. It was clear when your ideas differed from theirs/mine, but you allowed for multiple readings and analyses, as feminist criticism was not merely the content that we were discussing but also the process of our discussion. (Heather Braun)

Our pronouns slip, necessarily perhaps, as we try to negotiate non-traditional positions, as we question the traditional roles of teacher and student. We attempt to enact what scholars like Margo Culley, Frances Maher, and Paula Treichler have called feminist pedagogy: being inductive, cooperative, attentive to the subjective, student-centered.

I would love to be "lectured at." I know it goes against the inductive grain, but it would be so much easier if you could give the definitive word on "what Moi says about X." But we wouldn't want things to be easy, I know, for that might deny their complexity. (Elisabeth Stitt)

We are our own best experts. (Heather Braun)

Our thinking here—a moment of essentializing—is influenced by a strand of feminism that valorizes the personal, the experiential, the affective and that, paradoxically, given the subject of the course, resists theory. Maybe I can best express what I attempt in the classroom by refracting it through the comment of a male student in another course. He noted that he didn't feel as though the class invited rip-roaring arguments; other students—mostly women—responded that they therefore felt more comfortable about speaking up. Whether this mode is essentially feminine or feminist, I try to foster a collaborative climate in which students build on one another's thinking. We still challenge one another; as Nina Baym urges, "[T]he teacher needs to encourage her women students to say what she does not expect them to say and perhaps would rather not hear" (75). Yet we need not put one another down, need not score points off one another. The classroom climate can be both challenging and supportive.

I really appreciate the amount of class discussion because it helps me to understand what I have read. Sometimes, however, when I make a comment in class, I feel as if I get halfway through my statement and then I don't understand what I'm saying anymore. I find it difficult sometimes to grasp an idea and pin it down before it dissipates or changes. I feel like I'm trying to hold onto water. (Midsemester evaluation, anon.)

Being student-centered may be especially difficult in a theory course. How does one get students to articulate their concerns if they have read little theory before, if they are not yet comfortable speaking the language of "deconstruct" and "essentialize," if they are being urged to find unfamiliar ways of looking at the world?

Understanding theory means sometimes questioning when there are no answers. It means letting yourself be confused and accepting the frustration while hanging on to the belief that it will become clearer, more understandable in time. Sometimes I would be doing other course work or reading or even watching TV, and all of a sudden I would figure out how a theory worked or what an author or feminist critic meant in an article or book I had read days or even weeks earlier. (Heather Braun)

Somehow one has to build students' trust to enable them to take the risks that lead to true learning. I stress that we are all going through this educational process together, that it is difficult for all of us. I joke about how many hours I have had to spend wrestling with the piece by Julia Kristeva or how another piece gripped me in the gut or knocked my socks off.

Still, it was comforting for me to know that you understood the theory a little better than we students did. This kept us from feeling that all our questioning was futile, solving nothing. (Becky Hemperly)

We start the semester with get-acquainted exercises: each of us states her name and favorite fruit, after repeating the name and fruit of everyone who has gone before; as a group, we also reach consensus on answers to questions like who has had the most pets and who is wearing the most colors. These exercises both familiarize us with one another's names and start building a group feeling, as we do something a little silly together. Next time I teach the course, I want to share glimpses as well of our backgrounds and preconceptions—our racial, ethnic, and class backgrounds; our family situations; our reasons for being in the course (perhaps each of us could interview another and then introduce that partner). Each could develop a keener sense of her own positionality if she has a better sense of others' positions from the beginning. I know my own ideas are shaped by my having been the first member of my family to go to college, by being an adoptive parent, by considering myself a feminist.

I think background info as an icebreaker is good provided it does not lead to pigeonholing. Recently, I was in a nonfiction writing workshop that was part of my graduate program. Through something I had written, it became apparent to the class that I'm a lesbian. Now I did not mind sharing this fact with the class (after all, I wrote the piece), but after that, my classmates perceived me as the "resident expert" on all gay-related issues. (Becky Hemperly)

I also include frequent writing assignments as a way of learning, of grappling with difficult course materials, and of empowering students (though not all are equally empowered thereby).

I felt anxious as to whether I could write well enough, as a non-English person, to express ideas which I knew I could easily speak. (Heather Braun)

My own development raises the key issue of the difference between the passive "to be silenced" and the active "to be silent." Perhaps as a child I was silenced, but now I am silent. Perhaps, on the other hand, I am not silent at all. When the class first read about silencing, it was within the context of women writing, in which case I am neither silenced nor silent, for I get my ideas across in writing. (Michelle Henneberry)

Most important is the weekly writing assignment. Each week a student completes either three ten-minute journal entries or a one-page single-spaced paper. (I require three of the latter from each student during the semester.) In a one-page paper she can explore the extent to which the critics agree or disagree on an issue, the extent to which she agrees or disagrees with a critic, the extent to which a literary work illustrates or counters a theoretical insight. Students choose when they want to write their one-page papers, though I indicate final deadlines for each. This flexibility enables a student to write a polished essay when a week's topic particularly inspires her and perhaps when the demands of other courses are less onerous than usual.

The journals—which I grade with a check, check plus, or check minus —allow students to engage personally with the reading. The best entries, I tell students, often start by noting a question or problem and then explore possible answers and solutions. Or they connect a work with the student's own experiences or connect a work of criticism with a work of fiction. Students may thus query what they read, converse with it and with me. They can take risks in trying out ideas. They can feel comfortable about changing their minds in the course of the entry—or about revealing the contradictions that inhabit us all. Journals encourage students not just to prepare for class discussion but to work through shifting and contradictory thoughts and feelings. Usually the best way to explain to students what they can do with their journals is by giving examples, by having them read aloud from their journals in class. Sometimes I duplicate an entry from a previous class, perhaps one in which the process of writing pushes a student to explore self-contradictions.

Okay. I am coming out of the closet now. "My name is S— and I am a trashaholic." Well. I am not that bad. But I have to admit, frankly, that I have read some of this tripe. More than some. But I read the really trashy romances, the ones with the badly done lurid pictures on the cover. They're great for the recovery period after exams. I never buy them in the same store twice—just in case they remember me.

It was nice to read that so many women who read romances realize that this is not real life—I am tired of critics suggesting that women who read romances and watch soap operas are idiots who cannot make distinctions between fantasy and reality. But research shows that men who are shown a lot of films that depict violence against women are more apt to commit (or want to commit) violence against women. It should follow that women who read a lot of books that depict romance as simplistically as these do would then expect romance to be this simplistic. Sometimes I wonder what influence these books are having on me. Then I tell myself it can't be any worse than the message I learned from fairy tales as a child. (Journal entry, anon.)

Each week three or four members of the class distribute copies of what they have written and read them aloud. Such sharing not only provides models of writing but also builds bridges between writing and speaking, expanding the dialogue between reader and text into a conversation involving the whole class. This sharing ensures that classes start with students' concerns. I find it helpful, after students read their writing, to ask if they want to add anything, and often their descriptions of how they have struggled with the reading are revelatory. And I may ask other students whether they agree, whether they have felt similarly, whether their own experiences lead them to different views, whether there was a point that wasn't quite clear to them, whether there is a question they want to ask the reader.

Initially I felt awkward about speaking up about issues that could be so intensely personal. I felt much better, however, after my first journal-sharing time and after Heather engaged me, in class, in a conversation about why I felt the way I did. It was a subject that I was in the process of sorting through myself, which made it even more difficult, but to know someone else understood and respected my opinion was wonderful! (Karen Gennari)

For the term project each student creates an anthology of feminist criticism, usually on a single author.[1] This project enables students to build on their concrete experiences with literature by embracing theory and to appreciate a multiplicity of feminist approaches in their choice of articles. Early in the course, we have a library orientation session. We discuss MLA *Bibliography* CD-ROM searches; for example, students learn that while they can call up titles listed under both "feminist approach" and, say, "Toni Morrison," not everything that could be considered feminist criticism has necessarily been coded under "feminist approach." We discuss principles for choosing articles (has a student located the most recent criticism? represented a variety of approaches?) and for sequencing (chronological? topical?). Often students have a hard time grasping the principle of representing a variety of approaches: in writing term papers, they have sought criticism that supports particular theses; now I am urging them to feel comfortable with divergent thinking, with not tying everything into a neat, consistent package. For many students, this way of working is completely unfamiliar. We also brainstorm the kinds of topics they might address in an introduction, such as how they have defined feminist criticism, why they have chosen to include each piece, what common themes are addressed by the articles, what work has yet to be done and perhaps why it has not been done yet. About a month into the semester annotated bibliographies are due; the following month students make oral progress reports; a week before the final deadline students do peer reviewing of one another's drafts of the introductory essay (for some ideas on peer reviewing, see Beaven; Elbow).

The anthology project was a real change from the typical term paper. I thought it would be easy. Trying to understand and organize the materials, though, was one of the most difficult things I have had to do. It really tested my ability to interpret and differentiate among complex theories. (Michelle Henneberry)

All this student writing, especially the one-page papers and the journals, feeds into and is fed by class discussion. I want to undo the silencing that has hampered many women students. I feel strongly that all students should contribute to discussion—though not all agree.

One problem in any discussion about silencing is the assumption that talk is good and silence bad. This is just the type of duality that some feminists try to deconstruct. I am not saying that every class should be a rigid lecture; however, I am saying that verbal output is not the only gauge of "class participation" or the student's understanding and engagement. Individuals learn and process information in different ways. Some students gain a better understanding through discussion; others speak to prove to the professor that they grasp the material or to divert the professor's attention from the fact that they are not prepared; others absorb information and speak only when they have something important to say. (Michelle Henneberry)

Yes, you are right. But I would still like all students to benefit from airtime. I urge them to be sure, for instance, to speak up during the first class meeting. As I remember from my own undergraduate days, the longer one waits before speaking up, the more momentous a statement has to be.

Yes, but that is you. (Heather Braun)

I have also worked on extending my wait time—beyond the typical two seconds or less that an instructor waits after asking a question—before rephrasing or plunging on with an answer.

That also encourages those of us who are quick to speak to take time and reflect first. (Heather Braun)

I try to avoid calling on the first person to raise a hand. I look around the room before calling on anyone, making eye contact with as many students as possible. I provide mechanisms for students to do some thinking before talking, such as freewriting or listing ("Okay, we're resisting Duras's story, so let's freewrite for five minutes, this half of the room pretending to be the man in the story and that half the woman—let's just keep writing, using writing as a way of thinking, of trying to think like the characters, even if we can't think of anything to say and write over and over again, 'I can't think of anything to say'"). Or I may ask for a response from someone—anyone—who has not spoken yet that day. I may ask to hear from someone sitting on my right or against the far wall. Or I may call on someone who has not volunteered ("After Jane speaks, I want to hear from Emily"), especially if I am asking a question to which anyone should have an answer (Which work seemed most powerful? troubling? confusing?).

Sometimes that is the hardest kind of question to answer, because it is so personal. (Karen Gennari)

I continue to feel uncertain about how intrusive I should be. Some colleagues remind me that calling on nonvolunteers is for their own good. One colleague has an effective finger-snapping method for eliciting a rapid-fire variety of student responses. Yet I also want to respect students' space, their reticence; I want to respect Michelle.

Which is exactly what you did. You called on me enough to keep me on my toes, but, more important, you made it easier for me to speak up when I had something I really wanted to say. I found that if I could get your attention, make eye contact with you, you would ask for my opinion. You helped bridge the gap between silence and speech when I was having a hard time jumping into the discussion. (Michelle Henneberry)

It was also essential that we begin to speak to each other—a dialogue —which took a long time. I kept wanting to say, "But, Karen" or "So and so," but every time I spoke up (in the first half of the semester) they would instinctively look to you first. I'm glad that wore off. (Heather Braun)

Maybe I should do more small-group work in this course, as much as I would in a larger class: the advantage of such work is that I stay out of it; the interchanges are genuinely student-student, not teacher-student. I ask students to sort themselves into groups of about five—small enough so that everyone can participate, large enough to get some variety of opinion. And I unobtrusively monitor the interaction (which groups are laughing or animated? which have stalled?), remaining available for consultation, occasionally stepping in with a question or clarification. It is vital to give groups assignments that are well designed. Ranking exercises work well: I may ask students to reach a consensus on which readings speak to them most powerfully or which characters they like best (and each group sends someone to the blackboard to list the group's ranking). Reaching the consensus is not as important as fostering a group process attentive to each individual's viewpoint.

Finally we look at each group's results and try to find patterns. ("Okay, it looks as though we either loved or hated Angela Carter's story, nothing in between. Why did you love it? Why did you hate it? Did some of you find yourselves both loving and hating it?") In another course, I have also had some luck asking small groups to find a way of placing the week's readings in dialogue and then presenting something to the class; they might act out, as one group did, a group-therapy session for the marginalized children of *The Awakening* and *The Yellow Wallpaper*.

Occasionally I set up debates: each student chooses to argue for or against a certain proposition—that fairy tales are sexist, for example. I find, though, that the debate format does not always work for me, probably because the style of discussion I generally encourage is collaborative rather than confrontational. Debates work best if I encourage students to appreciate one another's arguments, even momentarily switch sides. The first time I taught Feminist Criticism, I tried pushing students to take provisional stands by asking them to raise their hands to indicate agreement or disagreement with a given statement ("Carter's story portrays a rape"). Recently, I have simply surveyed the room, getting everyone's response in all its complexity. I want to make it possible to express both the differences between students and the differences within each of us.

Both kinds of difference are important. With regard to the second kind, a course like Feminist Criticism engages students on a very personal level. I find that they are often working through the implications of feminism in their personal lives—a process especially acute, perhaps, for those of traditional college age, who are just embarking on adulthood, navigating new relationships with peers and parents. At times the personal focuses on the sexual.

It makes me angry that women's perspectives have been ignored. That women have had to adopt the male tradition. But if we women only read or relate to a women's canon, because it more closely reflects our experience, on what ground do we meet the males in our life? Surely men do not desire sex that is only a show of power and has nothing to do with caring and connection? If that is true, then how, why do we marry them? fall in love with them? desire them to fall in love with us? I don't like this stuff. (Elisabeth Stitt)

I remember my mother saying, "Don't bring this feminist mess into my home. You're confusing the issues." And my friends would say, "You're taking this too far. Let's be serious." We would all go on in class, but then we would talk to others and get confused again. (Ronnie Bernier)

It is important to address some of these issues in class, so that students know they are not alone. We do so not to delve into anyone's sex life but to acknowledge that the course is hard both intellectually and affectively. A lot of affect attaches, in particular, to the word *feminist*. I tend to assume that a student who signs up for a course called Feminist Criticism already considers herself a feminist. Not a good assumption. Once, halfway through the semester, I discovered that most of the students did not.

Perhaps the reason that women in my class, the last all-female entering class, were more cautious about labeling themselves feminist was because of the pressures Wheaton women faced for the first time. Men were no longer down the road or tucked away for weekend trips—they were on the green, in the sack, and in the classroom. It was less safe to be feminist —but in a very positive sense, it was more challenging and real to address and embrace these issues in this new, co-ed Wheaton. Still, I remember deep frustration when students glared at me for bringing up feminism or lesbianism in critiquing our reading. (Heather Braun)

I took the class because I had an interest in literature, and I knew I agreed with some women's issues, but I also had a curiosity to find out exactly what feminism was. That was no easy task. As I came to the realization that feminism was not a specific set of beliefs to which all feminists had to subscribe, I became more comfortable with all feminist theory and with calling myself a feminist—a big step. (Karen Gennari)

Even though I was one of the students who did label themselves feminists, I still felt the weight of that title. How in my creative writing out of class could I expect to live up to the label, to help create a women's canon? It was paralyzing. That is why I also call myself an individualist, a title that validates difference and is nonessentializing. (Michelle Henneberry)

In fact, such personal connections give life and meaning to theory. The literature we read also helps students find a personal connection to the theory. We read not just Hélène Cixous but also Clarice Lispector, not just Barbara Smith and Deborah McDowell but also Toni Morrison, not just Leslie Rabine and Janice Radway but also a Harlequin romance.

The fiction is definitely helpful in sorting out what the theoretical stances are really about. (Midsemester evaluation, anon.)

Yet reading theory and literature does not just connect the two: reading theory against literature constantly checks the theory, interrupts it, calls it into question, even as the theory checks, interrupts, and calls into question the literature. Maybe we should even unravel the opposition between the two. For much as some theorists want their work to be read as literature, literature can in turn be theory.

While Elaine Showalter, Adrienne Rich, and Ursula LeGuin call for readers to look within the body of women's writing to find the truths of the female tradition, LeGuin's and Rich's works present this point more effectively because the authors are practicing what they preach. By exploring the notion of "diving into the wreck" [Rich] of women's writings in their own work, they are forcing the reader to do what they prescribe, that is, explore the art. (Becky Hemperly)

Connecting literature and theory may be especially important in Feminist Criticism if, as Elizabeth Flynn and David Bleich both suggest, women tend to read literature differently than men do, if women tend to resist the abstract and theoretical.

It was somewhat of a shock to discover that men tend to distance themselves from fiction by trying to figure out what the author was trying to achieve and that women experience it more as reality. This morning, Mr. D. said, in response to someone's comment about the lovers in A Midsummer Night's Dream *being shallow, that we cannot assume that they are other than shallow, because after all, outside the play, they do not exist. That rather shocked me, because I always consider characters to be real—or, at least, as real as I am. And if the characters are not real—if within the world of fiction they do not live—what is the point? If I had protested this morning that I do consider those people to be real, would Mr. D. have smiled indulgently at that nice girl in his class?* (Elisabeth Stitt)

I try to be sensitive to each student's viewpoint and to foster growth through tactful questioning. Yet I need to be careful about expecting students to follow my own trajectory—basically from male-centered readings (what Judith Fetterley calls immasculation) to resistance (focusing on images of women) to celebration of a woman's tradition (what Showalter calls gynocriticism) to more deconstructive modes—from, in part, literature to theory. A given student (in my class, for instance, a French Canadian) may be able to bypass some "stages" and feel readily at home with French deconstruction. Others may want to continue to resist what Barbara Christian calls the "race for theory." Students majoring in the social sciences, rather than in English, may feel more at home with theoretical material than with literature—and so may not need to start with what I associate with the experiential.

I feel insecure when we talk about literature—a little less so when we talk about theory. (Midsemester evaluation, anon.)

I also make sure to include readings that I find unsettling, that keep me off balance, sensitive to difference; readings that I admit I have trouble with or am uncertain about. These readings empower the students, who sense that the questions I raise (Is the author endorsing violence? Is the character being cruel or just independent?) are genuine. They also realize that it's ok not to have all the answers. Usually these unsettling pieces, like Carter's "The Company of Wolves" and Morrison's *Sula*, are by women with backgrounds different from mine. And the pieces are more often literature than criticism.

Interesting and very alternative approach, Bev—but what if near the end of the semester we (students) pick a short article for the class to read—that is, one week's reading is chosen entirely by the students? (Heather Braun)

Beyond specifying the choice of readings, the syllabus is an important teaching tool in other ways. Yet I feel that students still need more guidance than I have thus far provided.

Bev, I agree with the rest of what you say, but I feel we did well in guiding ourselves. (Heather Braun)

You are right. My rhetorical control keeps slipping (who is guiding whom?) as I try to feel my way to a less controlling and condescending stance both on and off the page. Let me try again. It's not so much that students need more guidance as that I want to ease the approach to theory, provide more points of access. Next time, I plan to add study questions that students may address in their weekly writing, some questions relatively factual, some interpretive, others probing for affective response. For example, Which of the French feminists we've read essentializes least? What are the implications of their thinking for what we have so far understood as feminism? What are Sandra Gilbert and Susan Gubar's criticisms of their work? What criticism does Gayatri Spivak make? What is your gut response to Marguerite Duras's "The Seated Man in the Passage"? Why are we reading it? How would you have written it differently? How does Mary Lydon's framing of her translation affect your response? I have some misgivings about the way I will be channeling responses with these questions, but I hope the scaffolding will help students engage with difficult readings—and that they will then go on to find their own paths and questions.

These kinds of questions might be more important at the beginning of the semester—and when particularly difficult material is being read. (Susan Dearing)

The sequencing of assignments is equally important. We deal with issues of diversity—class, race, sexual orientation—throughout the semester, building toward the climax of reading *Sula*. The early discussions of women's traditions lay important groundwork.

Reading the essays on the topic of finding our writing tradition was difficult. Though I had no trouble understanding the essays, I found that I had to confront my own ideas of what is normal. My views would more than likely be representative of the feminists who are criticized, not because I am unwilling to accept what is different, but rather because of lack of exposure. The essays of Bonnie Zimmerman, Adrienne Rich, and Alice Walker were real eye-openers—all three women striving to open doors to their particular writing traditions, as either their sexual orientation or skin color had somehow invalidated the importance of their work. (Liz DeMarco)

We tackle the complexities of French feminisms early on, after only a week or two of dealing with relatively accessible material on, say, silencing—in part so that Continental thinking and language may inform our subsequent work. This timing also allows students to do some of the most demanding conceptual work before other courses make heavy demands. Then we shift to romance novels, and something happens that week to the feel of the course, something that makes the difficulty of getting thirteen copies of a Harlequin romance (try asking your bookstore) worthwhile. Students laugh. They open up personally. At the same time they are now able to bring new perspectives to a type of reading that they may hitherto have been enjoying in secret or to which they find themselves secretly drawn. The contradictory complexity of the theory we have been reading seems to enable us to recognize a contradictory complexity in our own responses, often differences within, sometimes differences between self and other.

The rapelike "love" scenes in Sunset at Izilwane *surprised me. Is this attractive to women? I thought that was a male misconception: "They really like it—they asked for it." I also was surprised that the women were carefully kept away from doing anything domestic—housework. And they had servants! The housework bit appeals to me. I had some trouble with faithful black servants, though.* (Marjorie Crowe)

The literature we read is key to uncovering difference—to recognizing that someone is left doing the housework if one character gets to live the fantasy of not doing it, and to recognizing who that someone is.

A given work may palpably connect with one student's experience yet uncover difference for another. It's one thing for a white middle-class heterosexual to read abstractions about middle-class attempts to ignore racial differences or about compulsory heterosexuality, quite another for a white woman to recognize herself in Jamaica Kincaid's Mariah or for a heterosexual woman to miss the lesbianism in Olga Broumas's "Little Red Riding Hood." And it's something else altogether for a woman who is black or lesbian or both to find her experiences validated. Literature can make the "differences between" concrete; can sensitize us to race, class, and sexual orientation; and can validate our individual differences in a way that no amount of theory can.

The first time I offered the course, my treatment of race, though serious, was not as central as it should have been: I was too eager to engage with French feminisms. I introduced the discussion of *Sula* (I'm embarrassed to admit) with the question "Do different women write differently?" I later revised it to "How does gender intersect with race and sexual preference?" The revised question may still assume a transcendent white, heterosexual norm, but it is less blatant.

Toni Morrison was on the Today *show back in October, promoting her new book. When Bryant Gumbel asked her if she wanted to "transcend" the label of being a "black woman writer," she laughed. She said that's what she is, and she wanted people to know it.* (Sydney Coutts)

We try to acknowledge that there is no universal woman's experience, that we are all positioned by, for instance, race and class.

I suppose it is easy for us, white middle- and upper-middle-class students at an expensive New England college, to sit in this classroom on Monday afternoons discussing issues related to feminism. We talk, for the most part, about what has been and might be happening to women other than ourselves. Not only do we study other women—we study the studies made by other women about other women! Are we like Anzia Yezierska's Hanneh Breineh, miserable in our riches—which others envy? Do we appreciate what has been accomplished for us by our feminist foremothers? Are we like Hanneh's ungrateful, selfish children—taking for granted a life of luxury she worked herself hard and bitter for?

I went to the career opportunity panel on Saturday with my father and listened to my peers talk about how the Filene Center helped them prepare for their futures by helping them write résumés, find and obtain internships, make them "marketable." As I thought about how lucky we Wheaton women are to have a center like this, I thought about other women who do not have this opportunity—women who will never see a college education and who may not see a high school diploma; who will never see a résumé because they don't need a résumé to work at minimum wage—if they can even get a job. Single parents who cannot provide adequately for their children because they cannot leave them to go out and work and who cannot afford a sitter because they do not have jobs. Other images came to mind as well—those of us in the Wheaton community who cannot get internships over Januarys and summers because we cannot afford to work without pay. Those of us who cannot go away for a weekend because that eight-hour workday on Saturday is critical. Those of us who cannot even go to the center to find out how to write a résumé because when we aren't working, we are studying or sleeping, and the center is closed by that time anyway. We are a fortunate few—even those of us who cannot take advantage of the center. Do we understand this? Do I? Do we understand the immense difference that class makes for women? Do we understand how other women had to fight for us to have this? Will we give back to what has been so boldly forged for us? Will I? (Kerry-Beth Garvey)

This attention to each individual's positioning brings me back to the student-centered classroom that I am committed to. I want now, at the close of this essay, to dismantle it—to dismantle the student-centered teaching I have been endorsing, to go beyond the essentializing implicit in feminist pedagogy, to admit the necessity and the desirability of the teacher retaining some authority: it is important to attend to the personal and the experiential as one builds theory, but it's not enough, for there is a conflict between being student-centered and, if one's students are virtually all white and middle-class women, plumbing diversity. How do all these mostly white students—sometimes only white students—build on their own experiences to come to terms with race? They—we—need to be jarred out of complacency. Acknowledging minority experience in a classroom dominated by the majority requires dismantling the student-centered and the experiential—not destroying or eliminating it but interrupting it, challenging it, with less tractable texts and interrogations. We must make connections and build bridges—between student and text, literature and theory, teaching and learning—but not so many that we erase difference, that those of us who are privileged start appropriating those who are not, the I-know-just-how-you-feel syndrome. The student-centered classroom may start dismantling the teacher's authority, yet it, too, must be dismantled.

Wheaton College

Note

[1] Here and elsewhere, I have cribbed ideas from colleagues, this one from Kathleen Vogt. Other colleagues who have contributed importantly to my thinking about feminism and pedagogy include Roger Clark, Bobbie Kauffman, Catherine Krupnick, Roz Ladd, Frinde Maher, Toni Oliviero, Dick Pearce, Itala Rutter, Sheila Shaw, other members of Wheaton's Feminist Theory Group, and other students in the courses Feminist Criticism and Introduction to Tutoring Writing.

Works Cited

Baym, Nina. "The Feminist Teacher of Literature: Feminist or Teacher?" 1988. *Gender in the Classroom: Power and Pedagogy.* Ed. Susan L. Gabriel and Isaiah Smithson. Urbana: U of Illinois P, 1990. 60–78.

Beaven, Mary H. "Individualized Goal Setting, Self-Evaluation, and Peer Evaluation." *Evaluating Writing: Describing, Measuring, Judging.* Ed. Charles R. Cooper and Lee Odell. Urbana: NCTE, 1977. 135–56.

Belsey, Catherine, and Jane Moore, eds. *The Feminist Reader: Essays in Gender and the Politics of Literary Criticism*. New York: Blackwell, 1989.

Bleich, David. "Gender Interests in Reading and Language." *Gender and Reading: Essays on Readers, Texts, and Contexts*. Ed. Elizabeth A. Flynn and Patrocinio P. Schweikart. Baltimore: Johns Hopkins UP, 1986. 234–66.

Broumas, Olga. "Little Red Riding Hood." 1977. *Don't Bet on the Prince: Contemporary Feminist Fairy Tales in North America and England*. Ed. Jack Zipes. New York: Methuen, 1986. 119–20.

Carter, Angela. "The Company of Wolves." 1979. Rpt. in Gilbert and Gubar, *Norton Anthology* 2326–34.

Christian, Barbara. "The Race for Theory." 1987. Rpt. in *Gender and Theory: Dialogues on Feminist Criticism*. Ed. Linda Kauffman. Oxford: Blackwell, 1989. 225–37.

Cixous, Hélène. "Sorties: Out and Out: Attacks/Ways Out/Forays." 1975. Trans. Betsy Wing. Excerpt rpt. in Belsey and Moore 101–16, 229–30.

Culley, Margo. "Anger and Authority in the Introductory Women's Studies Classroom." *Gendered Subjects: The Dynamics of Feminist Teaching*. Ed. Culley and Catherine Portuges. Boston: Routledge, 1985. 209–17.

Eagleton, Mary, ed. *Feminist Literary Theory: A Reader*. Oxford: Blackwell, 1986.

Elbow, Peter. *Writing with Power: Techniques for Mastering the Writing Process*. New York: Oxford UP, 1981.

Fetterley, Judith. *The Resisting Reader: A Feminist Approach to American Fiction*. Bloomington: Indiana UP, 1978.

Flynn, Elizabeth A. "Gender and Reading." 1983. *Gender and Reading: Essays on Readers, Texts, and Contexts*. Ed. Flynn and Patrocinio P. Schweikart. Baltimore: Johns Hopkins UP, 1986. 267–88.

Gilbert, Sandra M., and Susan Gubar, eds. *The Norton Anthology of Literature by Women: The Tradition in English*. New York: Norton, 1985.

———. "Sexual Linguistics: Gender, Language, Sexuality." 1985. Excerpt rpt. in Belsey and Moore 81–99, 225–29.

Kincaid, Jamaica. "Mariah." *Lucy*. New York: Farrar, 1990. 17–41.

Kristeva, Julia. "Women's Time." 1981. Trans. Alice Jardine and Harry Blake. Excerpt rpt. in Belsey and Moore 197–217, 240–42.

LeGuin, Ursula K. "Sur." 1982. Rpt. in Gilbert and Gubar, *Norton Anthology* 2007–22.

Lispector, Clarice. "The Imitation of the Rose." *Family Ties*. Trans. and introd. Giovanni Pontiero. Austin: U of Texas P, 1972. 53–72.

Lydon, Mary. "Translating Duras: 'The Seated Man in the Passage.'" *Contemporary Literature* 24 (1983): 259–75.

Maher, Frances. "Classroom Pedagogy and the New Scholarship on Women." *Gendered Subjects: The Dynamics of Feminist Teaching*. Ed. Margo Culley and Catherine Portuges. Boston: Routledge, 1985. 29–48.

McDowell, Deborah E. "New Directions for Black Feminist Criticism." 1980. Excerpt rpt. in Eagleton 163–69.

Rabine, Leslie W. "Romance in the Age of Electronics: Harlequin Enterprises." Rev. and rpt. in *Feminist Criticism and Social Change: Sex, Class, and Race in Literature and Culture*. Ed. Judith Newton and Deborah Rosenfelt. New York: Methuen, 1985. 249–67.

Radway, Janice A. "Women Read the Romance: The Interaction of Text and Context." 1983. Excerpt rpt. in Eagleton 128–31.

Rich, Adrienne. "Compulsory Heterosexuality and Lesbian Existence." 1980. Excerpt rpt. in Eagleton 22–28.

———. "Diving into the Wreck." 1973. Gilbert and Gubar, *Norton Anthology* 2032–35.

Showalter, Elaine. "Feminist Criticism in the Wilderness." 1981. *The New Feminist Criticism: Essays on Women, Literature, and Theory*. Ed. Showalter. New York: Pantheon, 1985. 243–70.

Smith, Barbara. "Toward a Black Feminist Criticism." *The New Feminist Criticism: Essays on Women, Literature, and Theory*. Ed. Elaine Showalter. New York: Pantheon, 1985. 168–85.

Spivak, Gayatri Chakravorty. "Feminism and Critical Theory." *In Other Worlds: Essays in Cultural Politics*. New York: Methuen, 1987. 77–92.

Treichler, Paula A. "Teaching Feminist Theory." *Theory in the Classroom*. Ed. Cary Nelson. Urbana: U of Illinois P, 1986. 57–128.

Walker, Alice. "Saving the Life That Is Your Own: The Importance of Models in the Artist's Life." 1976. Excerpt rpt. in Eagleton 28–31.

Yezierska, Anzia. "The Fat of the Land." 1920. Gilbert and Gubar, *Norton Anthology* 1424–42.

Zimmerman, Bonnie. "What Has Never Been: An Overview of Lesbian Feminist Literary Criticism." Excerpt rpt. in Eagleton 15–22.

Practicing Theory, Theorizing Practice: Critical Transformations of *The Marble Faun*

Evan Carton

Any purposeful introduction of critical theory into the literature class must engage three related assumptions that undergraduates typically bring to literary study. The first is that the text is (or is meant to be considered) a masterwork, an original composition distinguished by the perfection of its form and the coherence of its thought. The second is that an author invests the text with its meaning through his or her freely intentional creative act. The third is that a reader's interpretation is a freely intentional— that is, a subjective—critical act. Most contemporary theory, in different ways and to different ends, calls these assumptions into question. The literature class that explicitly elicits and tests these assumptions, then, provides a practical occasion for the introduction of theory and for students' examination of theory's methods, values, and stakes.

The assumptions I have enumerated share a commitment to the idea of integral, autonomous identity, whether of the literary object or of the writing or reading subject. While this familiar Western idea is often experienced as a source of comfort and power, its underwriting of the incompatible notions of an authoritative author and a subjective reader betrays its tendency in the literature class (as, I believe, in life) to promote powerlessness and alienation. According to this model, reading is either fated subordination to realized authorial will—in which case readers comprehend the text by becoming what the text is assumed to be, a receptacle for the author's design—or free association, the reader's arbitrary (and necessarily alienated, or disengaged) assertion of his or her own design. The self-conscious and comparative use of theory in the classroom to construct, deconstruct, and reconstruct various readings of a literary text can dissolve this double bind by showing students how texts, authors, and readers exist not integrally and autonomously but through relation to one another, through the discursive conventions and analytical paradigms that they apply or that are applied to them, through the material conditions and historical contexts that they inhabit or are imagined to inhabit.

Nathaniel Hawthorne's last novel, *The Marble Faun* (1860), offers a particularly rich opportunity for theorizing practice and practicing theory in the teaching of literature. To begin with, it is a novel that revolves around works of art, their creation, and their interpretation. Its characters are all producers and interpreters of art, models for artistic compositions, or even living incarnations of art objects. Moreover, the ontological integrity and autonomy of authors, readers, and texts (or artists, viewers, and artworks) and the epistemological grounds for claiming or assigning identity are at issue throughout the novel. Formally and thematically, *The Marble Faun* presses the question of whether meanings are determined or indeterminate, the world fatal or chaotic, and explores the entailments of both positions.

The Marble Faun also occupies a suggestively vexed position in the American canon and in the generic history of the novel, the social history of the nation, and the personal history of its author. It is the work of a quintessentially canonical writer, arguably the writer around whom the idea of an American canon coalesced. Yet, although always held to be deeply Hawthornean, it has typically been judged not a masterwork but a breakdown, a failure. Because literary evaluation often involves measuring texts against unconscious or at least unself-conscious standards, a work that claims canonicity yet fails or refuses to meet conventional criteria for excellence may usefully prompt the articulation and scrutiny of the criteria themselves. Disparaging evaluation of *The Marble Faun* has tended to accompany thwarted classification. The narrative itself challenges the distinction between criticism and imaginative literature by incorporating large swatches of art criticism taken directly from Hawthorne's Italian notebooks. Henry James observed in 1879 that "the book is positively neither of one category nor of another" (134), but its generic instability was already evident in the two most characteristic responses of its earliest readers: some took it as an allegory of the loss of Eden; others took it along to Rome as a travel guide.

James's remark specifically refers to the categories of "romance" and "realism," and Hawthorne's last completed fiction (which, in its preface, laments the probable death of the gentle reader of romance and apologizes for its own tendency toward journalistic description) may be seen as the locus of transition in American literary history, a key site of romance's disintegration and realism's incipient rise. More generally, *The Marble Faun* appears at a transitional moment in American history and cultural consciousness. In the year of its publication, Lincoln's election to the presidency and South Carolina's secession shattered the union that the United States Constitution had established in 1787, and succeeding events effected America's ideological transformation from innocence to experience, from unity to diversity, from a romantic or mythic self-conception to a more realistic and historical one. Critical theory today provides means of recognizing the novel, despite its billing as an Italian romance, to be a product of and an index to this transitional moment.

Finally, Hawthorne wrote *The Marble Faun* at a time and in circumstances in his personal life when he felt his national, familial, and vocational identities to be less secure than they had ever been before. For six years, he had lived abroad and had come to feel increasingly estranged from his rapidly changing country. During those years, Europe had bombarded his provincial New England sensibilities with evidence of difference, otherness—not only different sights, sounds, and customs but also people whose lives suggested different orders of experience and different understandings of the workings of history and culture. Not for seven years had Hawthorne been an active writer, nor was he any longer a man of public affairs, a representative of the American government. His work on the novel also coincided with the nearly fatal illness of his daughter Una, the person he both powerfully associated with the idea of the female and foreign other (her affliction was malaria, known then as Roman fever) and uneasily identified with his own character and gender position as a writer.

Hawthorne could not decide on a title for his book, and his British publisher chose, out of a dozen possibilities that the author proposed, *Transformation*. Although this title disconcerted Hawthorne, his novel in fact is organized around a series of acts of critical vision and the numerous transformations of meaning and identity that they produce. Readers have also made *The Marble Faun* an object of frequent and thoroughgoing interpretive transformation. In using the novel to teach literary theory, then, I begin with the word *transformation*, which designates an operation the text repeatedly performs and an operation its critics have repeatedly performed on it. I ask students to list the transformations—of character, meaning, scene, perspective, reader expectation—that they noted or experienced in their reading and to describe as well the different identities the novel assumes in a sampling of its interpretations. What I seek to introduce here is the principle that a literary work generates and delimits multiple critical judgments and inquiries and is itself multiply constituted and delimited by them.

I proceed from this point by eliciting from the students various readings of *The Marble Faun*. We then seek to theorize our practice by aligning these readings with different critical schools or orientations, by comparing their different powers and limitations, and by noting the different values they give to, or relations they assume between, author, reader, text, and world. A simple way to stimulate multiple interpretations that may later be shown to entail different critical vocabularies, priorities, and consequences is to divide the class into groups, each of which is given a character or pair of characters and asked to construct a reading in support of the proposition that the novel is principally "about" the designated character or characters. The American title, *The Marble Faun*, directs us toward Donatello, but Hawthorne's own proposed titles also include "Hilda: A Romance" and "Miriam: A Romance," as well as others—such as "Marble and Mud" and "Transformation"—that seem to accord primacy to relations rather than to individual figures, and not only relations between characters but also those between processes (art and history), between concepts (permanence and change, ideality and degradation), and between different national, religious, gender, and racial affiliations. Students quickly discover that readings radically different in kind, not simply in emphasis, may proceed from choosing as the novel's central focus the living faun, Donatello; the three artists, Miriam, Hilda, and Kenyon; the two women, Hilda and Miriam; the protean figure, Miriam's model; or Hawthorne himself.

In the remaining pages of this essay, I outline five such readings and show how the process of producing, critiquing, and comparing them provides undergraduates with a practical introduction to the leading methods, claims, and controversies of contemporary criticism. These readings may be labeled "plotting the fall," "the morality of form," "writing as a woman," "the deconstructive world of the model," and "racial purity and American history."

Plotting the Fall

To what do we commit ourselves when we take the title's cue, as most readers of *The Marble Faun* have done, and make Donatello, the innocent faun, the focal point of our interpretation? We commit ourselves to rely more heavily on the plot than on anything else about the text and, in fact, to privilege the mythic elements of the plot or to construe it in archetypal, rather than more socially and historically situated, terms. When our center of interest is Donatello, whose impulsive murder of his beloved Miriam's shadowy model and tormentor initiates him into the knowledge of good and evil and transforms him from a state of animal simplicity and innocence to one of human complexity and guilt, *The Marble Faun* becomes an allegory of the Fall of the human race. This reading is explicitly authorized, even dictated, by Hawthorne in numerous pointed references to his novel's enactment of the Fall; for example, at one point Miriam flatly says to Kenyon, "The story of the Fall of Man! Is it not repeated in our Romance of Monte Beni?" (434). The reading is reinforced, moreover, by the plot's engineering of a secondary fall from innocence that is the direct consequence of the first: the American copyist Hilda, a "daughter of the Puritans" (54) whose "angelic purity" (366) has set her apart from the other characters, accidentally witnesses Donatello's crime and thereby comes to share the human burden of the consciousness of sin. Stained by this knowledge, Hilda loses her aloof self-sufficiency and her capacity to reproduce the paintings of the old masters in their "pristine glory" (59). In exchange, she is invited to enter into the community of human sympathy and need that is established through the acknowledgment of our common imperfection.

Directed by the title, by the novel's specific references to Eden and to the Fall, and by a tendency to read principally for the central plot element, my students have little difficulty sketching out this archetypal reading. But once they have done so, I ask them to, in effect, deconstruct it—to find its problems or weaknesses and to list everything they can think of that the allegory of the Fall in *The Marble Faun* and corresponding critical interpretations ignore, suppress, or abstract. This class exercise—establishing a consensus around the text's most apparent or conventional meaning and then undermining it—is a good alternative or complement to the strategy of dividing the class into groups assigned to interpret from different vantage points. Both methods show interpretation to be not so much a reception as a selective reconstruction, a process that may make use of different textual materials and different organizational and evaluative principles but that, at the same time, is neither arbitrary nor private.

Consolidated and elaborated under my guidance, the problems and weaknesses of the archetypal reading that my students list usually generate some provocative questions: Do Hawthorne's own religious attitudes and practices or his earlier works indicate that his concerns are theological, or does the myth of the Fall more likely serve as a useful and culturally resonant way of organizing, controlling, and perhaps deflecting more-concrete and topical concerns? How close is the fit between the biblical story of Adam's first disobedience to a perfect heavenly Father who has given him paradise in exchange for filial reverence and a novel that abounds in illegitimate father figures whose evil exists apart from and long precedes Donatello's sin? How is this plot of filial disobedience further complicated by the association of the bond between Miriam, the model, and Donatello with the story of Beatrice Cenci, the renowned sixteenth-century Italian noblewoman who was executed for conspiring with her brother to kill the brutal father who may have raped her? And what about the novel's treatment of its class of spiritual "Fathers" and ostensible representatives of God, the Roman Catholic priests who are described as "pampered, sensual" (411) servants of "an irresponsible dynasty of Holy Fathers" (100)?

This last question points to a particularly glaring inadequacy of the critical tradition that proceeds from James Russell Lowell's identification of *The Marble Faun* as "a parable of the development of the Christian idea" (Cohen 77): the novel's representation of Christianity as fractured into the starkly contrasting ideologies and aesthetics of Catholicism and Protestantism. The biblical theme of the Fall provides no insight into the historical context of this contrastive analysis: the popular concern of mid-nineteenth-century guardians of American Protestant culture with the threat of European Catholicism. It also belies the primary filial relationship in the novel, which is that between fathers and daughters, a relationship underscored by the greater prominence and more frequent occurrence of the painted image of Beatrice Cenci (whose features are mirrored repeatedly in those of both Miriam and Hilda) than of the sculpted figure of the faun. Another unacknowledged challenge to "the Christian idea" is the pervasive presence of the Jew. Hawthorne's American Protestants are not only immersed in a Catholic culture but also spend much of the latter half of the novel traversing Rome's Jewish ghetto. And Miriam, whose secret past precipitates all the action and whose raven hair emanates "a dark glory such as crowns no Christian maiden's head" (48), is conceived as a Jew and modeled on a Jewish woman who deeply unsettled Hawthorne in England. Finally, while the novel's plot may correspond to the story of the Fall, its local attention tends to focus on the production, reception, and effects of works of art in various visual and verbal media, and often its central issue seems to be artistic originality, rather than original sin.

The Morality of Form

Because students' first interpretive impulse is generally to examine the story for a summary message, they easily "plot the Fall" in *The Marble Faun*. But, having done so, and having then subjected the fruit of that impulse to an initial critique, they are in a position to recognize that much of the novel is devoted less to a cosmic message than to a self-reflective examination of artistic media—to a formal debate, in fact, on questions of artistic form and value. In this debate, the contest between Catholicism and Protestantism is aestheticized through its incorporation into a series of analogous tensions between opposing styles, principles, and forms of art. Students assigned to explore the relationship among, and argue the centrality of, the novel's three artists soon see that their importance lies in the carefully juxtaposed descriptions of their studios, their works, and their personalities (with Hilda as, in all respects, the mediatory figure between Miriam and Kenyon), which communicate these aesthetic tensions and their moral correlatives. Again, asking students to list the traits associated with the environments, creations, and characters of Miriam and Kenyon enables them to recognize at once the terms of Hawthorne's contest between the arts and between the two divisions of Christianity. What students report is that chromatic or prismatic light, emotion, warm corporeality, mutability, and painting are aligned against unrefracted white light, intellect, cold idealism, permanence, and sculpture. Hilda's progress from angelic ice maiden (pervasively associated with whiteness and purity), through a reactive susceptibility to the comforts of Catholicism and attraction to the most de-idealizing painting, to a final sanctified yet earthly union with Kenyon anchors the interpretation of *The Marble Faun* as a work whose formal organization and moral resolution are achieved in the balance of these opposites.

Having established this reading, first by rehearsing the Miriam-Kenyon polarity that the students have discovered and then by performing a class exercise in which we trace Hilda's physical, moral, and ideological shuttlings between the two, I again elicit its critique. First, I ask, what textual evidence challenges the notion that the marriage of painter and sculptor constitutes a resolution of the novel's moral and aesthetic antitheses? Second, how is this supposed resolution transformed if we approach it as feminists rather than as formalists? We soon see that Kenyon and Hilda's union is predicated on their flight from Rome, the "home of art" (214), and, implicitly, from their own artistic vocations, and it is their explicit refuge from the mediatory aesthetics and morality that is emblematized by Kenyon's unfinished clay bust of Donatello, a work whose synthesis of the text's constitutive oppositions both Hilda and Kenyon ultimately reject. From a feminist standpoint, moreover, the notion of Hilda's progress—and even that of her difference from her ostensible opposite, Miriam—is an illusory effect of patriarchal discourse. The "daughter of the Puritans" who becomes captivated by "the Old Masters" and is later arrested by church fathers happily ends her career, according to Kenyon's image, imprisoned in her husband's heart and home (395). The task of tending the Virgin's flame (which Hilda, living in a "dovecote" just beneath a rooftop shrine, has performed in Rome) is replaced by that of keeping the home fires burning; the small Protestant contributor to the Catholic cult of the Virgin assumes her own place as the idol in the American cult of true womanhood.

Writing as a Woman

Through its organization, my course prompts students to theorize their critical practice by taking any proposed textual interpretation and questioning the kinds of evidence, vocabulary, research, and contextualization on which it depends. Transforming *The Marble Faun* from a Christian allegory or an aesthetic debate to a work built around the threat (embodied in Miriam) and the containment (effected, in different ways, on both Hilda and Miriam) of the female other, for instance, requires a distinct shift in the terms, research, and contexts that we bring to bear on the text. Feminist criticism both inclines and enables us to ground this reading in the sexual politics of Hawthorne's class and culture and to support it through the analysis of gender relations and psychology in his earlier work and personal history. As I have shown elsewhere, writing, femininity, childhood, and homelessness were intimately interrelated for Hawthorne from early adolescence to the end of his career, and his romances are in some sense always sites of his ongoing crisis of sexual identity, a crisis that was more acute during the writing of *The Marble Faun* than at any previous time in Hawthorne's adult life (Carton).

Once in possession of the information about Una's illness and its powerful effect on Hawthorne's imagination during his composition of *The Marble Faun* (an effect rooted in his guilt over his forsaken intimacy both with his daughter and with the part of himself that she had always emblematized and the literary vocation that gave it expression), my students see the conflict among Hawthorne's "patriarchal" and "daughterly" characters, values, and selves everywhere in the novel. On this reading, *The Marble Faun* is a work haunted by treacherously intimate daughter-father relations and by their collapse into two stark alternatives: utter filial submission to (and perhaps incestuous incorporation by) the father's imperial identity or symbolic (perhaps actual) patricide. This ultimate choice is suggested by the narrator's only entrance into the narrative in the first person just as both the rebellious daughter, Miriam, and the submissive daughter, Hilda, are exchanged for each other, each taken into the custody of the appropriate patriarchal institution and representative of the patriarchal order.

The Deconstructive World of the Model

What, for all the differences, do the first three readings have in common? What shared assumption about the text as an object of interpretation and about the project of interpretation itself, I ask my class, supports each of these readings as a valid representation of *The Marble Faun*? These questions may be greeted with blank stares at first, but eventually someone will say that the readings all assume that the text can be read, that one meaning can be demonstrated and decided on. What underlies them all, then, is our common and generally unarticulated faith in the determinateness of textual meaning. In its own terms, each reading I have outlined, by applying particular contextual information and critical vocabularies to the language of Hawthorne's novel, offers a persuasive account of the meaning of that linguistic construct. But how do we determine which of these readings is the right or even the best one? What if the linguistic construct that we call *The Marble Faun* inherently neither precludes nor confirms any one of an infinite number of potentially persuasive readings? Hawthorne betrays, perhaps, his own uneasy awareness of this instability in his dismay at the English title, *Transformation*, which revealed the one (anti-) truth of his book or of any book: the indeterminacy—or the limitless constructibility, deconstructibility, and reconstructibility—of its meaning.

Indeed, it may be argued that in the person of the model Hawthorne gives bodily form to the deconstructive principle of sourceless and endless transformation, or "freeplay," of ontological and epistemological indeterminacy. It is the model, after all, as students assigned to argue his centrality observe, who initiates as well as falls victim to the novel's plot. And, above all, this character is associated with unstable and fictive identity, "being no other than one of those living models . . . whom artists convert into Saints or assassins, according as their pictorial purposes demand" (19). The model seems to pass freely between art and life and between life and death. He steps out of niches carved for statuary, his features turn up on the face of the demon subdued by the archangel Michael in Guido Reni's seventeenth-century canvas, he enters the narrative as an avatar of the mythical specter of the catacombs, and after Donatello hurls him from the parapet, he is discovered lying in state in the Church of the Capuchins, identified as the holy Brother Antonio.

The model is a shifting signifier, a model of a world of models, a sign of a world of signs, in which no depth is plumbed, because there is only representation all the way down. The mysteries of Miriam's and Donatello's identities are not resolved but ramified in a series of speculations, legends, analogs, images. The chapter in which the model and Miriam presumably speak the secret that drives the action is entitled "Fragmentary Sentences." In it the narrator assumes the position of a reader, in fact a secondhand receiver of information, who has heard "but a few vague whisperings of what passed" and, in forging a representation, assumes "a task resembling, in its perplexity, that of gathering up and piecing together the fragments of a letter, which has been torn and scattered to the winds" (93). As the image suggests, meaning in *The Marble Faun* is a matter of arbitrarily systematizing difference, of presenting absence. And, as the entire chapter suggests, the novel's language creates difference and "absents" presence as well. This linguistic function is exemplified in the transaction whereby a young Italian artist paints Hilda, as she looks at the portrait of Beatrice Cenci and thinks of the fallen Miriam. The artist calls his picture "Innocence, Dying of a Blood-Stain" only to have it transformed by his market-conscious dealer's substitution of the title *The Signorina's Vengeance*. Here, language makes and differentiates the martyr and the assassin as it creates and erases the apparent difference between the innocent Donatello and the evil model himself—for the model is at once Donatello's fate and his origin. Donatello not only reconstitutes the model's bond to Miriam through his murder of the model. More subtly, the opposition between the two collapses in the reader's recognition that, despite differing connotations, *faun* and *satyr* (the model, who first appears in goatskin breeches and a buffalo cloak, is repeatedly associated with the latter) are actually the Latin and Greek names for a single sylvan deity, conceived as being part human and part animal.

Racial Purity and American History

In this final reading, the principal meaning of *The Marble Faun* is not located in the novel's most prominent thematic or formal concerns or in the psychosexual dynamics of Hawthorne's life and previous work or in the text's subversion of any determinate meaning. Let us assume instead, I suggest to my class, that the meaning is located in what the Marxist critic Fredric Jameson calls "the political unconscious," on which Hawthorne and his novel may be seen to draw. What if we attend to the particular historical moment of Hawthorne's 15 October 1859 preface, in which he familiarly and ingenuously rehearses the suitable conditions for romance? Don't we find curious his characterization of the United States as a country in or about which it is "happily" impossible to write romance because of its absence of "shadow," "gloomy wrong," or "anything but a common-place prosperity, in broad and simple daylight"—its freedom, that is, from the scourges of division and darkness? Don't these same images inevitably call forth the shadow and gloomy wrong that, as everyone in 1859 knew, had bitterly divided America and threatened to destroy it?

At this point some students object that the issue of slavery is nowhere taken up in *The Marble Faun*, but I ask them to play along. According to the theory of the unconscious, I remind them, the issue would emerge only indirectly, either because Hawthorne was thinking about it during the composition of a book he imagined had to do with something else or because in 1859 it generally conditioned his thought and that of other Americans in ways of which he was unaware. The students now discover that once we admit the possibility that slavery is an issue in *The Marble Faun*, we find that its presence—as well as that of the larger issue of racial identity and race relations—is significantly marked. Students are quick to notice numerous images of master-slave relations, and they soon recall that on the night of the model's murder the specter of American slavery does pointedly arise. Observing the swirling Trevi Fountain, one of a group of artists with whom the principals are strolling suggests that in America this water might "turn the machinery of a cotton-mill," to which another responds—and the context permits little doubt about his meaning—that it might also be used in "cleansing the national flag of any stains that it may have incurred" (146).

I now introduce contextual information that may help us make something more of these textual details. Both in a campaign biography of Franklin Pierce (for which the consulship in England and subsequent opportunity for European travel had been Hawthorne's reward) and in letters home during the middle and late 1850s, Hawthorne had discussed the Union's claim to sacredness and unity in the light of slavery and racial difference. Comparing passages from some of these writings with passages from the novel proves fruitful. The author's political characterizations are curiously displaced in *The Marble Faun*, where the terms used to evaluate the paradoxically sacred and profane union of Donatello and Miriam are the same ones with which, in correspondence and nonfiction, Hawthorne characterizes the United States. What is it about Miriam and Donatello, I ask, that might logically connect them to the American crisis? A vision of the novel that was virtually unavailable before now appears to many of my students with the force of revelation. Miriam and Donatello are linked to the slavery question and the question of America's future in one striking way: in their individual persons and in their union, they embody the problems of racial difference and racial mixture.

The mystery and moral ambiguity that attend both Donatello and Miriam are tied up in the two characters' racial identity. Each at once signifies racial purity and racial mixture. Two prominent speculations about Miriam hold her to be a Jew in flight from a symbolically incestuous forced union with a close associate of her father and "the offspring of a Southern American planter" who has recoiled from the discovery of her "one burning drop of African blood" (23). Donatello's "race of Monte Beni" (231) is at once a pure race of fauns, innocent of human sinfulness, and an already mixed race, combining "the characteristics of the brute creation . . . with those of humanity" (9). That *The Marble Faun* is significantly "about" the crisis of American identity as it revolved around the issue of race on the eve of the Civil War is supported by two astonishing passages in Hawthorne's nonfiction writing that I have no space to quote or analyze here. One, from the 1862 essay "Chiefly about War Matters," contains a description of a party of escaped slaves as "a kind of creature by themselves, not altogether human, but perhaps quite as good, and akin to the fauns and rustic deities of olden times" (318); the other, from his *English Notebooks*, records Hawthorne's encounter with Emma Abigail Salamons, sister-in-law to the Jewish lord mayor of London and the extratextual model for Miriam in *The Marble Faun*. The most striking aspect of this passage is Emma Salamons's insistent unrepresentability for Hawthorne, his sense of her as a figure who unsettles the grounds and disables the media of representation themselves and who renders the very blackness of black and the whiteness of white uncertain and problematic propositions (319–20).

What have we learned through our five readings about the theoretical entailments of our critical practice? For one thing, we have learned that each reading entails different assumptions about what, where, and how meaning is or comes to be. To privilege the theme of the Fall in *The Marble Faun* is to assume that what is important about the novel is some central propositional statement that it may make. Further, it is to assume that the author, Hawthorne, is in full control of the ideas and the language involved in formulating and articulating the proposition. This critical approach takes the primary materials of the novel to be the biblical myths and historical archetypes on which Hawthorne consciously drew. Its general orientation is humanistic in that it implicitly understands a work of literature to be an individual's creative effort to affirm some meaning—in this case, the moral significance of human existence itself.

To focus instead on the novel's juxtaposition of opposing values in both religion and aesthetics is to take a more formalistic approach. More than any of the other readings, "the morality of form" restricts itself to the analysis of textual patterns and structures and to the evaluation of their degree of synthesis or polarization. It casts its critical light, we might say, not so much on what the author says as on what the work does. While this approach tends to present the work as illustrating a problem or a tension, rather than the author as stating an answer, it continues to grant intentional authority to the author through the work; it assumes, in other words, that the novel's more or less overt and conscious concerns define the meaning of the text.

Subsequent readings depart significantly from the approaches and assumptions of the first two. According to these views, Hawthorne's novel shares the character of Miriam's compulsive paintings of biblical murderesses, paintings that she deems "not things that [she] created, but things that haunt [her]" (45). "Writing as a woman" portrays *The Marble Faun* as a product of Hawthorne's complex personal relations to gender roles that are deeply embedded in and powerfully reinforced by the larger society. This reading represents the novel not as a vehicle of humane wisdom or as an object in and of itself but as a vivid site of Hawthorne's lifelong struggle—and the struggle of American culture at an important moment in its development—with the psychology and politics of gender.

In the last two readings, the authority of the author and the centrality of the literary object are further eroded as the relative power of language and of the world increases. "The deconstructive world of the model" emphasizes the constant transformations of the meanings of words and images and even of the identities of characters in *The Marble Faun*. It also suggests the impossibility of uncovering origins or of grounding interpretations in the novel. "Racial purity and American history" offers a historicization of such ontological and epistemological chaos by linking it to the destabilization of traditional understandings of personal and national identity that was brought about in mid-nineteenth-century America by new social and economic conditions and especially by the political crisis over how race was to be understood and racial relations organized. Following contemporary trends in cultural criticism, or in the new historicism, this final reading is concerned more with what the novel silences than with what it speaks. Its purpose is to expose the stamp of the culture's dominant ideology on the text and to reveal the covert and even unconscious ways in which that ideology is passed on.

Each of these readings has its particular power and particular limitations. In pursuing them as far as they will take us, we may never reach a single point of intersection or discover any harmonizing principle. But, I conclude in my class, even if we are ultimately left to choose among competing interpretations, our choices will be meaningful and not purely subjective ones because, knowing what they entail and what they exclude, we will be obliged to explain them and to see how they explain us.

University of Texas, Austin

Works Cited

Carton, Evan. "A Daughter of the Puritans and Her Old Master: Hawthorne, Una, and the Sexuality of Romance." *Daughters and Fathers*. Ed. Lynda E. Boose and Betty S. Flowers. Baltimore: Johns Hopkins UP, 1989. 208–32.

Cohen, B. Bernard, ed. *The Recognition of Nathaniel Hawthorne: Selected Criticism since 1828*. Ann Arbor: U of Michigan P, 1969.

Hawthorne, Nathaniel. "Chiefly about War Matters." 1862. *Tales, Sketches, and Other Matters*. Ed. George Parsons Lathrop. Boston: Houghton, 1883. Vol. 12 of *Hawthorne's Works*. 15 vols. 1881–84.

———. *The English Notebooks*. Ed. Randall Stewart. New York: MLA, 1941.

———. *The Marble Faun*. Columbus: Ohio State UP, 1968. Vol. 4 of *The Centenary Edition of the Works of Nathaniel Hawthorne*. Ed. William Charvat et al.

James, Henry. *Hawthorne*. London: Macmillan, 1879.

The Pedagogy of the Depressed: Feminism, Poststructuralism, and Pedagogical Practice

Laurie A. Finke

> *I fall to pieces.*
> —Harlan Howard, lyricist
>
> *History begins at ground level, with footsteps.*
> —Michel de Certeau

Every year, about halfway through my feminist theory class, students begin to complain about being depressed. To be sure, not every student becomes depressed, but many do, enough to affect negatively the dynamics of the classroom. After my first naive attempt at teaching this often contentious course, I have come to understand that feminist students' resistance to theory results from their perception that theory is aridly intellectual, "masculinist" in its preoccupations, and irrelevant to the political activism that drives them (sometimes impatiently). They are just as frequently daunted by the difficulty of some of the readings I choose, finding the language impenetrably "academic." But just as often, students' malaise results from a feeling that what the class may be unintentionally teaching them is that women have always been oppressed, continue to be oppressed, will always be oppressed and that nothing anyone can do will change anything because that oppression has always been "the same." The following comment from one student is characteristic: "What I find very scary . . . is that very little has changed in the 250 years since Rousseau's time. . . . Why should we have any hope that things will ever truly change? . . . I really don't see changing in the future."

I suspect that such reactions may be more or less peculiar to the relatively privileged students who attend private liberal arts colleges like the one at which I teach. Unlike Paulo Freire's "oppressed" students (*Pedagogy of the Oppressed*), these students seem more accurately characterized as "depressed," overwhelmed by the disparity between their own relative privilege and their perceived inability to act effectively for change. Understandably, the overwhelming problems they want to solve constitute a disheartening checklist of social ills that might depress anyone: rape, sexual violence, abortion, racial inequality, the degradation of the environment, intolerance, misogyny. Nevertheless, I am puzzled by this pervasive sense of hopelessness and powerlessness, which is the opposite of the empowerment I had wanted them to gain from the class.

As the teacher, I assume that the readings are designed to help them see that women have always been agents of social change. This course begins with an examination of the natural rights political theory out of which liberal feminism historically emerged. Zillah Eisenstein's reading, in *The Radical Future of Liberal Feminism,* of Locke and Rousseau—as well as her account of early feminist theorists like Mary Wollstonecraft, John Stuart Mill and Harriet Taylor, Susan B. Anthony, and Elizabeth Cady Stanton—provides an account of feminism's long history of theorizing. This background is designed to enable students to understand the roots of their own ideological commitments to Enlightenment liberal individualism. From there the course moves to an examination of the challenges to this model posed by such theoretical paradigms as poststructuralism, psychoanalysis, ecofeminism, and what Chela Sandoval has called the "oppositional consciousness" of Third World American feminists.

I have decided, however, that their depression, far from being implicit in the material they read, has much more to do with their ideas about what, for them, would constitute effective social or political change, the central problem addressed in the course. For many students, women would cease to be oppressed only following some drastic, revolutionary social change within every institution, one preferably achieved overnight. These notions, I found on probing, are related to their ideas about what a society is and how it changes, notions that have little to do with the poststructuralist theories I introduce in the class. For them a society is monolithic, static, autonomous, and homogeneous, a conception strikingly similar to their own liberal-individualist notions of the self. This philosophy understands society as basically static until drastic events occur to change everything: revolutions, wars, protest movements, marches, new statutes. As a result, for many students, their perception that political activism or legal remedies have failed to effect change in women's lives is an occasion for depression and despair since these practices seem to them the only mechanisms for change.

To confront this depression, I have devised as accompaniments to the course readings some pedagogical strategies that would make the abstractions of poststructuralist theory a material reality for students. I now consciously attempt to enable my students to understand that societies are heterogeneous and fragmented fields, constantly changing and shifting. I want to encourage them to engage in debates—including poststructuralist formulations of them—on the mechanisms of that change (Hodge and Kress 182–92). In this conception of social formations, the trick is not overcoming inertia to initiate change, but, within a formation that is always changing, controlling the direction and velocity of change. I want students to see that societies have to expend a great deal of energy—what I call cultural or ideological work (Finke 191–96)—to create the illusion of stasis that is so depressing for them. This essay outlines some of my strategies, which I hope will empower students by encouraging them to rethink their understanding of social change through the poststructuralist argument that knowledge about the world is socially constructed and not simply found ready-made, that knowledge produces what it claims to represent. My aim is to move away from what is often characterized as the moral nihilism of poststructuralism to investigate its potential as part of a political agenda for social change and liberation. That change, I argue, following Teresa de Lauretis, cannot be sought in some utopian fantasy of the future or in a nostalgic romancing of the archaic past; rather, it will be found in the material and symbolic practices that have been marginalized by the cultural work of dominant institutions and practices, including those of teaching (25).

Feminists, while proclaiming the social construction of both gender and knowledge as a major theoretical tenet, have often had difficulty articulating the implications of that claim for feminist practice, and I fear that we often bequeath this ambivalence to our students. If it is true that all knowledge is socially constructed, what follows from this assertion? For some feminists, potential answers to this question are troubling. How are women empowered by the belief that knowledge about the world is really nothing more than narrative, that the world is really only a contestable text? If it is, then the stories feminists tell would seem to have no greater claim to authority than the old ones they have rejected. As Donna Haraway puts it, "We would like to think our appeals to real worlds are more than a desperate lurch away from cynicism and an act of faith like any other cult's" (185). The problem, then, as Haraway articulates it, is

> how to have *simultaneously* an account of radical historical contingency for all knowledge claims and knowing subjects, a critical practice for recognizing our own "semiotic technologies" for making meanings, *and* a no-nonsense commitment to faithful accounts of a "real" world, one that can be partially shared and that is friendly to earthwide projects of finite freedom, adequate material abundance, modest meaning in suffering, and limited happiness. (187)

It is one thing to proclaim the radical historical contingency and social contestability of all knowledge claims and quite another (as Haraway knows) to devise a critical practice for recognizing our "semiotic technologies" for making meanings as a way of empowering ourselves and our students. Such a critical practice (a microtheory), which would trace the specific and practical day-to-day construction and implementation of the "hegemonic ideology" of gender (Moi 1019), may help our students understand which strategies of resistance will be the most effective. Such an approach may be empowering insofar as it suggests that those everyday practices of gender which we generally understand as deriving from an already constituted "fact" of gender (or even biological sex) may be reread more productively as an attempt to hold together what is at best a fragile construct in need of constant reinforcement. The pedagogical strategies I propose are designed to suggest a critical method for understanding the practices of everyday life that create gendered subjects and to imply a theory of social power and agency radically different from the monolithic and catastrophic theory of social change so paralyzing for my depressed students. This theory would describe the ways in which apparently monolithic structures of domination are created by practices of domination—in this case of gender domination—as well as the ways in which these hegemonic practices coexist with alternative practices, practices of resistance.[1] This exercise might be useful to teachers of literature as well as teachers of theory in its unmasking of the "semiotic technologies for making meaning" (Haraway 187) that inhabit both literature and everyday life.

I begin my lesson in the microtheory of social constructivism by asking students to consider a campus map and then taking a leisurely and aimless walk around the campus. I am indebted to an essay by Michel de Certeau called "Practices of Space" for this idea. In it, he attempts to describe a "rhetoric of walking," constructing an elaborate parallel between discourse and walking in which a map functions as *langue* (language as system) and the act of walking itself as *parole* (individual speech). The campus map I ask my students to consider represents an aerial view of a social formation (a college campus in this instance) that is homogenized, rationalized, disciplined, and surveyed. The map, in other words, is emblematic of students' conception of society as basically static. The walk enacts a different perspective, providing glimpses of those complexities that escape such rationalization and, I hope, suggesting a re-*vision* of the whole problem of social change. My goal is to use a trivial, even mundane, event to get students to grasp in a concrete way (pun intended) the social technologies designed to contain and control "docile" subjects and the countless modes of everyday resistance to those technologies.

The map functions as a totalizing representation that enables the viewer—situated in a godlike relation to the object of representation—to take in the entire campus at a single glance. The map is produced by a social authority,[2] an instantiation at the level of everyday life of the monolithic society my students imagine. The map presents the appearance of permanence, of a static and unchanging object of knowledge. Any changes in its appearance would be costly and presumably would coincide with a substantial shift in social relations (at least at the campus level): the gift of a new building, the addition of a new parking lot, or, alternatively, the closing of the campus to automobile traffic. To make its meaning, the map employs the semiotic technologies of authority and order, including print, graphic design, alphabetical order, and numeration to represent buildings, streets, sidewalks, parking lots, traffic patterns. Another, less obvious technology crucial to the authority of this text is its suppression of authorship. Unlike the literary text, the map appears to have no author; it is produced not by any particular man or woman but by nameless, faceless—and presumably genderless— authority, by "the college." Because the map assumes a purpose and a teleology, it encourages certain kinds of uses (readings) while discouraging others. The map is designed to move people—bodies—from one place to another by locating destinations. On the map of my campus I use for this exercise, individuals can locate a site only if they have a particular destination in mind and only if they know the correct name of that destination. The reader cannot easily find out, for instance, what the name of a particular building is because buildings are represented by numbers and are then listed in the key alphabetically rather than numerically. The spatial equivalent of browsing is not encouraged by this map. Because it presumes prior knowledge, the map discourages such readings.

Aerial representations like maps transform the complexity of social formations—which may be made up not only of buildings, streets, parking lots, and sidewalks but also of people, animals, architectural curiosities, trees, gardens, dirt paths, grass, hills, and all sorts of other things I can't even imagine—into "readability." As de Certeau suggests, they freeze "opaque mobility into a crystal clear text." The cost is "forgetfulness and a misunderstanding of process. Beneath the discourses ideologizing [space] there is a proliferation of tricks and fusions of power that are devoid of legible identity, . . . that are without any rational clarity—impossible to manage" (124)—at least from the perspective represented by the map. But de Certeau's "tricks and fusions," I suggest, are not simply random, meaningless individual acts but variable—and even manageable—social practices that constitute an alternative reading of space from ground level, one that might be organized into an effective political resistance. To begin to tease out such alternative representations—and potential spaces of resistance to rationalization—and to account for what the map has had to erase to perform its social function, we go for a walk.

A group of twenty-five out for a leisurely class stroll together is admittedly a strange sight, even on a college campus. But the artificiality of the situation itself provides occasion for analyses. Why do students find it so strange to be walking together instead of sitting together in a classroom? This question lends itself to an analysis of the institutional functions of classrooms and the ways in which they structure particular kinds of intellectual exchanges while discouraging others. During the walk, we talk about the social meanings of the sights we encounter. If we are walking on a sidewalk, we might consider the sidewalk as a social construction produced by the social relations of labor and production. Usually students understand that the sidewalk is intended to "control" the flow of foot traffic. I then ask them to consider the ways in which it constrains them, as well as the ways in which they resist such constraint. We might then move on to discover all those footpaths that have worn away the grass or hillsides where countless pedestrians, resisting sidewalks, have found shortcuts to their destinations. We watch people cut across the grass. We consider the cars legally and illegally parked. We talk about obstacles in our path, both permanent (buildings) and temporary, planned (construction) and unplanned (fallen trees), as well as their social meanings. Like de Certeau's urban walker, we can make "only a few of the possibilities set out by the established order effective" (we go here and not there). At the same time, we can increase "the number of possibilities (e.g. by making up shortcuts and detours) and the number of interdictions (e.g. by avoiding routes regarded as licit or obligatory)." In short, we select. In so doing, we create discontinuity, "either by choosing among the signifiers of the spatial language or by altering them through the use [we] make of them" (130), illustrating the ways in which individual and chaotic events may coalesce into alternative—and even counterhegemonic—practices.[3]

During our walk, then, we attempt to discover the ways in which the "perambulatory gesture" (136) transforms the spatial signifiers of panopticism into something else. The map can preserve only the "traces" of those social significations that describe process, change, heterogeneity, conformity, and resistance and that can be discovered only at "ground level." Only at ground level, in the act of walking itself, can we discover the "effect of successive encounters and occasions that are constantly altering [the landscape] into the advertisement for the other, the agent of whatever may surprise, cross or seduce its route" (136). This other establishes—and even defines—a new rhetoric of social change. This microtheory of social process does not exist in dialectical opposition to the monolithic and totalizing view represented by the map and articulated by depressed and angry students in feminist theory classes. These phenomena are not either-or alternatives. Rather, the two exist in a dialogical relation in which effective social critique must account for both the apparent coherence and stability promised by institutional representations and the countless unrecorded and often taken-for-granted activities that challenge, resist, and even alter that order.

This demonstration introduces students to the deconstructive notion that meaning can never be fixed once and for all but is endlessly deferred through the disruptive "free play" of signifiers, in this case the social signifiers of space.[4] It suggests that a society, far from being a fixed entity, is a contestable process by which meanings are produced, a process in which our students already participate as agents. But for this insight to become politically useful, students must also come to see that free play does not constitute some relativistic never-never land in which meaning and truth are self-determined, whatever anyone believes them to be. And they must understand that the political consequences of such transformative free play cannot be determined in advance. While it can certainly

disrupt structures of social order, it can also constitute structures of domination, coexisting with powerful social practices that attempt to close
off this free play and create the illusion of fixed meanings. The contested
areas between practices of domination and practices of resistance must
be a focus of our microtheory of social process as we apply the insights
gleaned from our walk to the social construction of gender, examining
the countless everyday practices that instantiate the hegemonic ideology
of gender.

Common sense tells us that we bleach our "facial hair" *because* we are
women and shave our "mustaches" *because* we are men. But common sense
is thoroughly ideological (Eagleton 108), and I like to encourage my students to think against or outside common sense—at least occasionally, for
the practice. I ask them, What if, in fact, cause and effect worked in the
opposite direction, if they became women through repeated acts like wearing dresses and shaving their legs and became men through acts like
wearing ties and growing mustaches? Of course, it isn't quite that easy;
one obviously cannot decide to change gender just by changing clothes.
The process is more complicated, however, not because the assignment
of gender is biological and fixed but because the social processes by which
we are assigned gender are so multiple and complex. At this particular
moment I want to blur the conventional sex-gender dichotomy to which
feminists have generally subscribed because I want to destabilize students'
commonsense notions about biology as the limit of gender. I do this not
because I want them to reject biology or biological sex once and for all;
rather, I want them to try out the position, to think about their own ideological investments in biological sex.[5] Gender is created by a massively
plural system of practices—cultural and ideological work—that are sometimes redundant, sometimes contradictory, but always shifting and changing, adjusting and readjusting to account for new information and new
changes. Many of these practices are nearly invisible because we do not
often think about them for the purposes of analysis. In *Outline of a Theory
of Practice*, Pierre Bourdieu describes the importance of those social practices that "exhort the essential while seeming to demand the insignificant."

> If all societies and, significantly, all the "totalitarian institutions" . . . that
> seek to produce a new man through a process of "deculturation" and "recul-
> turation" set such store on the seemingly most insignificant details of *dress,
> bearing*, physical and verbal *manners*, the reason is that, treating the body
> as a memory, they entrust to it in abbreviated and practical, i.e., mnemonic,
> form the fundamental principles of the arbitrary content of culture. . . .
> [N]othing seems more ineffable, more incommunicable, more inimitable, and
> therefore, more precious, than the values given body, *made* body.   (94)

There are countless practices of dress, bearing, and physical and verbal
manners (movement, facial expression, gesture) that both produce and
express gender through our very bodies. Bourdieu seems to suggest that
these bodily practices are beyond conscious analysis, that they cannot be

deliberately transformed or even made explicit. I would argue, however, that as part of the minutiae of everyday life, such practices might most productively be characterized as part of a practical or nondiscursive consciousness that, while not yet part of discourse, is available for critical reflection. Furthermore, a feminist "body politics" can coalesce around attempts to make this tacit knowledge conscious and discursive. "The socially produced body is thus necessarily also a political body, or rather an embodied politics" (Moi 1031).

To encourage my students to think about the political body, about the ideological work that makes them gendered individuals by "organizing" their bodies, I ask them to keep for one twenty-four-hour period a diary of every act that genders them. This diary focuses their attention on everyday practices of gender rather than structures of dichotomous sex. I ask them to record in this diary everything they notice themselves doing that makes them a particular gender, male or female. In addition, I ask them to record the things that others do to them that assign them gender. And, since they most likely will find themselves resisting at least some of those cultural markers, I ask them to record these events as well. At other times they might find themselves uncertain whether a particular act creates gender or not. I ask students to record those events too and try to figure out why they are confusing.

The exercise begins by creating confusion, but that confusion often reveals the usually totalizing assumptions about gender that students bring to this class. For this reason, it is useful to examine how students interpret (and misinterpret) the assignment. One student, for instance, wrote, "The way I interpret this is . . . which of my activities could be different if my gender were different. . . . These things, collectively, are not things that happen to the typical man in a day." This student assumes that gender is fixed and "what happens" to us on a daily basis is the result of that fixed identity. Initially, at least, she does not consider the extent to which the minutiae of everyday life create, as well as reinforce, her gender. To understand this assignment, students generally fall back on the sex-gender distinction that they have learned in other classes. "What genders me? By that I take you to mean what is making me a social, rather than merely a biological, female." As a result of these two common, if contradictory, assumptions —that gender is a fixed part of identity (what you are, which determines how others treat you) and that it is separate from biological sex—students often further assume that they should be recording only instances of sexist behavior and negative instances of gendering and that the goal is to create what one student called "gender neutral behavior" (i.e., nonsexist behavior).

This totalizing perspective colludes with the ideology that encourages men to think of themselves as genderless. Many men in the class initially cannot respond to the assignment. One man wrote, for instance, "I have trouble considering myself of a gender. Am I a man because I do like other men, or follow social constraints of what it means to be masculine?"

Another said, "I must admit that I have some difficulty identifying events during the past day that have gendered me. Even the concept of being gendered and using gender as a verb seems alien to me." Yet, forced by the terms of the assignment to write about something, most are able to think of many events in their lives that marked them as men, particularly as they thought about the "sexual boundaries" that limit male-to-male relationships but that, to them, seem absent in female-to-female relationships. Some even begin to think self-reflexively about the narrative of the diary itself as a technology of gender, as did the student who wrote at the end of his diary, "I am now writing about men's things."

As the assignment unfolds, these initial assumptions begin to lose their explanatory power. Since what we usually think of as the biological markers of sex—the genitalia—are invisible in most social encounters, to make determinations about gender we have to rely on other visible markers—clothing, hair, voices, bearing, posture, and so forth—and these largely redundant systems of codes and practices that signal (or create) gender are highly context-bound. This quickly becomes clear as students explore the incidents they record. In the particular context of this exercise (a contemporary American small liberal arts college), the most obvious marks of gender are conspicuously absent, so much so that students often feel at a loss for something to record in their diaries. Stereotypically, we might expect women to record putting on dresses, panty hose, high heels, and makeup, shaving their legs, and wearing jewelry, while men would record wearing short hair, pants exclusively, and shaving their facial hair. Most college-age adults, as my own students never hesitate to point out, do not dress in such clearly gender-marked ways. Women wear pants much of the time, and men never wear ties. Some women shave their heads, while men may grow their hair long. Women may refuse to shave their legs; some men wear earrings. The earring, in fact, has become a fascinating example of a contested practice of gender. Once a sign of effeminacy in men, it has now become, at least among college students and other cultural rebels, practically a mark of machismo, suggesting the chameleonlike capacity for change of gender's body politic. What students' initial confusion suggests is the variability of the cultural work of gender: the possibilities for appropriation, redistribution, crossover, and conflict, as well as the importance of context in determining the "meaning" of any specific incidence of gendering.

But the androgyny of college students at a small liberal arts college is the result of a specific context, one that does not represent all situations, as students invariably discover when they examine other, noncampus contexts. One student described an incident that occurred during a restaurant brunch:

> There was a line where you could be served with a made-to-order omelette and the man that I am dating decided he wanted one. So, he stood in the

> very long line and when he finally reached the very busy omelette chef, the chef glanced up at him and said, "What can I get you, ma'am?" . . . You see, the man I am dating has long hair. Both men were embarrassed by the situation. The chef was terribly sorry and even went so far as to buy my boyfriend a drink from the bar.

She concluded that "the chef was making amends so as not to offend the masculinity, the manhood of another man."[6] She speculates about the fear and anxiety generated when the signs that were sufficient in one context to distinguish gender fail in another so that both parties feel the need to restore the boundaries of male-male interaction through an act (buying drinks) designed to mark unambiguous masculinity. What further probing of this anecdote might reveal is the writer's own policing of gender by her reconstitution of her own sexual identity—firmly heterosexual—in the somewhat anxious repetition throughout the narrative of the word *boyfriend* and of phrases like "the man I am dating." This anecdote suggests that a feminist analysis of the social text of gender requires a dual perspective accounting both for the totalizing structures that enforce gender dichotomy and for the countless and shifting practices of everyday life, practices that are highly context bound and instantiate the dichotomy while providing the prospect of change. But the story also enables us to understand something about the productive capacity of institutional structures of power, both the ways in which the regulative strategies of gender produce the subjects they come to subjugate and the specific mechanisms by which power produces gender in the context of even the simplest narrative (Butler 96–100).

This "confessional production of the self" (Butler 99) within even such simple autobiographical narrative is at once highly visible and deeply invisible, recalling Bourdieu's remarks about the power of physical and verbal "manners" to produce the subjects they seek to regulate. Consider, for example, the spectacular and specular use of metaphor in the following excerpt from a diary describing how the writer applies cosmetics:

> I am putting on my war paint, carefully in front of the big mirror which my mother bought for this ritual. Every day I go to fight the world but never without my armor. This is how I feel. I think I am at odds with everyone around me. The enemy can never see me with my guard down.

The martial metaphors—war paint, ritual, armor—that structure this remark about a quintessentially female activity constitute a striking example of the production and reproduction within narrative of both totalizing structures of dichotomous gender (even in their confusion, male and female activities—war and makeup—are conceptualized oppositionally) and everyday acts of resistance to those meanings. At the same time, the very invisibility of such practices in everyday activities led one student to remark that he recognized the absence of gender marking more easily than its presence. For instance, in a preparatory LSAT class, he was surprised to notice that the class's response to practice questions which employed gender-neutral language was to attribute gender—male gender—to both the authors and subjects of the questions: "What I noticed most from this incident was the construction of a male voice. I mean that there is such a thing as the male voice. [The questions] could have been written by a woman, however, the topic and tone were characteristically male." The absence of gender marking within a narrative (here, a legal case study) is itself gender-marked.[7]

The analyses get more complex as students begin examining in greater detail their daily encounters with subtler forms of gender marking. One student described her experiences buying a used car in an essay about the discourse system of car sales:

> I found that car sales was a field dominated completely by males and geared toward male buyers. Not all of the men were as rude as [the salesman in the incident described] but they all created an environment that was intimidating for two major reasons: first, because I was a woman entering into a strictly male territory and secondly because I didn't know much about cars. Whether I don't know much about cars because I am a woman . . . or because I was truly never interested in knowing is a valid question. Perhaps I was never interested in knowing about them because it would be too intimidating to violate the . . . system.

This student is beginning to explore the ideological foundations of her common sense, of what Bourdieu calls *le sens pratique*: those inarticulate norms and values that determine what can legitimately be said—or perceived—in any social encounter. Suddenly her lack of knowledge about cars has become more than simply a benign gap in her education. She is questioning the relation between her learning and her gender. Did she not know about cars because of her gender? Or had part of her learning how to be female entailed not learning about cars because "it would be too intimidating to violate the . . . system"?

Following is the same student's description of the nonverbal details of this encounter. What is most interesting about her analysis is her recognition that the nonverbal exchanges assigned both gender and value to her before any words had been uttered and that these same attitudes were reinforced during the verbal exchange. She is beginning to discover the extent to which gender codes are reinforced and made to seem holistic through their sheer redundancy. Indeed, this semiotic redundancy may be the primary means of maintaining the illusion that societies are seamless, static, and more or less permanent.

> On the grounds, there were three or four adult males working or watching TV, the guys that came along with me, and myself. Obviously I was the only female. The salesman is sitting down behind a desk, when Jeff [one of the male friends she had brought along] and I entered the place

soaking wet. Already, there are signs of cohesion and order. I am the only woman among a fairly large number of men, most of whom are older than I am. There is the separation of gender and age. The level of solidarity between Jeff and me is lower because the ratio of men to women creates a gender separation. In other words, despite the difference in age and in class between Jeff and the men at the place, identifying with them in terms of sameness or maleness has a high affinity because of the predominance of men. Jeff and I can identify with each other as friends despite gender differences, but . . . our solidarity is lowered because of the "maleness"of that territory.

This student's intuition that she has been isolated because of her gender and is being nonverbally intimidated is validated by her verbal exchange with the salesman. When she complains that a car she has test-driven stalled, the salesman attacks her driving ability, implying that because she is a woman she must be a poor driver:

"Well it stalled on me two or three times."
"Well you know, sometimes it's the driver. I noticed when you were pulling out that you weren't a very good driver."

None of the male friends she has brought with her offer any support, either verbal or nonverbal, during this exchange, which ends in the student's doubting her own driving capabilities and even her own experience, despite statistical evidence (which she herself mentions) that women are better drivers than men are. I am suggesting not that the statistical evidence is necessarily "truer" than the salesman's perception but that such uncertainties cannot be resolved by recourse to any facts because the facts are precisely what are at issue. At this point we might wonder if the exchange happened *because* the student was a female or if its purpose was to reinforce, and even re-create, her femininity when that attribute was very much in doubt. The difference may seem subtle, but it is crucial to my argument that this kind of microanalysis empowers students. This exchange is depressing if it occurred simply because this student was female. It would then be one more instance of the intransigence of gender relations, their resistance to progressive change. If, however, this incident was designed (whether consciously or unconsciously) to create gender at a moment when it was in doubt, the situation is much less depressing because it suggests the instability of "normal" gender relations. This student's violation of an ideologically male domain—car sales—required a strategy that, in effect, reproduced clear gender marking. Gender separation is so fragile and so unstable that it requires constant policing, constant ideological work to maintain the illusion that it is "natural." Furthermore, the student's analysis exposes the ideological work of gender at the moment of its production, suggesting the ways in which such analyses are empowering to the extent that they return at least some control and agency to the analyst.

My purpose in asking students to keep gender diaries is to expose the constant cultural work that must go into the maintenance of gender and gender relations. I designed the exercise to suggest that, far from being a single, monolithic, and clearly delimited entity that is decided once and for all, gender is an ongoing, highly complex, and fragmented process that cuts across almost all social fields and that is variously and even contradictorily represented in those fields. Gender is a contested area of culture in which both old and new meanings are constantly being produced, and students, however powerless this ideological work has made them feel, are agents actively engaged in those contests. Such an analysis makes social change at once more difficult and more conceivable. It certainly suggests different strategies of social change. It becomes more difficult (perhaps even more depressing, I'll admit) because we can no longer hope for a onetime global change in gender relations that will liberate everyone once and for all. Instead, effective political actions will be local, particularistic, and plural, perhaps even contradictory. Furthermore, we can anticipate no Marxist "withering away" of the state of gender oppression. Rather, new "fronts" must be opened everywhere. In particular we need more analyses of the minutiae of everyday life, of the ways in which we can instill "a whole cosmology, an ethic, a metaphysic, a political philosophy through an injunction as insignificant as 'stand up straight'" (Bourdieu 94–95). At the same time, such a theoretical conception makes change more conceivable because there is no longer the illusion of some massive inertia to overcome. Change is constant once we shift our perspective from the aerial to "ground level." Our tasks become less monumental and global, more local and manageable. No longer is it necessary for individuals to bear total responsibility for a massive transformation of an essentially static social formation—an understandably daunting prospect. What we hope to do instead is to influence the direction and velocity of changes that are already in progress by exposing those areas within culture in which gender is being contested. In the final analysis, it is not poststructuralism's claims for the indeterminacy of social meaning that liberate us but, rather, the corollary claim that this indeterminacy makes us all agents responsible for harnessing it to serve progressive social ends.

Kenyon College

Notes

I am grateful to Dorothy Berkson, Anne Dawid, Deborah Heath, and Kristi Williams for their perceptive comments on an earlier version of this essay.

[1] My argument draws on Raymond Williams's, and ultimately Antonio Gramsci's, definition of *hegemony* as those social meanings, practices, and values that must be continually "renewed, recreated, and defended" and so can be continually "challenged, resisted, modified" (R. Williams 112).

² I recommend leaving aside, for the moment, the question of whether this authority is gendered in any way. My focus at this stage of the exercise is on the illusion of permanence created by all technologies of social control, not simply those technologies that produce gender.

³ One suggestion for an adaptation of this exercise is to ask the students to construct an "antimap" or alternative map that reflects their own use of the campus. While recognizing that such an exercise might be valuable, I recommend it guardedly. I take students on an actual walk in part because I want students to be able to see the differences between social constructionism and relativism. Asking students to construct their own map corresponding to their idiosyncratic uses of the campus would, I think, encourage their already too-easy relativism in which anyone's representation of space (or of the social) is as good as anyone else's. This conclusion would distort the point of the exercise. Clearly the campus map, with its print technologies and suppressed authorship, has an authority that students' maps could not have. Furthermore, their maps would be yet another kind of totalizing representation, encouraging them to continue in their belief that social formations are essentially static. Instead I want them to catalogue firsthand those things that escape the rationalizations of social authority—that is, change, heterogeneity, and flux. As it turns out, the walk itself, as a "social text," changes significantly from outing to outing, term to term, even when we retrace the same path.

⁴ Given the counterintuitive force of deconstructive claims about meaning, such an exercise would be valuable in any class that attempts to understand and even critique the Derridean notion of free play because it puts into practice the often abstract theoretical insight.

⁵ For a historical examination of the limits of biological sex, see Laqueur. For a critique of the sex-gender dichotomy, see Butler, esp. 6–25. A particularly compelling film to accompany this exercise, which should encourage students to extend its observations to literary and cultural texts, would be Jennifer Livingston's documentary on drag, *Paris Is Burning.*

⁶ As I read this scene, I think of Lacan's notorious quip "You can't make an Hommelette without breaking eggs" (Clément 97). For a psychoanalytic perspective on such identities, see Clément 96–101.

⁷ For a discussion of neutrality in the language of the law, see Patricia Williams 8–14 and 98–121.

Works Cited

Bourdieu, Pierre. *Outline of a Theory of Practice.* Trans. Richard Nice. Cambridge: Cambridge UP, 1977.

Butler, Judith. *Gender Trouble: Feminism and the Subversion of Identity.* New York: Routledge, 1990.

Clément, Catherine. *The Lives and Legends of Jacques Lacan.* Trans. Arthur Goldhammer. New York: Columbia UP, 1983.

de Certeau, Michel. "Practices of Space." *On Signs.* Ed. Marshall Blonsky. Baltimore: Johns Hopkins UP, 1985. 122–45.

de Lauretis, Teresa. *Technologies of Gender: Essays on Theory, Film, and Fiction.* Bloomington: U of Indiana P, 1987.

Eagleton, Terry. *Literary Theory: An Introduction.* Minneapolis: U of Minnesota P, 1983.

Eisenstein, Zillah. *The Radical Future of Liberal Feminism*. Boston: Northeastern UP, 1981.

Finke, Laurie A. *Feminist Theory, Women's Writing*. Ithaca: Cornell UP, 1992.

Freire, Paulo. *Pedagogy of the Oppressed*. Trans. Myra Bergman Ramos. New York: Herder, 1968.

Haraway, Donna. *Simians, Cyborgs, and Women: The Reinvention of Nature*. New York: Routledge, 1991.

Hodge, Robert, and Gunther Kress. *Social Semiotics*. Ithaca: Cornell UP, 1988.

Laqueur, Thomas. *Making Sex: Body and Gender from the Greeks to Freud*. Cambridge: Harvard UP, 1990.

Moi, Toril. "Appropriating Bourdieu: Feminist Theory and Pierre Bourdieu's Sociology of Culture." *New Literary History* 4 (1991): 1017–49.

Sandoval, Chela. "U.S. Third-World Feminism: The Theory and Method of Oppositional Consciousness in the Postmodern World." *Genders* 10 (1991): 1–24.

Williams, Patricia. *The Alchemy of Race and Rights*. Cambridge: Harvard UP, 1991.

Williams, Raymond. *Marxism and Literature*. Oxford: Oxford UP, 1977.

An Introductory Texts and Theory Course

Jonathan Arac

The texts and theory course I describe and discuss assigns literary and critical works that might be called canonical, but the issues I emphasize are of current critical concern. I have taught the course about ten times since 1980, at the University of Illinois at Chicago, in the School of General Studies at Columbia University, and at the University of Pittsburgh. It has been required of English majors at all three institutions, though in each department it has a different relation to other requirements. My course is designed for students who have in some serious sense committed themselves to reading literature but are not necessarily very knowledgeable or much trained. I understand *theory* as the deliberate thinking about the principles of activities that are already somewhat familiar. In this course, I assume that students are already familiar with preferring one work over another. My purpose in the course, then, is to help students gain strength and confidence in exercising their judgments by introducing them to some notable ways in which other readers have thought about what makes a work of literature valuable and by giving them practice in these ways of thought.

I thus acknowledge from the beginning, as a given of my students' experiences, the overriding emphasis our culture has placed on readers' emotional and personal relations to the arts, but I make these relations the basis for thought and reasoned argument, rather than treat them as an unarguable zone of privacy. In teaching students the study of literature, I am not just "exposing" them to a power that can make them swoon; I aim to engage their powers of attention. The works we study are meant to be intelligible. They are highly, usually deliberately, structured, yet they are small enough wholes that it is possible to grasp and analyze with some precision the particulars that make them up. This part of our task is itself a valuable intellectual practice, but it is not sufficient. Above all, I want to engage students in comparative evaluation as part of fundamental pedagogy—that is, to begin relating the small system of individual works to a range of larger systems.

In my course, I use a broad spectrum of authors, drawing works from at least five centuries and four national literatures (but mostly written in English). I choose, with a few significant exceptions, critical writings that do not directly address the literary writings: this is one major respect in which it is a course in theory. From the critical texts, certain theoretical issues emerge, which are then discussed in relation to specific works. For the classroom, these works are largely of my choosing, but the students may choose others for their papers. Since students overwhelmingly choose twentieth-century, usually contemporary, works, I do not include twentieth-century literary works in the basic syllabus. Some five times in the course, students have the freedom, and responsibility, to respond to the following assignment for a short essay: "Choose a work that you know from somewhere other than this course and that you value; bring it into relation with the theoretical issue we are now exploring." (This is the common skeleton of the assignments; in each, there are more specifics.) Students' choices include not only poems, plays, and novels of various genres, by writers of both genders and diverse ethnicities, but also songs, movies, and TV shows. Although the works I assign, as opposed to the ones students choose to explore in their essays, are fairly traditional and canonical, it is not my intention to assert a coercively restrictive definition of literature. Whenever a student asks whether he or she may write about a given work, I say yes, as long as it is in some sense a verbally based work (since I do not want the course to become simply aesthetic, rather than literary).

The critics I assign include Aristotle, Longinus, Samuel Johnson, William Wordsworth, T. S. Eliot, and Virginia Woolf; the literary works may include *Oedipus, King Lear, Madame Bovary*, poems by Emily Dickinson, plus one or two others from each of six or eight additional poets. In presenting the critical texts, I draw attention to theory as itself a work of writing (the fictional form of *A Room of One's Own* illustrates this point well). Procedures for reading literature are not restricted to novels, poetry, and drama (such restrictions being one of the most destructive educational effects of the New Criticism).

The overall concern of the course is to introduce students to ways of thinking about works of fiction and about argument. These ways have historical standing but are also relevant to current thinking about current works. These ways have both formal and contextual dimensions. Throughout the course, the two emphases prove distinguishable but rarely separable. The emphasis in the first weeks is relatively more formalist than the course later becomes. In beginning with Sophocles's *Oedipus the King* and Aristotle's *Poetics*, I emphasize Aristotle's definition of a plot, especially such distinctions as the simple versus the complex plot and the contrast of plot (as the imitation of a single action) to biography and history. The goal is to renew for students the intellectual respectability of a mode of analysis that has been crucial to most twentieth-century varieties of structuralism and narratology but that most students have been taught in high school to reject as childish, in favor of such (nineteenth-century) concerns as character and theme.

The first writing assignment begins from Aristotle's summary, in section 17, of the plot of the *Odyssey* (even more impressive in the Greek, in which it is a single sentence). I discuss with students the implications of this more-than-thousandfold reduction of the work, an astonishing feat of abstraction. Sometimes I characterize Plato's *Ion* and other works which suggest that before Aristotle Greek culture lacked the conceptual tools for plot summary. I ask students to choose a work of a "certain magnitude" they know from elsewhere in their reading (or viewing), summarize its plot in no more than one hundred words, and then write a brief essay in which they reflect on what may be learned, and what gained or lost, by such an intellectual exercise. Most people do not like this exercise, but it may accomplish a great deal of valuable preliminary work. For instance, several times a student has been distressed by the exercise because, when reduced to its plot, so admired a work as *Jane Eyre* becomes indistinguishable from a Harlequin romance. Class discussion of such an observation leads to questions about the social analysis of cultural characteristics, which anticipates later discussions of Wordsworth and Flaubert, but it also highlights students' usual preference for "detail" as a value, in contrast to Aristotle's prime emphasis on plot.

As we are concluding this first phase of the course, I distribute a handout of Wordsworth's "A Slumber Did My Spirit Seal." The purpose of our discussion is to determine whether there is a plot to be found in this eight-line poem (for example, a change of fortune for "her": she lived, but then she died). The question now becomes, What about me—that is, the "I" of the poem? A complex plot may be defined, in which I considered her immortal, but I was disappointed. This exercise begins to make Aristotle's arguments more engaging, as their application moves farther from his home ground.

Next we read *King Lear*. As the first topic for discussion, I ask students to define—"as grossly as possible"—the most important ways in which this play differs from *Oedipus* and, from there, to consider the applicability of Aristotle's ideas to it. Students recognize *King Lear* as bigger, in many specifiable ways, and more complicated than *Oedipus*. The double-plot structure provokes vigorous debate about whether it is good in Aristotelian terms. The reunion of Lear and Cordelia (4.7) has often been a focus for discussion because it may be read as perfectly exemplifying, in quite a literal sense, what Aristotle describes and values as "recognition."

To shift the ground of critical debate, I assign "The Imagination," a chapter from I. A. Richards's *Principles of Literary Criticism*, which begins its constructive argument by quoting a paragraph from chapter 14 of Samuel Taylor Coleridge's *Biographia Literaria* on "the reconciliation of opposites." I find it much more workable to ration the dose of Coleridge in this way and to focus on Richards, who has been more directly influential in the literary pedagogy with which students are (somewhat) familiar. Richards presents an interpretation of Aristotle that places in the foreground the affective element and explicitly downplays the formal element. As part of our working with Richards's notion of an openness to all the ramifications of an experience, I ask students to investigate the various meanings they can find for the term *nature* and its affiliates in *King Lear*.

From Richards we turn to Johnson's preface to his edition of Shakespeare and his comments on *King Lear*. For my purposes there are two crucial points here. First, Johnson takes Richards's affective emphasis and opens it to the vagaries of actual experience. He was shocked, painfully, rather than exalted by *King Lear*. As a result, Johnson prefers the stage version of Nahum Tate (in which, among many other changes, Cordelia survives to marry Edgar) to Shakespeare's original text. This notorious crux is always extremely provocative for theoretical debate. In his preface, Johnson summons the authority of Shakespeare's practice to refute theorists who claim that great plays must observe unity of time, place, or genre, but at this moment in his commentary he overrides Shakespeare by granting authority to the audience. I ask students whether they agree with Johnson, and most do not. Their reasons touch on major theoretical and institutional issues: students defend authors' rights to have their work seen as they wrote it; students claim that the horror of Shakespeare's ending is truer than the poetic justice that pleased Johnson; students attempt to determine whether there are formal grounds for claiming that one way of ending the play is more coherent with the first four acts than is the other.

Johnson's challenge to New Critical organicism is heightened by our reading of Longinus's *On the Sublime*. Longinus combines extravagant critical language, intense emphasis on the emotions of author and audience, and a belief that the strongest effects come from moments that destroy unity, yet he also deploys a rhetorician's precise array of terms and minute local effects. Students find reading Longinus an extraordinary experience; this is the critic that students never thought they would meet in a course. The term's second paper moved from the unfamiliarity of Aristotle on plot to an exercise much closer to one that many students have done before: the analysis of a single brief work as a whole from the viewpoint of Richards's argument. The third paper is again disorienting: I ask the students to emulate Longinus by choosing a brief excerpt from a work, where the excerpt (not necessarily the work itself) is one of the high points of their literary experience, and to try to explain, as precisely as they can, how the words make this excerpt outstanding. In preparation, I circulate for discussion brief passages from *Paradise Lost* and *Titus Andronicus* (a great moment from a play most students have never heard of), and then, over one or two more class meetings, students bring in the passages they are thinking about.

In our next reading, Wordsworth's Preface to *Lyrical Ballads*, the arguments about the language of poetry also invite close verbal attention to particular texts. We start discussion of the Preface, however, by focusing on its polemic about what is now called mass culture and on the social role that Wordsworth envisions for his own favored kinds of writing, which he presents as avoiding the perversions of elitism no less than the "gross and violent stimulants" (449) of modern life. Then the classroom exercises return to close reading. We look at Thomas Gray's sonnet on the death of Richard West, which Wordsworth quotes to criticize in the Preface, and we consider whether there are other ways of reading it that might make it seem more valuable than Wordsworth finds it. (For example, is there what Coleridge, and Richards, called a "reconciliation of opposites" between the lines Wordsworth italicizes for approval and the lines he rejects?) For a wider sense of the possibilities and obstacles in a type of poetry that, contrary to Wordsworth's wishes, works with personified abstractions, we read Johnson's "On the Death of Dr. Robert Levet." Juxtaposing this work with Gray on West and "A Slumber Did My Spirit Seal," we stage a fruitful comparison of three poems of mourning from a fifty-year period. We begin by noting in the three poems the very different emphases between focus on the speaker (almost total in Gray) and focus on the deceased (almost total in Johnson). Wordsworth might then seem to reconcile the extremes of his two predecessors, but in his poem students usually find, frustratingly, less of the detail they value about either speaker or deceased. I then change this line of discussion by asking the question "Which would you prefer to have as your memorial?" Students are often surprised to find that they prefer Johnson.

The last classroom exercise in the wake of discussing Wordsworth contributes to the examination of verbal differences among historically divergent English poetic styles. There are two versions of Sir Thomas Wyatt's lyric beginning "They flee from me," each with contemporary authority. Editors now prefer to print the version from Wyatt's Egerton manuscript, but for centuries the version known to readers was that entitled "The Lover Showeth How He Is Forsaken of Such as He Sometime Enjoyed" and published among the "songs and sonnets" of Tottel's *Miscellany* in 1557, some fifteen years after Wyatt's death and a long way from him in the rapidly shifting expectations for English prosody. I begin, as did Richards in *Practical Criticism*, by presenting the poems as bare texts. I ask students to underline the differences between the two versions, reproduced face to face; to try to imagine reasons for the changes; to propose a hypothesis linking the two versions; and to develop an argument for the superiority of one version over the other (i.e., the reasons for one's preference).

I read the two versions aloud, emphasizing iambic regularity for Tottel and four-stress speech intonation for the Egerton manuscript, to highlight the differences in their metrical practices. Both the New Criticism and the newer criticism tend to underemphasize this technical, material dimension of poetry, yet without attention to prosody, poetry may seem like arbitrary magic rather than a codified technology of verbal power. Metrical study makes poetry more like something one can do oneself and also increases respect for poets because their ability looks more like a conscious skill than like a mere gift. Nonetheless, the most vigorous discussion tends to focus on a more semantic issue. In the concluding couplet, the two versions seem to represent opposing senses (an Empsonian seventh-level ambiguity): the manuscript reads "kindely," Tottel "unkindly." I ask students whether they believe that the speaker has reversed his feelings about the situation. Some think yes, but others suggest that the apparent reversal occurs because *kindely* is ironic. The notion of irony may then be used to help students find a term to characterize the tone of the Tottel version, in which *unkindly* is more straightforwardly aggressive, biting, or as the students put it, "sarcastic."

This comparison of two versions enables students to enjoy a much more flexible, attentive discussion of the poem than would be possible if we studied it in a single text. In reading only the manuscript version, most students I have known would characterize it as sarcastic (too) and would not readily accept any distinction between irony and sarcasm as applied to the solitary poem. Having arrived at a possible distinction between sarcasm and irony still does not determine for students which version is preferable. Some praise the sarcastic version for being more sincere and straightforward (praising also its metrics, for greater smoothness and regularity). Perhaps more to the point, having chosen to prefer one version, at least some students will then ask whether this poem is enjoyable at all, for it seems an instance of male sexual degradation of women. I ask students whether they know of other love poetry in which this issue may also be present. Some claim to know no other love poetry, but they all prove to know many current songs dealing with love, which are highly relevant to this discussion. These issues of the relations between aesthetics, psychology, ethics, and the social regulation of gender return a few weeks later in the sequence that runs from Dickinson through Woolf and *Madame Bovary* (including the trial).

The next critical reading is Eliot's "Tradition and the Individual Talent." With this essay, literary history as a theoretical problem is foregrounded, and I try to help the students begin to organize their knowledge by introducing and distinguishing from one another the categories of imitation, influence, convention, topos, genre, and tradition. I also assign the first class exercise. Wyatt and Henry Howard, Earl of Surrey, both translated the same sonnet by Petrarch, and I offer a current prose translation of the Petrarch along with the two sonnets. To begin with, I do not identify any of the texts. I ask students to compare them and to pose hypotheses on the relations among the three. The further discussion brings categories of literary history back to Eliot's essay. Eliot somewhat obscurely distinguishes between "emotions" and "feelings," attempting to one-up Wordsworth's "formula" (as Eliot calls it) of "emotion recollected in tranquillity." I offer the sonnets by Wyatt and Surrey, after revealing their actual relation, to try out a claim that since they are translations, the "emotion," in Eliot's sense of biographical experience of the "man who suffered," was Petrarch's and that the diference between the two English sonnets may be accounted for in Eliot's terms by the differing "feelings" of the translator-poets. That is, Eliot's distinction acknowledges the poet's active agency through the institutionalized media of language, while denying that the poem "reflects" or "expresses" the poet's soul. Eliot emphasizes that the poet's "feeling" will often be located in an especially striking "image" (41). As we look over the sonnets again with this hypothesis in mind, students often single out Wyatt's phrase "the heart's forest" (an image not in Petrarch or Surrey) as a complication in meaning that seems to bring an added range of suggestiveness and intensity to Wyatt's development of the pregiven allegory.

The final exercise related to Eliot's essay specifies tradition as a matter of convention and genre, comparing John Keats's "To Autumn" with Percy Bysshe Shelley's "Ode to the West Wind." Both poems are formal odes, addresses to seasonal deities, written in the same English meter, in the fall of 1819, by poets who knew each other; both poems are typically presented in teaching anthologies with biographical attestations tying the composition of the poems to particular moments in particular landscapes. The assignment is to look for differences in the "movement" of the two poems. Assisted by preliminary discussion of basic English metrics—including such matters as end-stop versus run-on, the variations possible in the iambic norm of unstressed-stressed, and what a caesura is (matters previously discussed in the term)—students with little experience in reading traditional English verse become capable of making fairly elaborate distinctions between the two, rather than simply saying of each, as they might if they addressed the poems separately, "It flows." Their sharpened feel for versification helps them respond vividly when asked to consider the once authoritative judgment that Keats's poem, because it avoids the first-person singular, is much more impersonal than Shelley's, which, notoriously, does employ the first person. After students have closely analyzed the difference between Keats's heavily end-stopped, heavily spondaic verse and Shelley's long loops of syntax that make verse-paragraphs even out of closely rhymed tercets, it seems pointless to judge one less personally marked than the other.

Our work in Romantic lyric traditions looks forward to the complex relations to these traditions in the writings of Woolf and Dickinson. Woolf, like Wordsworth, emphasizes both social and psychological concerns in her understanding of valuable writing and its possibilities, and while Wordsworth looked to vocabulary as a standard for both local and global evaluation of particular works, Woolf offers the sentence. In reading Dickinson, we try out some of Woolf's hypotheses. Can we arrive at ways of understanding Dickinson's work that depend on her being a woman? Does the condition of being a woman produce angry sentences, as Woolf argued it did in Charlotte Brontë, a contemporary of Dickinson's? Does such anger mark Dickinson's strongest work, or is her best work impersonal, as Woolf, in an adaptation of Coleridge much like Richards's, suggests is so for the greatest authors, such as Jane Austen and Shakespeare? (See Woolf 71, 76, 102–08.)

It is common, I think, for theory-oriented courses that include *Madame Bovary* to use the wonderful anthology of criticism of the novel that Paul de Man assembled in his Norton critical edition. I prefer, however, to have available the trial of the novel, which de Man omitted, without explanation but in perfect harmony with his mature critical position. The trial brings the question of the social dimension of criticism most dramatically to the forefront, and it emphasizes even more thoroughly the questions of responsibility that one undertakes as a writer, whether of fiction (poetry) or criticism. The debate between defense and prosecution allows us to replay issues from the whole course of the term: Is the work's power to be felt in its whole or through fragments (Aristotle versus Longinus)? What role in evaluation may a reader's shock play (Johnson)? What is the relation between Flaubert's language and the problems of the social uses of language in his time (Wordsworth)? Do the apparent contradictions of tone, feeling, and stylistic register in the book permit "reconciliation"? Does the work exploit women, instruct women, or offer opportunities for women who read it? Students are usually surprised by the good sense of much of the prosecution's case, even when they do not favor censorship, and they are distressed by the combination of formal sophistication and ideological benightedness in the arguments of the defense. Having worked through the trial, we return to the very first words of *Madame Bovary*, Flaubert's dedication of the book to his defense attorney. What do students make of this? Does it show that Flaubert himself accepted the argument, made in his defense, that the novel shows the social damage produced by educating farm women beyond their station? Is it a further example of Flaubert's ironic relation to the bourgeois culture that he mocked yet depended on? Students who supported Shakespeare against Johnson do not necessarily wish here to grant Flaubert the authority to determine their judgment of his text.

Enough examples. Now I would like to offer some reflections. First, it is an enabling premise of the course that even students who have not pursued much college literary study are nonetheless already experienced with "poetry and fiction," in the various combinations of popular music, movies, and television that for many of us as well are a major part of our current cultural experience. Teaching these students may thus rely on familiarity and place primary emphasis on topics of "analysis"—that is, of description and evaluation. At the same time, many of these students, however experienced they may be with poetry and fiction, have read almost no traditional belles lettres, and eventually their reading will require a great deal of support with regard to the language, references, and institutions (or, in a word, the history) that separate them from these works, even as other histories join them to the works.

The various verbal enactments that make up the works of older writing we wish our students to read are alien forms of life, which have proved empowering to some who have read and written in them. We may invite students to try them on, hoping for some cooperation, but how hard can we make someone try? That is why I present so many of the materials of this course in the form of exercises—like teachers of creative writing who try to get around the combined inhibition and bombast that cripple much student workshop writing by assigning formal exercises in imitation. The diminished commitment ("It's not me") often allows for an enhanced engagement with the actual work of writing. So in my course students choose the works on which they write, and the works I choose are presented primarily not as "the masterpieces" of English literature but as interesting places to consider problems that have arisen from our discussions of the critics.

This issue is all the more significant because the major traditions of thinking about literature hold that it affects the reader. Plato, Aristotle, and Longinus are here at one with Johnson, the Romantics, and current theorists about the formation of subjectivity. The encounter with powerful, and powerfully alien, works is threatening. If you simply swoon, you acknowledge the work's power, but you have probably not gained any of it for yourself. The study of literature aims to concentrate the reader's attention and to provide a discipline that may make the encounter more valuable because not wholly overwhelming, a use of knowledge to gain power.

My language of discipline, knowledge, and power acknowledges the influence of Michel Foucault on my thinking, even if I have not always used his "tool-kit" in the ways that have become conventional. A further Foucauldian dimension of my course is its attempt to start from the present even while focusing direct attention on older materials. My course ranges over a wide chronology, and it frequently aims to provoke dialogue, often polemical or antagonistic, between present concerns and concerns of older writers. Nonetheless, there is a further dimension of history that I believe must be addressed in response to current theoretical concerns. The study of English has never been authoritatively defined as a discipline in the same way that most other academic units have been, nor has it even been defined by a canon. It has, rather, been defined by a subject matter: writings in a certain language from certain times and places, plus whatever materials we can prove relevant to those writings. Period courses and survey courses are still the fundamental building blocks of undergraduate English departments that attempt to provide more structure than a simple amassing of elective credits, and theory has yet to galvanize this institutional mass toward reaching a new consensus on a historical introduction to the subject. Until this happens, a course like mine, however valuable in itself, remains marginal rather than central to a curriculum.

University of Pittsburgh

Note

My thanks to David Laurence, whose invitation to a 1991 ADE Seminar provoked a first version of this paper.

Works Cited

Aristotle. *On the Art of Poetry. Classical Literary Criticism*. Trans. T. S. Dorsch. Harmondsworth, Eng.: Penguin, 1965. 31–75.

de Man, Paul, ed. and trans. *Gustave Flaubert:* Madame Bovary; *Backgrounds and Sources; Essays in Criticism*. New York: Norton, 1965.

Eliot, T. S. "Tradition and the Individual Talent." *Selected Prose of T. S. Eliot*. Ed. Frank Kermode. New York: Harcourt, 1975. 37–44.

Flaubert, Gustave. *Madame Bovary*. Trans. Mildred Marmur. With "The Trial of *Madame Bovary*." Trans. Evelyn Gendel. New York: NAL, 1964.

Howard, Henry, Earl of Surrey. "Love, That Doth Reign and Live within My Thought" [trans. of poem by Petrarch]. *The Norton Anthology of English Literature*. 4th ed. Vol. 1. Ed. M. H. Abrams et al. New York: Norton, 1979. 474.

Johnson, Samuel. Excerpts from "Preface to Shakespeare" and notes to *King Lear*. *King Lear*. By William Shakespeare. Ed. Russell Fraser. New York: NAL, 1963. 212–24.

———. "On the Death of Dr. Robert Levet." *Samuel Johnson*. Ed. Donald Greene. Oxford: Oxford UP, 1986. 35–36.

Longinus. *On the Sublime. Classical Literary Criticism*. Trans. T. S. Dorsch. Harmondsworth, Eng.: Penguin, 1965. 99–158.

Richards, I. A. "The Imagination." *Principles of Literary Criticism*. New York: Harcourt, 1925. 239–53.

———. *Practical Criticism*. New York: Harcourt, 1929.

Woolf, Virginia. *A Room of One's Own*. New York: Harcourt, 1929.

Wordsworth, William. Preface to *Lyrical Ballads* (1800). *Selected Poems and Prefaces*. Ed. Jack Stillinger. Boston: Houghton, 1965. 445–64.

Wyatt, Sir Thomas the Elder. "They Flee from Me." "The Lover Showest How He Is Forsaken of Such as He Sometime Enjoyed." "The Long Love That in My Thought Doth Harbor" [trans. of poem by Petrarch]. *The Norton Anthology of English Literature*. 4th ed. Vol. 1. Ed. M. H. Abrams et al. New York: Norton, 1979. 464, 467–68.

A Theorized Poetry Class

Cary Nelson

I want to ground my remarks about theory and social responsibility in undergraduate teaching in a specific material context: a course in modern poetry that I taught recently. I was returning to the undergraduate literature classroom after several years' absence, having taught mostly courses and seminars in theory. Because I wanted my students to treat critical books and essays as texts, rather than as mere exportable systems of ideas (and because no one else in my department was teaching courses in pure theory at the time), I considered it important to exclude literary texts from my theory courses and to require students to write directly about theory, not to apply it to literature. That was a requirement I maintained for both graduate and undergraduate students. Except for a graduate seminar in contemporary poetry, I thus had not taught literature at all for some time. But now I was writing a book about modern poetry—*Repression and Recovery: Modern American Poetry and the Politics of Cultural Memory, 1910–1945*, published in 1989—and I did not want the book to be impoverished by lack of contact with student opinions and reactions. Moreover, I had acquired a sense of mission about overturning the modern poetry canon and giving new cultural life to dozens of forgotten poets; it was time to share that mission with our undergraduates.

My long sabbatical from literature meant that it was time to begin thinking seriously about what I thought a literature class might do in the late 1980s. In a way I had no choice. The texts I had used years earlier were either out of print or so narrow in their representations of women and minorities as to be totally alienating. The most obvious new anthologies—such as the current revisions of *The Norton Anthology of Poetry* (Allison) and *The Norton Anthology of Modern Poetry* (Ellmann and O'Clair)—could hardly have been less generous in their representation of the expanded canon. I no longer remembered the details of the modern poetry courses I had taught years ago, and I didn't want to think about the effort that would be required to find any of my old syllabi. And indeed literature itself—in a classroom—seemed a foreign and uneasy prospect.

Having spent years trying to persuade students who had never read anything other than literature in an English class that they ought to stop reading it for a time, I was now required to reverse that policy. Little remained of the inertial energy that so often shapes our plans for literature classes.

But there was a good deal of motivating energy of other sorts, from convictions about the centrality of theory in literary studies to nearly a decade of frustration with the Reagan-Bush era. A series of contexts (local, national, disciplinary)—along with my own research commitments—colored what I thought it necessary and appropriate to do. What I was not particularly interested in doing was letting the course be shaped primarily by an effort to honor my students' initial sense of their own needs. I had an agenda for them, an agenda determined by my sense of where the country and the profession were culturally and politically, an agenda shaped by the cultural work I thought it was most useful for me to do as a teacher. I was prepared to adjust and redirect my plans as the semester proceeded and as I found what did and did not excite them, but even though the students spent most of their time in discussion, the course was clearly shaped by my agenda, not theirs. Some, it turned out, responded enthusiastically; others resisted. A few have since told me or my colleagues that it was one of the two or three best courses they took here, but the evaluation form that complained "If this was to be a left-wing indoctrination course, we should have been warned" no doubt captured the views of other students. For they had no choice about going along with the general program, which was a product of the readings I assigned and the topics I raised. Indeed, though it was essential that they talk through the poems and the theoretical issues at stake, this process was important not so much to extol the virtues of self-articulation as to create a theater of contesting interpretations and to draw out the values I was encouraging through discussion rather than authoritarian rule.

Except that we did a lot of oral performing of poetry—sometimes individually, sometimes in chorus—there was, however, nothing surprising about the classroom structure. Many of these students were students of rather unreflective prosperity, unaware that their privileges were class specific and that education might serve other—and more critical—functions than those associated with facilitating careers. Under the influence of the 1960s and 1970s, some faculty members still believe that simple changes in the classroom structure can revolutionize education by empowering students to take control of their own education. But that faith in self-determination is underwritten by faculty members' confidence in students' basic values. I admired some of my students' values but not others. Certain classes of the 1980s might regard sitting in a circle and taking charge of the class as an opportunity to talk about how to invest the money they hoped to earn after graduation. That situation is less likely to happen in a poetry class, to be sure, than in many others, but it is nonetheless fair to say that today's students are less critically engaged with American culture and their place in it than were their peers of twenty years ago.

As for the poems my students would have chosen to read, those who knew anything about modern poetry knew only the conventional canon. Some of them—especially women and minority students—were more than ready to read outside the canon, but they would not have been able to name many poets to meet that need. Those women who had an interest in feminist poetry knew only the work of a few poets who came to prominence after the Second World War. Once they had been through the bulk of the course, the students would be able to define their own special interests within noncanonical modern poetry, but at this stage they needed me to guide them toward material they had never heard of in previous classes.

I was teaching different sections of the course to what turned out to be two very different audiences: freshmen and upper-class undergraduates. The differences were at once cheering and depressing. The first-year students were much more open to an unconventional reading list. Most of them saw nothing wrong with a course in which the white male canon occupied less than half their time. Yet these students also knew little or nothing about modern poetry. Many of the students who had been on campus for a few years, however, were anxious about the course. Not merely resistant to noncanonical poetry, they were often puzzled and frightened by it. The idea that poetry could be pervaded by social issues rather than by speculations about the imagination undermined the investments they had made in the study of literature. And they were flatly uncomfortable with the large number of women and minority poets in the syllabus. While this pattern made the prospect of teaching freshmen appealing, it offered little reason to be happy about the socialization process in either the department or the university.

Twenty years earlier a theorized classroom had meant in part an experimental classroom, where participants tried multiple different formats, met away from the university, followed agendas set in part by the students. I had taught such classes in answer to the politics of those days. But today's students are not the students of twenty years ago. There was a time when leftist teaching meant collaborating with a sense of cultural, political, and educational necessity shared by a majority of the students. Now I was fighting a different action; I was doing resistance teaching in a conservative department under a reactionary government. I had allies among the students, to be sure, including some who were extremely happy finally to be reading poems that had more direct bearing on their lives. But I did not have the kind of leftist consensus that was possible in the 1960s and early 1970s, a consensus that made structural changes in the classroom environment both possible and helpful. Although I made certain that all students could air their views and I frequently helped articulate positions with which I disagreed, it was generally clear where I stood and clear as well that I was politically allied with some students and not others. For some of them, therefore, I was a figure to resist or reject. I could live with the resulting tensions more easily than I could live with suppressing my values in the classroom, but I nonetheless definitely preferred the class section in which the students were more sympathetic.

That our culture has changed and thus requires different pedagogical strategies does not, however, render the politics of an earlier moment meaningless. Nor is it a sign of defeat that we must adapt to different political contexts. The notion that politically relevant teaching will always take the same form does not survive historical analysis and reflection. The attempt—not only by some radical faculty members but also by faculty members influenced by various traditional humanisms—to impose on all of us one politically correct form of teaching is the tyranny of an empty idealism, not any plausible, realistic politics. Even at one moment in history there are likely to be a variety of classroom structures appropriate to different material conditions. Now the content of the course and the cultural purposes I articulated for it seemed far more important than a critique of classroom hierarchy. The students would go through the experience whether they wanted to or not. Thus they would be required to write essays about race or gender, essays about poems on working-class experience, whether or not they shared these concerns. They need not come to conclusions I agreed with, but they had to take on these issues.

Having encouraged all the students to express themselves as openly as they could, it would hardly have been appropriate for me to penalize them once they did so. Some students, to be sure, made appallingly sexist or racist remarks in class. On those occasions, I did my best to wait for others to object before stating my own views. Such hesitation was not always easy, but it was sometimes rewarded. I still remember with embarrassment the day when a basically liberal student was led by a poem written in a black woman's voice to begin generalizing about black people's physique and sexuality; the other students were too mortified to speak, so I had to intervene. But on another occasion, the student who responded to one of Countee Cullen's concise poems about racism by complaining irrelevantly about "welfare cheats" was resoundingly reeducated by his peers. Similarly, a student who launched into an attack on unions after reading a poem about workers being injured in factories may not have understood what this connection revealed about him and his culture, but a number of the other students made it clear that they did.

The problem of how to deal with papers was somewhat different. Since the papers were essentially private communications to me, I did not have to be so concerned with their public impact, but I also lacked the advantage of group reeducation. In the end I let students know that I would comment on objectionable remarks in papers but that such remarks would not influence my grading. A witty and outrageously reactionary student thus knew he could write what he pleased and still get an A in the course. None of these strategies left me altogether comfortable, but they were the best I could devise. My aim, after all, was to expose students to alternative literary traditions and to explore the kind of work those traditions might do now in our conflicted culture, not to demand a false conformity that would have vanished once the course was over. Unlike some faculty members, I do not believe that penalizing students for racism or sexism will cure them of those attitudes.

I also had a theoretical agenda that directed what I said about the readings we did. In fact, although the course was called Modern American Poetry, I am unsure whether it was a course in theory or in poetry. All our readings were poems, in part because the particular theoretical texts that informed my lectures—such as Ernesto Laclau and Chantal Mouffe's *Hegemony and Socialist Strategy*—were too difficult for beginning undergraduates and in part because teaching them to read contemporary theory would require a separate course. Contrary, however, to the widespread beliefs of a decade ago, undergraduates *can* read abstract theory, but not every undergraduate can handle the most difficult texts. Certainly juniors and seniors can deal with a theory course covering a wide range of recent theoretical texts. I have taught Roland Barthes's *S/Z* in an undergraduate honors seminar by going through portions of the book sentence by sentence and explicating it, but I have not attempted Jacques Derrida's *Of Grammatology* with the same group. I have also assigned essays by Michel Foucault, Luce Irigaray, and Georges Poulet to undergraduates, but I would not expect them to read all of Foucault's *The Order of Things*. For this course, moreover, some of the most pertinent work was quite far from literary analysis. Rather than read, say, Stuart Hall's book on Thatcherism, *The Hard Road to Renewal*, summarize the history of cultural studies, and then explain how Hall offers a model of discursive politics that can illuminate the history of modern poetry, I chose simply to use his concepts to talk about cultural processes and about the texts we were reading.

Teaching theory only by way of lecture and discussion meant largely betraying my own commitment to critical textuality. Yet in some ways that betrayal was less troubling than the realization that the students had no awareness that theoretical concepts and problems come with their own intellectual and political history. Both classes—not only the first-year students but also the juniors and seniors—were inclined to assume that ideas exist in a freely accessible space of contemporaneity. No one ever asked what critics or what disciplines had developed various notions—like "relative autonomy" and "rearticulation"—that I was using in my lectures. I supplied some of this background because I felt it was necessary, but I would never have been asked for it. This was also the only area in which I consistently felt uneasy about my authority in the classroom. The students were quite willing to criticize my arguments about the profession and about the canon, and they continually offered inventive alternative readings of the poetry we discussed. But they were in no way inclined or prepared to contest the effects of the theoretical concepts I used. That limitation in their acculturation was one I never overcame.

Nonetheless, I spent a good deal of class time at the blackboard writing down theoretical terms and defining them. I frequently gave twenty-minute lectures on theoretical issues; sometimes we spent entire class periods discussing just theory. That the class was generically unstable, a hybrid of theory and literature, seemed to me one of its strengths. Indeed, I think it is fair to say that the theory and the poetry had shifting relations of priority; neither consistently served the other. Sometimes an overview of cultural issues introduced a discussion of poetry; on other occasions the poems served as sources of theoretical concerns.

What counts as theory and what cultural functions we understand theory to serve vary historically. Through the 1950s and 1960s—and into the early 1970s—theory came in discreet units like psychoanalysis, Marxism, and feminism that could be learned and applied to literary texts. In the course of the 1970s, however, these theories began to define themselves in relation to one another. At the same time, we began to realize that taking up theory entailed taking up certain writing practices as well. But we could still study theory, it seemed, without putting intense pressure on the social and political institutions of which it was a part. But then, in the 1980s, it became increasingly impossible to teach theory without also reflecting on and theorizing the social mission of English studies. Consequently I could not imagine teaching an introductory literature course that would not also introduce students to current debates in English and to the politics and social positioning of the discipline. I was as concerned to get them thinking about what it means to study poetry as I was to familiarize them with the poetry itself.

The mutual implication or contamination of poetry, theory, and politics was made apparent on the first day. We studied five improbable poems: Mike Quin's "The Glorious Fourth," Irene Paull's "Ballad of a Lumberjack," Lucia Trent's "Parade the Narrow Turrets," Henry Tichenor's version of "Onward, Christian Soldiers" from his *Rhymes of the Revolution*, and Kenneth Fearing's "Dirge." There is a good chance that none of these texts would open other modern poetry courses; indeed, they would probably fall into a nervous, degenerate academic category that my colleagues call occasional verse. They are all explicitly political and all satiric, but their form and style vary. Quin's 1941 poem, nine stanzas long, describes a hollow, opportunistic, reactionary politician:

> Senator Screwball would nearly die
> If he couldn't make a speech on the Fourth of July;
> If he couldn't stand up there beside Old Glory
> And blow off his mouth like a damned old tory.

I told the students that they could, if they liked, think of it as a prophetic poem about Dan Quayle. Trent's 1929 poem is an attack on academic escapism:

What do you care if blacks are lynched beneath a withering sky?
What do you care if two men burn to death in a great steel chair
. . . .
Thumb over your well-worn classics with clammy and accurate eyes,
Teach freshman to scan Homer and Horace and look wise.

Fearing, in his distinctive frenetic rhythms, takes on a modern businessman destroyed by the commodified culture he serves: "O executive type, would you like to drive a floating-power, / knee-action, silk-upholstered six? Wed a Hollywood star?" Tichenor's "Onward, Christian Soldiers" straddles poetry and song in an international economic lesson that is no less pertinent now than it was in 1914:

Big Business is behind you
In your fight for kingdom come—
It is sailing with its cargoes
Of Gatling guns and rum—
Just fill the heathen with your creeds
To keep them out of hell—
And tell them of the shoddy goods
Big
  Business
    Has
      To
       Sell.

Taken together, these poems amount to an irreverent critique of American culture, an uncivil burlesque of the high modernist canon and, in Trent's poem, a witty but savage attack on the English profession, a convenient way of making the politics of literary study an unavoidable topic. The poems are also thoroughly accessible, and thus the students formed opinions about them immediately. I announced that we would have a vote to determine which poem seemed most "literary" or "poetic" and which the least. I then asked the students to discuss the reasons for their votes, having deliberately made no effort to define what I meant by literariness. Some opinions were predictable. The few students with sensibilities shaped by experimental modernism, for example, thought Fearing's poem the most literary. Surprisingly, however, Paull's "Ballad of a Lumberjack," even less popular than I expected, did not receive a single vote as most literary. Originally included in a leaflet distributed during the 1937 Timber Workers strike, its seven stanzas lay out the realities of industrial exploitation:

We told 'em the blankets were crummy
And they said that we like 'em that way.
We told 'em that skunks couldn't smell like our bunks,
But they said that our bunks were okay.

I cast my vote for this orphaned text and prepared to defend it.

Although the students did not quite have a category for "Ballad of a Lumberjack," they were pretty sure it wasn't poetry; it just wasn't respectable enough. So I asked the key question: Would the workers who picked up the leaflet in 1937 have been likely to think it was poetry? There was a moment of genuine surprise, followed by some sputtering, but general agreement developed: they would. Unwilling to opt for overt snobbery, most students had to admit that this text might have functioned as a poem for that audience; it wouldn't do simply to assert our superiority and exile the poem to some extraliterary category. Nor was the poem as simple as they all initially argued it was. It condensed some fairly complex notions of class difference and rhetorical deception into common-sense language. In combination with the overall spread of votes—which differed in the two sections I was teaching—it became clear that literariness is not self-evidently inherent in poems. This quality is to a degree one that the culture invents and reinforces in various selective ways. I talked for a while about the different kinds of cultural work poems might do at different times. And I concluded by talking about the canon and about why none of these poems are in it. Mine would be a course, it was clear, not only about modern poetry but also about the English profession, about key issues in current theoretical debates, and about the varying cultural roles poetry has played in our history. In the end it was a course in cultural studies, with poetry granted only a relative autonomy, a relative autonomy in which poems were variously reinforced and challenged by other cultural forces.

In the light of these five poems, the next ones we discussed, though also largely forgotten, would seem almost conventionally poetic. This strategy was one I would also use in my book: exposure to a series of bluntly rhetorical political poems would win tolerance for poems in which the language was more appealingly literary. We dealt with a series of depression-era poems on working conditions among the working class. Included were Edwin Rolfe's "Asbestos" and Tillie Olsen's "I Want You Women Up North to Know." If the students had doubts about whether we needed to remember Irene Paull, they had no doubts about the value of remembering these metaphorically inventive poems. Olsen calls on women in the North to recognize

> how those dainty children's dresses you buy
>   at macy's, wannamaker's, gimbels, marshall fields
> are dyed in blood . . .

She asks them to think of women like "Maria Vasquez, spinster, emptiness, emptiness / flaming with dresses for children she can never fondle." Rolfe tells us in a chilling conceit how a dying worker's body becomes his deathbed:

John's deathbed is a curious affair:
the posts are made of bone, the spring of nerves,
the mattress bleeding flesh. Infinite air,
compressed from dizzy altitudes, now serves

His skullface as a pillow.

The only plausible reasons for eliminating these poems from literary histories and anthologies were ideological. The class began to feel a sense of injustice about the profession's selective memory; it was a feeling I had wanted them to have, but I was still surprised by its intensity. Working-class experience and economic exploitation were apparently not acceptable poetic subjects for the profession. Olsen's poem is based on a letter to *New Masses*; comparing the poem and its source also gave us an opportunity to develop the earlier discussion about literariness.

The students were now involved in looking at the broader range of texts from which the modern poetry canon was selected; they began to establish a position from which to evaluate and critique the discipline's politics and its sense of social mission. That poems about the dangers of factory life were no longer dated was an advantage. After years of indifference to reporting Reagan's failure to enforce job safety laws, newspapers were beginning to carry stories about the people being injured and killed in the workplace. These poems thus seemed highly relevant again. And it seemed appropriate that the values they espoused have a place in the sometimes rarified domain of the poetic.

From there on, the syllabus was structured as a dialogue between the canon and its alternatives. In fact, I did end up assigning *The Norton Anthology of Modern Poetry*, along with a 300-page photocopied selection of noncanonical poems now in the public domain, though I also gave them the table of contents of the previous edition of the Norton so they could see how little progress it had made in expanding the canon. The course thus included two texts in explicit competition. About half of the poems we read were well known; the others were not. We were also therefore shuttling back and forth between rereadings of canonical poems and readings of poems that were now out of print. Neither of these commitments would be sufficient on its own. We need to teach the traditional canon because we cannot otherwise understand either our profession or the place of literature in the dominant culture. The shaping of the exclusionary modern canon is a part of our history that we need to know. But the modern American poetry canon—which now emphasizes T. S. Eliot, Ezra Pound, Wallace Stevens, and William Carlos Williams—excludes so many important perspectives on race, class, and gender, and so many forgotten versions of modernist experimentation, that it gives a false view of our literary history. And it offers no evidence of the cultural work women and minorities accomplished in poetry in the first half of this century. If we focus only on rereading the narrow postwar canon, we omit a wide range of social functions for poetry, along with an incredible variety of poetic forms and styles. Finally, the modern canon deprives women, minority, and working-class students of the full range of relevant subject positions historically available to them in modern poetry. As a result, the traditional canon distorts and impoverishes the potential meaning of poetry in their lives. It is not, therefore, condescending to argue that women and minorities deserve a chance to see how their particular interests have been taken up in poetry.

In explicitly moving back and forth between canonical and non-canonical poems, always asking why any given poem was or was not canonical, I was to a certain extent also following Gerald Graff's oft-repeated slogan to "teach the conflicts" in the profession. But I was not indulging in any fiction of liberal neutrality. And I was also addressing a number of theoretical issues that were not widely debated in literary studies, such as the competitive relations between literature and other discourses and institutions within the culture. We treated poetry not as a secure and preexisting category but, rather, as a changing and contested cultural space. We looked repeatedly at how poetry won and lost various powers and social functions in the course of the modern period and at its critical reconstitution in the decades to follow.

The course would not have worked at all if I had been obsessed with the issue of coverage. I decided to leave claims about coverage to paint companies and to concern myself more with the course's intellectual aims. I do not mean to say that people who are concerned with coverage necessarily lack intellectual commitments, though a focus on coverage can, at the very least, displace other issues of importance. Sometimes, moreover, people obsessed with coverage do use it as a way to avoid dealing with more-threatening theoretical and political problems.

My own sense of what merited time and attention did not, however, always carry the day. When the students were not interested in a topic, I generally abandoned it. Perhaps my only complete failure was my effort to win some sympathy for the most blatantly pro-Soviet revolutionary poems of the early 1930s. The choral classroom readings that worked extraordinarily well for some of the sound poems of the 1920s—turning sound poems by Harry Crosby and Eugene Jolas into ritual incantations—were no help here. Reading 1920s sound poems outside class, students considered them mere nonsense. But by reading them aloud in class—sometimes in unison and sometimes contrapuntally—students discovered uncanny power and humor in texts that had previously seemed meaningless. I could not, however, save many of the explicitly revolutionary proletarian poems of the 1930s. I can still remember the dull, flat sound of thirty-five students unenthusiastically reading the line "All Power to the Soviets!" from Sol Funaroff's "What the Thunder Said: A Fire Sermon." Nor would the revolutionary Communist poems of the 1930s be helped now by recent events in Europe and the Soviet Union. So I cut my losses and eliminated other such poems from the course.

I was learning something about the limits of my students' cultural sympathies. In a course devoted exclusively to the 1930s, there would have been time for a much more thorough historical grounding in the realities of the depression. We would also have been reading many more depression-era poems. The line "All Power to the Soviets," we might have noted, also appears in Richard Wright's "I Am a Red Slogan." That comparison would have given us an opportunity to talk about the role of explicit, preexisting political slogans in 1930s poetry, a discursive element we like to think has no place in poetry whatsoever.

The one text with which we made some progress on this issue was Tillie Olsen's 1934 poem "I Want You Women Up North to Know." The bulk of the poem deals with the impossible lives of Mexican-American women in Texas who earned at most a few dollars a week hand-embroidering children's dresses for sale up north. Not until about two thirds of the way through the poem does Olsen refer to "a heaven . . . brought to earth in 1917 in Russia." The students talked enthusiastically about the poem simply by avoiding any mention of the offending line. When it did finally come up, the class fell silent, and we were then able to discuss and evaluate the silence itself.

When students wanted to spend more time on a topic, we adjusted the syllabus accordingly. For example, when a week on poems about race by white authors stretched to two weeks, something had to go. I looked at the syllabus and decided that Wallace Stevens was expendable. In a moment he disappeared from modernism. I felt a passing sensation of guilt, apparently myself still a pathetic victim of the very ideology I was trying to overturn, but shortly thereafter I experienced a certain bemused pleasure at Stevens's local erasure, and that emotion has happily ruled since.

While teaching poems about race, I felt the strongest sense that this teaching mattered. We had read work by Angelina Weld Grimké, Countee Cullen, Sterling Brown, and Langston Hughes and then moved on to a series of poems by white poets: Sol Funaroff's "Goin Mah Own Road"; Charles Henri Ford's "Plaint"; E. E. Cummings's "Theys SO Alive"; V. J. Jerome's "A Negro Mother"; Carl Sandburg's "Nigger," "Mammy," and "Jazz Fantasia"; Kenneth Patchen's "Nice Day for a Lynching"; Genevieve Taggard's "To the Negro People"; and others. Especially in the 1920s and 1930s, many white poets felt it important to write both poems protesting racial injustice and poems sympathetic to black culture. Most remarkable of all, a surprising number of white poets tried to write poems in black dialect, something it would be difficult to imagine a white poet daring to do today. Some of these poems I find powerful and effective. Others, though trying to give a positive picture of black culture, end up perpetuating offensive stereotypes. But sometimes we could not agree whether a poem was or was not racist, a shockingly fundamental matter on which to differ. The subtle duplicities of racism in the poems gave these students a start at thinking about racism in their own lives, as did the revealing and sometimes heated class discussions.

I found it interesting that opinions about these poems did not divide predictably along racial lines. The white students, for example, assumed Sandburg's "Nigger" to be an unredeemably racist poem. But one black student argued that its startling, accusatory, self-assertive conclusion could do important cultural work:

> Brooding and muttering with memories of shackles:
> I am the nigger.
> Look at me.
> I am the nigger.

The epithet we all found offensive, he argued, was after all probably the right word for that moment in history (see also Nielsen). Nervous, the white students were looking for the quick, correct response. The black student called them to more sustained reflection.

Most striking overall was the students' eagerness to debate the strengths and weaknesses of these poems. In the midst of a racist culture these poems —especially the ones by white people—enabled the class to deal openly with issues they badly needed to discuss. I had assigned the poems in part because I considered it part of my social responsibility to spend class-room time discussing race in America. I wanted the white students in the class to feel the special ethical pressure they would feel only if they heard white poets speaking out against racial injustice. And I wanted the minority students in the class to hear white poets engaged in the kinds of racially reflective, committed cultural work those students might not have imagined possible for members of the dominant culture. For all the students it was a revelation—about the discipline and about American cul-ture—to hear white writers far more intricately and thoughtfully engaged in questions of race sixty years ago than they are in our supposedly more progressive contemporary culture. Sometimes the class came to a con-sensus about a particular poem. Other times they did not. I made no effort to impose a resolution. Theories of textual indeterminacy—theories we had often talked about in the course of the semester—here had not only the most intractable material support but also powerful and sometimes painful social and emotional consequences. But if these students were going to live in America, then by any sane standard of what matters they needed to read these poems more than they needed to read T. S. Eliot and Wallace Stevens. That very few of my colleagues would agree with me says, in a way, all one needs to say about the politics of English in America.

University of Illinois, Urbana

Works Cited

Allison, Alexander, ed. *The Norton Anthology of Poetry*. New York: Norton, 1990.

Cummings, E. E. "Theys SO Alive." *Complete Poems, 1913–1962*. New York: Harcourt, 1972. 622.

Ellmann, Richard, and Robert O'Clair, eds. *The Norton Anthology of Modern Poetry*. New York: Norton, 1973.

Fearing, Kenneth. "Dirge." *Poems*. New York: Dynamo, 1935. 43–44.

Ford, Charles Henri. "Plaint." *The Garden of Disorder*. London: Europa, 1938. 60.

Funaroff, Sol. "Goin Mah Own Road." *Exile from a Future Time*. New York: Dynamo, 1943. 8–10.

———. "What the Thunder Said: A Fire Sermon." *The Spider and the Clock*. New York: International, 1938. 25–32.

Hall, Stuart. *The Hard Road to Renewal: Thatcherism and the Crisis of the Left*. New York: Verso, 1988.

Jerome, V. J. "A Negro Mother." *The Rebel Poet* 15 (Aug. 1932): 1.

Laclau, Ernesto, and Chantal Mouffe. *Hegemony and Socialist Strategy*. London: Verso, 1985.

Nelson, Cary. *Repression and Recovery: Modern American Poetry and the Politics of Cultural Memory*. Madison: U of Wisconsin P, 1989.

Nielsen, Aldon Lynn. *Reading Race: White American Poets and the Racial Discourse in the Twentieth Century*. Athens: U of Georgia P, 1988.

Olsen, Tillie. "I Want You Women Up North to Know." *Partisan* 1.4 (1934): 4.

Patchen, Kenneth. "Nice Day for a Lynching." *The Poetry of the Negro*. Ed. Langston Hughes and Arna Bontemps. Garden City: Doubleday, 1949. 272.

Paull, Irene. "Ballad of a Lumberjack." *We're the People*. Duluth: Midwest Labor, [c. 1941]. 49.

Quin, Mike. "The Glorious Fourth." *More Dangerous Thoughts*. San Francisco: People's World, 1940. 91–92.

Rolfe, Edwin. "Asbestos." *Collected Poems*. Ed. Cary Nelson and Jefferson Hendricks. Urbana: U of Illinois P, 1993. 62.

Sandburg, Carl. *The Complete Poems of Carl Sandburg*. New York: Harcourt, 1970.

———. "Jazz Fantasia." *Complete Poems* 179.

———. "Mammy." *Complete Poems* 17.

———. "Nigger." *Complete Poems* 23–24.

Taggard, Genevieve. "To the Negro People." *Long View*. New York: Harper, 1942. 49–55.

Tichenor, Henry. "Onward Christian Soldiers." *Rhymes of the Revolution*. St. Louis: National Ripsaw, 1914. n.p.

Trent, Lucia. "Parade the Narrow Turrets." *Children of Fire and Shadow*. Chicago: Packard, 1929. 85.

Part IV
Theory and Culture

Living History: The New Historicism in the Classroom

Huston Diehl

The new historicism has always had an uneasy relation to literary theory. Stephen Greenblatt, one of its most influential practitioners, notes, "One of the peculiar characteristics of the 'new historicism' in literary studies is precisely how unresolved and in some ways disingenuous it has been—I have been—about [its] relation to literary theory" (*Learning* 146). Although, as Greenblatt points out, "an openness to the theoretical ferment of the last few years is precisely what distinguishes the new historicism from the positivist historical scholarship of the early twentieth century" (*Learning* 146), its insistence on both "the constitutive presence of the historical reader" (Lentricchia, "Foucault's Legacy" 233) and the historical contingency of every theoretical assumption fosters in its practitioners a skepticism about the abstractions, generalizations, and even the explanatory power of theory. Because the new historicism seeks to position both the literary text and the critical text in a history (or histories) that is itself conceived of as textual (White 294–97), it destabilizes both positivist assumptions about history and the very theories that enable it to critique those assumptions.

Teaching the new historicism therefore involves, on the one hand, engaging students in the ways theories of culture currently advanced by semioticians, symbolic anthropologists, cultural materialists, and Foucauldians have reconceptualized history and, on the other hand, helping students situate their own interpretive acts, as well as the literature they read, in history. My experience teaching the literature and culture of early modern England has convinced me that students will engage the past with a remarkable intensity if they are encouraged, first, to think of history as "a multiplicity of 'histories'" (Lentricchia, *New Criticism* xiii–xiv) that are "kinds of 'texts'" (White 294) and, second, to see themselves as historical subjects implicated in the very history they are examining.

To perceive history in this way is, however, precisely what most of my undergraduate students—who arrive at this university already having

internalized the critical assumptions of an earlier generation of teachers—
are not trained to do. They typically employ interpretive strategies from
either the New Criticism or what has come to be called an "old" historicism.
That is, they either privilege the literary text, isolating it from its historical
context and analyzing it as if it were a thing unto itself, or they assume
that a work of literature is a transparent reflection of its age, merely re-
iterating the assumptions and beliefs of the "great" philosophers, theolo-
gians, political thinkers, and scientists or passively mirroring the "major"
events of history. In general, undergraduates enter my classroom predis-
posed either to ignore questions about the relation between literature and
history or to misconstrue that relation.

The new historicism challenges both their ahistorical assumptions
and their sense of a stable, monolithic, and fully knowable past. Because
it adopts a dialogic model of historical inquiry, it fosters in students an
awareness of the multiple voices of the past and teaches them to listen
for the ways those voices might resist, qualify, or illuminate their own
attempts to make sense of that past (Kramer 103). Because it asks, with
the cultural anthropologist, "how the deeply different can be deeply
known" (Geertz, *Local Knowledge* 48), it nurtures the historical imagination, enabling students to encounter the strange without reducing such
territory to a false familiarity. Because the new historicism requires its
practitioners to become self-reflexive about the historical embeddedness
of their own interpretive acts, it enables undergraduate students to confront
the phenomenon in their critical reading and writing that they are most
apt to ignore: their own historicity. And because it assumes that the study
of history is a study of the "forces of heterogeneity, contradiction, frag-
mentation, and difference" (Lentricchia, *New Criticism* xiv) and views
literary texts as "places of dissension and shifting interests, occasions for
the jostling of orthodox and subversive impulses" (Greenblatt, *Forms* 6),
it discourages totalizing views of history and encourages instead a more
open-ended inquiry into the past. Such an inquiry, I have found, surprises
and delights, excites and energizes students who experience, often for the
first time, the wonder of encountering the strange and mysterious, the
exhilaration of discovering the unknown and forgotten, the pleasure of
recognizing their own participation in history.

This essay describes four classroom exercises I have developed to help
my students explore the relation between literature and history. In each exercise I attempt to enact in the classroom a set of theoretical commitments I
would identify as new-historicist. The first seeks to engage students in a
lively dialogue with the past; the second asks students to encounter a strange
artifact on their own and encourages them to examine their efforts to make
sense of it; the third playfully constructs the students and their culture in a
totalizing way, thus disrupting their tendency to totalize history; and the
last attempts to foreground internal contradictions in students' thinking, to
help them understand the complexity of ideological inscription.

Although these exercises are designed to teach certain theoretical assumptions about history, I typically do not ask undergraduates to read theory, choosing instead to locate my inquiry in the historical particulars of the texts we examine and the present we inhabit. Inasmuch as my methods derive from cultural theories that textualize history and yet require students to historicize their own interpretive texts, I replicate in the classroom Greenblatt's "unresolved" relation to theory. My pedagogical goal is to enable students to experience their own historicity. That experience, I believe, helps them imagine a past that (in the case of early modern England) is profoundly different from their present and yet shapes, in part, their constructions of it and themselves.

Engaging in a Dialogue with the Past

To "converse" with the past, students must become attentive to their own listening, as well as receptive to the voices of strangers. To facilitate such a dialogue in the classroom, I frequently set up a comparison between an artifact from the students' own culture (e.g., a Hollywood film, a popular song, a public ceremony) and a related artifact from early modern culture. Anchoring the students in their present, I ask them to converse—in Clifford Geertz's sense of that word (*Interpretation* 13)—with a particular voice from the past. My students explore the historicity of pleasure by comparing their responses to a baroque painting with their reaction to a work of minimalist art; they address the cultural construction of revenge by comparing questions of justice in *Hamlet* with like questions in such films as *Walking Tall* and *Death Wish*; they examine the possible ways in which art shapes national identity by comparing myths of war in Shakespeare's *Henry V* with those in the film *Gone with the Wind*. These comparisons drive students more deeply into the past by freeing them to examine their resistances to it, their preconceptions of it, and their culturally conditioned responses to it. They begin to recognize how the present they inhabit is shaped by the past they study and at the same time to acknowledge how their own historical narratives inevitably reshape and reconstruct that past.

Let me demonstrate more fully how this strategy works. In a course on Elizabethan literature, I once asked students to compare a portrait of Marilyn Monroe by Andy Warhol with a portrait of Queen Elizabeth I by Marcus Gheeraerdts the Younger. Focusing first on the Warhol painting, my students eagerly discussed this representation of a famous woman they all recognized as a central icon of their own time and place. Why had Warhol appropriated an image and a style from popular culture? What was the rhetorical effect of his replicating the same bold image twice on one canvas? What did his representation of this Hollywood idol reveal about contemporary American attitudes toward women, beauty, sexuality, fame, and power?

Turning to the second painting, the Rainbow Portrait of Queen Elizabeth, I urged my students to consider how it differed from the pop art
image of Monroe and what those differences might suggest about the two
cultures that produced them. I asked them to identify elements in the Tudor
painting that impeded their understanding or appreciation of it and
elements in the Warhol painting that made it accessible to them. Conversely, I asked them to imagine what might puzzle or confound an Elizabethan about the Warhol painting and what might give an Elizabethan
viewer access to the Gheeraerts portrait. Able immediately to engage and
appreciate Warhol's portrait but baffled and frustrated by the Rainbow
Portrait, the students directly experienced the cultural embedding of images
and of their own ways of seeing. By focusing on the differences between
these two representations of famous women, they were able to historicize
both paintings as well as their own aesthetic responses to them. At the
same time, they were able to identify points of connection between their
present and this past culture.

Comparing the exaggerated lips and breasts of Warhol's Marilyn
Monroe with the disembodied eyes and ears ornamenting the gown of
Gheeraerts's Elizabeth, one student raised questions about the social construction of the body. Another argued that Gheeraerts idealizes Elizabeth
as a woman destined to greatness, thereby celebrating and affirming a
Tudor belief in the divine right of kings, whereas Warhol explores—and
interrogates—the power of the popular media in modern American culture
to elevate an ordinary woman to a cult status. A third student commented
that the four-hundred-year-old image more closely articulated her feminist
beliefs than the thirty-year-old image did. She was intrigued that a woman
in the 1580s represented an all-powerful, all-knowing, godlike sovereign
and embodied the ideal of political reason, whereas a woman in the 1960s
represented female sexuality, valorized for her vulnerability, her
sensuality, and her dangerous allure. This student wondered whether Elizabeth I and the idealized myths about her reign contributed to the Anglo-
American feminist tradition, and she began to raise questions about the
historical origins and generic conventions of the Hollywood sex symbol.

Administering Culture Shock

When I was an undergraduate in the late 1960s, my teachers worked within
a humanist tradition, assuming that great works of literature transcended
their culture and contained universal truths. Many students in my
generation, however, failed to see how these works were pertinent to their
lives and began to demand "relevance" which was generally (although
I think mistakenly) understood to mean "about us" or "of our own times."
The new historicists reject both positions. Denying the humanist belief
in universal truths, they nevertheless believe in the value of encountering

the strange and other. Rather than deny difference, they seek it out. "When you realize that you are not getting something—a joke, a proverb, a ceremony—that is particularly meaningful to the natives," explains Robert Darnton, "you can see where to grasp a foreign system of meaning in order to unravel it." He argues that historians and cultural critics continually need to be "shaken out of a false sense of familiarity with the past, to be administered doses of culture shock" (78).

I have developed a two-part exercise designed to help students confront the differences between their own and early modern culture. First, I bring to class a particularly complex, strange, or puzzling artifact from a past culture and, without giving students any clues or assistance, ask them to interpret it. Then I ask them to analyze—from a third-person point of view—their own interpretations. Such self-reflexive assignments are extraordinarily effective ways of heightening students' awareness of their own historically based assumptions. My students often tell me that this exercise provided the first opportunity they had ever had to think about the ways in which they think.

I once used this strategy at the beginning of a freshman humanities course. On the second day of class and without any preparatory discussion, I asked the students to write an in-class analysis of Diego Velázquez's *Las meninas* (*Maids of Honor*, 1656), a complicated painting that is itself a highly self-reflexive text. The next day I engaged them in an analysis of their own texts and encouraged them to reflect on the ways in which they went about making sense of this seventeenth-century Spanish painting. While they looked again at it, I summarized their collective responses. My students were by no means ignorant of history. Participants in an accelerated academic program known as the Unified Program, they entered my course having already completed—together—an intellectual history course in which they had read major texts of the Hebraic, classical, and medieval cultures. But for all their knowledge of Genesis and Job, Plato and Euripides, Augustine and Dante, they were quite unable to imagine the past or to comprehend its otherness.

To some, the interior room of the palace was not a place for the royal or wealthy but a dark and depressing, gloomy and oppressive setting, a cavernous basement or a poor person's home. For quite a few others, the kneeling maid of honor was no maid at all but an adoring male lover, proposing marriage to the central female figure. The dwarf, despite her feminine dress, also appeared to some as a boy—because "girls are not supposed to be ugly"; one student thought the dwarf was a jealous brother, seething in anger at the attention lavished on the little girl. The princess herself was, for the most part, not admired for her regal appearance but, rather, criticized as spoiled, pampered, selfish, and arrogant. To some she was not even a child, despite her small size, but a sexually mature and coy woman scornful of the "man" proposing marriage. For many of my students, the dog was the central figure of this painting: noble, faithful, beautiful, and protective, a family pet superior to all the human figures. Two students thought the large canvas on which the artist gazes was not a painting in progress but a gigantic television screen. Most of the others could not process this image at all: it was a door, a mysterious object, a white line slashed through the painting.

Taken together, the responses of sixty American freshmen—all bright, committed, "culturally literate" students—revealed culture-bound assumptions about interior design, dress, gesture, human behavior, femininity, masculinity, sexuality, social class, power relations, family, animals, and material culture that impeded and distorted their interpretation of this painting. Although I focused on their misreadings, especially those that to an art historian would seem most naive, outrageous, absurd, or bizarre, I consciously avoided being judgmental or critical. I wanted my students to recognize the *logic* of their interpretations, and I wanted them to see how they had, with remarkable consistency and a good bit of ingenuity, read their own culture onto this representation of a past culture.

I then asked each student to write—from a third-person point of view—a close analysis of his or her in-class essay. Required to treat their writing as a cultural artifact and asked to discover how it was a product of its historical time, the students found that they could identify and analyze cultural paradigms, assumptions, biases, and "truths" that they had just a few days earlier taken to be universal, natural, and uncontestable. Because this assignment required them to become self-reflexive about their own, twentieth-century ways of knowing, it changed dramatically the way they looked at seventeenth-century texts. Having "denaturalized" their assumptions, they experienced an exhilarating awareness of the Velázquez painting. Newly attentive to its strangeness, they wanted to know about princesses and dwarfs and court painters and nuns, about Velázquez's position in the Hapsburg court and the Infanta Margarita's relationship to her parents, and they were eager to engage in discussions about seventeenth-century theories of monarchy, childhood, art, knowledge, and power.

Disrupting Totalizing Constructions of the Past

From time to time I have intentionally constructed my students as they tend to construct the people of early modern England: not as individual men and women from various social, economic, political, and educational backgrounds who hold widely divergent views on controversial issues but as "Elizabethans" or "the people of the Renaissance"—or, in reference to my students, "contemporary Americans." I make this generalization so that they can begin to see how, on the one hand, they are shaped by the dominant ideologies of their own time and place and how, on the other, they can and do take any number of positions relative to those ideologies, some of which may be hostile, oppositional, or conflicted. This strategy enables my students not only to grapple with the ways in which they have internalized, and perhaps also resisted or subverted, their culture's central ideological paradigms but also to avoid monologic or totalizing perspectives on earlier cultures.

When, in an honors seminar devoted to the study of *Hamlet*, I wanted my students to imagine a culture in which one of the dominant paradigms was theological, I used this strategy to prevent students from assuming that the writings of Luther or Calvin directly and unproblematically "influenced" Shakespeare or that this play simply "reflects" mainstream Protestant thought. In a move calculated to arouse passions and stimulate debate, I proposed that the dominant paradigm in our time and place is economic, and I argued that, whether or not students are aware of it, current notions of "economic man" shape who they are, how they behave, and even how they relate to their family and friends. Reading excerpts from the writings of the Chicago school of economics and from the law and economics movement, I pointed out how influential these economists are and how fully Americans have embraced their theories.

Most students, as I had expected, adamantly resisted my totalizing construction of them. They emphatically denied that they see people as driven by self-interest, that all acts may be explained as attempts to maximize wealth, and that relationships may be seen as acts of exchange. They were outraged when I read a passage from Richard Posner in which he discusses the parental care of children as "investments" that "create a stock of 'human capital' . . . that yields earnings" (103), and they were dumbfounded when I quoted Posner's advocating the sale of babies because "it is unlikely that, in a free market, the price of babies would substantially exceed the opportunity costs . . . that the adoptive parents would have incurred had they produced rather than purchased the child" (115).

While I had identified a cultural paradigm that I could demonstrate was shaping the political, economic, social, and legal decisions being made in the late 1980s, my students consciously and vehemently denied that it adequately reflected their sense of who they were. Although they protested, I persisted. How, I asked, might this particular economic paradigm shape our ideas about marriage, children, human relationships—even if we are unconscious of it? even if we reject it? How does the widespread use of economic language and metaphors affect the way we define ourselves? What evidence can we cite for our ability to live free and separate from such a pervasive paradigm? What evidence can we cite that illustrates how we are implicated in this ideology? To this last question, I presented an Ann Landers column from that morning's newspaper. Complaining that her ailing and elderly mother-in-law has come to live in her house, a woman writes, "She does not pay us one red cent for her room, board and care. . . . I think I am entitled to something for the time and energy I am investing in her care." My students responded to the above questions, and especially to the Ann Landers column, with recognition, confessions, anecdotes. Posner's paradigms are, they admitted with great consternation, operative in their private lives as well as in the realm of American politics.

Once my students acknowledged that they indeed could not escape the shaping force of this dominant economic paradigm, yet recognized that they had some power to resist, critique, and counter it, I raised another series of questions that I hoped would give them some perspective on their interpretation of religious issues in *Hamlet*. I asked them to imagine that they were scholars—cultural historians—four hundred years from now and reminded them that four hundred years separated them from *Hamlet* and Elizabethan culture. Suppose they discovered texts by American economists, legal theorists, and newspaper columnists. What conclusions about our society might they draw? How might they misinterpret or distort the lives of ordinary people during this era by focusing on just these documents or examining just this one paradigm? What, in other words, may scholars accurately infer from a study of a single cultural paradigm, and what eludes them?

Turning from late twentieth-century American culture and its economic paradigms to sixteenth-century English culture and its theological ones, I found that my students were now prepared to grapple with early Protestantism as an emerging ideology and to think about the ways in which Shakespeare internalizes and resists, appropriates and subverts the religion of the reformers. They could see how Hamlet's connection to the Wittenberg of Luther and Melanchthon might be significant without concluding that Shakespeare advocated religious reform. They could examine Hamlet's "death of a sparrow" speech in the context of Calvinist discussions of Providence without equating a work of the theater with a theological doctrine. They could locate Hamlet's interest in plays and players in Reformation debates about the nature and function of images, the role of the imagination, and the power of representation without assuming that Elizabethan audiences held a uniform set of religious beliefs about these issues.

Foregrounding Contradictions

Sometimes I seek to foreground contradictions within or among the dominant ideologies of contemporary American society so that my students will experience directly the instability of their ways of knowing and begin to reflect on the complexity of their ideological inscription. As someone who teaches the literature of early modern England, I am particularly interested in getting students to think about the ways in which they have been shaped by ideologies that emerged in the sixteenth century.

I suspected, for instance, that the students in a course I taught on sixteenth-century English culture might well view the iconoclasm of the

Protestant Reformation from multiple and conflicting perspectives that would reveal to them historically inscribed contradictions in their own thinking. I decided to see if I could foreground these contradictions. I began by asking my students to examine Matthias Grünewald's powerful Isenheim altarpiece (c. 1510–15) from the perspective of the art historian. How, I inquired after they had carefully and thoughtfully analyzed it as an art object, would they respond to the willful destruction of this painting? How would they view the Protestant iconoclasts who defaced and burned such precious objects of art? My students expressed horror, disbelief, contempt. They condemned the iconoclasts for violating the beautiful, stealing property, wasting the artist's labor, and robbing them of their cultural heritage.

After they had unanimously asserted the sanctity of art and the inviolable rights of property, I directed their attention away from the art object and toward the particular social conditions that motivated the reformers to abolish sacred images and angry mobs to smash them. I read excerpts from polemical tracts that deplored the money lavished on "dead" images while the poor—those "living images of God"—went hungry and unattended on the streets. I read from sermons that ridiculed rich donors for thinking they could buy salvation through these works of art. I read exposés of priests who had staged fake miracles, tricking the faithful into believing images efficacious. My students immediately reversed their position and fully supported the very acts of iconoclasm they had condemned just minutes earlier. They angrily denounced the greed, privilege, elitism, selfishness, and materialism of the clergy and the wealthy and empathized with the iconoclasts, whom they now constructed as courageous radicals overthrowing an oppressive and corrupt system.

From this exercise, they understood—because they had directly experienced—how competing ideologies might exert pressures that create shifting perspectives and internal contradictions, and they saw how their own assumptions about art were unstable and informed by contradictory ideologies: one mystifying, the other demystifying, the object of art.

Such exercises help my students develop a historical imagination. When they understand history as "an attempt to reimagine the past" (Biersack 76), they become attentive to what Louis Montrose calls "the textuality of history" (20). They discover with great excitement the fictive, imaginative, metaphorical, and symbolic dimensions of historical narratives, including their own, and they are able to apply their skill in literary analysis to primary documents and historical anecdotes as well. When they begin to see how all cultural forms—rituals and ceremonies as well as plays, histories and anthropological texts as well as novels, sermons and political speeches as well as poems, adolescent fads and subway graffiti as well as essays—are symbolic actions, woven together in intricate "webs of significance" (Geertz, *Interpretation* 5), they become intrigued as well with what Montrose calls "the historicity of texts" (20). They cease to think of literature as a privileged, autonomous activity, its authors isolated creative geniuses, and they are motivated instead to explore the complicated and fascinating ways in which a literary text relates to its (and to their own) culture.

University of Iowa

Works Cited

Biersack, Aletta. "Local Knowledge, Local History: Geertz and Beyond." Hunt 72–96.

Darnton, Robert. *The Great Cat Massacre*. New York: Random House, 1984.

Geertz, Clifford. *The Interpretation of Cultures*. New York: Basic, 1973.

———. *Local Knowledge*. New York: Basic, 1983.

Greenblatt, Stephen. Introduction. *The Forms of Power and the Power of Forms in the Renaissance*. Spec. issue of *Genre* 15 (1982): 3–6.

———. *Learning to Curse: Essays in Early Modern Culture*. New York: Routledge, 1990.

Hunt, Lynn, ed. *The New Cultural History*. Berkeley: U of California P, 1989.

Kramer, Lloyd S. "Literature, Criticism, and Historical Imagination: The Literary Challenge of Hayden White and Dominick LaCapra." Hunt 97–128.

Landers, Ann. Newspaper column. *Des Moines Register* 8 Mar. 1990: 4T.

Lentricchia, Frank. *After the New Criticism*. Chicago: U of Chicago P, 1980.

———. "Foucault's Legacy: A New Historicism." Veeser 231–42.

Montrose, Louis A. "Professing the Renaissance: The Poetics and Politics of Culture." Veeser 15–36.

Posner, Richard. *Economic Analysis of Law*. 2nd ed. Boston: Little, 1977.

White, Hayden. "New Historicism: A Comment." Veeser 293–302.

Veeser, H. Aram, ed. *The New Historicism*. New York: Routledge, 1989.

Teaching the Social Text: England, 1859—Brushing History against the Grain

Cannon Schmitt and Donald Ulin

As literary and cultural theory has moved toward a more self-consciously historical perspective, theoretically informed pedagogy has faced a series of problems in addressing the relations between history and literary texts. These problems can be summed up, briefly, as follows: First, it is difficult to avoid an attitude toward theory which itself escapes theorization—that is, to avoid treating theory as simply one more collection of texts to be mastered. Second, the distinction between (presumably interpretable) literary and (presumably factual) nonliterary texts is a tenacious one; even well-meaning efforts to break down this distinction tend to repeat the text-context model. Third, and closely related to the first two problems, the imaginary divide between teachers who "know all" and students who "know nothing" may become larger as the amount of history and theory brought into the classroom grows. To address these problems, we designed a course, entitled England, 1859—Brushing History against the Grain, that draws on a variety of texts written in England and published around the year 1859. It was our hope that students, once presented with a question about the relations between diverse texts from a single year, would naturally seek out alternative ways of characterizing cultural phenomena, investigating their production, and describing their imbrications with one another—in short, would look to theory. At that point theory, far from a list of required readings, might take on the character of genuine intellectual investigation; as the distinction between literary works and their contexts gives way to a conception of history as a collection of interpretable texts—taken together, a social text—teachers and students could engage in a joint effort to make sense of this new text.

"Always historicize!"—Fredric Jameson's opening words to *The Political Unconscious*—might be followed by a second imperative: "Always theorize!" Together, they are the two rallying cries behind much of recent literary scholarship. One important result of this scholarship has been a reshaping of the relations posited between texts and the social milieus in which they are produced, distributed, and consumed. In particular, the distinctions between text and context have been reformulated by recent critical approaches that treat history as a collection of texts—some legal, some literary, some architectural, some medical, but all susceptible to various modes of textual analysis. The differences among these various sorts of text are not effaced, but the texts themselves are seen to interact in some striking new ways.[1]

Pedagogy, however, has been slow to follow scholarship in this area. Translating the impulse to historicize into classroom practice poses a whole new set of difficulties and, when it is attempted at all, often produces simply an additional tool in the conventional critical toolbox.[2] One of the primary impediments to a theoretically and historically informed approach to teaching literature is the departmentalization of existing literature courses. To the instructor attempting to modify a course to include an honest assessment of the position of literary texts in history, modification often simply means addition. It soon becomes apparent that the large amount of necessary extra reading cannot easily be accommodated in the tight syllabi of most courses on either literature or literary theory. Thus, even where interdisciplinary work is encouraged, the courses themselves continue to reflect a persistent departmental paradigm. What we find are courses in literature that may occasionally refer to, say, history or political science, but only as evidence or background for what remains a separate and distinct subject. It is all too easy for students and teachers alike to view the world in this way, imagining reality as a set of compartments and finding uncomfortable those methodologies that challenge such an assumption.

Despite these serious impediments, historically and theoretically informed pedagogy has had its advocates. In his book *Textual Power*, Robert Scholes lays some significant groundwork for such an approach. Scholes argues first of all that we need to make an effort, in the classroom as much as in our scholarship, to break down such distinctions as those between literature and nonliterature, between textual production and textual consumption, and between the "real world" and the academy. "To put it as directly, and perhaps as brutally, as possible," he writes, "we must stop 'teaching literature' and start 'studying texts.' . . . All kinds of texts, visual as well as verbal, polemical as well as seductive, must be taken as the occasions for further textuality" (16). For Scholes one's ability to read, interpret, and criticize these texts depends on "a knowledge of the codes that were operative in the composition of any given text and the historical situation in which it was composed" (21). That numerous codes are operative at any given moment and therefore all contribute to the meanings of a text makes reading an extremely complex activity, for the reader not only must be familiar with the codes themselves but also must be able to judge which codes are most relevant in the reading of any given text.

Again, a major stumbling block here, and one that Scholes himself recognizes, is the need to bring into the classroom the extra material necessary for any conscientious attempt at historicizing. Scholes offers a choice in dealing with this necessary information: "either to send students to the library or to provide it as a handout" (43). In his sample critique of Hemingway's *In Our Time*, Scholes draws on a wide range of disciplines, including art history, Hungarian and Spanish history, Spanish and Italian etymology, and mythology. The difficulty here, as we see it, involves not so much the type of material Scholes employs as the status of that material. Despite his desire to break down the distinction between literary and nonliterary texts and to "open the way between the literary or the verbal text and the social text in which we live" (24), the material he brings to his analysis of Hemingway never achieves the status of a social text. Instead, it remains extra, occupying a kind of auxiliary position—elucidating the primary, fictional text while remaining free from the critical scrutiny applied to the fiction. In this way Scholes's practice fails to critique the distinction between literary text and nonliterary context. Furthermore, the distinction between teacher and student widens when the codes by which a student is expected to perform readings on primary texts are distributed by the instructor in the form of handouts. The idea of history as something given (i.e., taken for granted or given out by the instructor) is precisely what we need to call into question.

England, 1859, our own effort at teaching theoretical approaches to the relations between literary texts and history, draws on work such as Scholes's while remaining attentive to some of that work's shortcomings. In placing texts from various discourses—literary, historical, political, scientific, medical—on the same footing by studying the textual productions of a single year, we address several of these shortcomings at once. The text-context distinction can be maintained only with difficulty when there is no single discipline by which to determine the proper object of study. This violation of departmental organization certainly evokes discomfort in students; such discomfort, however, could prove productive, laying bare the assumptions behind much traditional scholarship (including the very categories such scholarship generally deploys: historical, literary, Victorian, etc.). When there is no text outside the complex social text, whose construction is the responsibility of the entire class, the gulf between student and teacher, like that between text and context, is blurred. Theory, then, takes its place neither as required reading nor as a tool to be correctly applied but as a common conceptual vocabulary with which we as a class may begin to make sense of the textual-historical construct produced by our own practice.

Why England? Why 1859? In a traditional historical sense, 1859 was an important year. It can be seen as the culmination of much that had taken place in the decades before; it can also be seen as a starting point for much that marks our own time. In 1859 Darwin's *On the Origin of Species* intensified the crisis in religious faith that had been building in England; the book also promoted a new kind of faith, that in the value of science. In 1859 the British were recovering from a war with Russia (the Crimean War) and the suppression of the most serious attempt at rebellion to date against their rule in India (the Sepoy Mutiny). Political ideologies of lasting importance were taking shape, as evidenced by the publication of Karl Marx's *Contribution to the Critique of Political Economy* (an early attempt at what was to become *Capital*) and John Stuart Mill's *On Liberty*—key documents for Marxism and liberalism. In the world of literary history, the success of Wilkie Collins's *The Woman in White* established the "sensation novel" as a recognizable and extremely popular genre.

Thus, 1859 provides a rich collection of primary materials to work with, texts significant enough to various academic disciplines to be canonical, allied with pivotal historical events. In this sense our choice of year was not arbitrary. Yet there is a peculiar irony here. Characterizing certain events and texts as pivotal takes for granted the received notions of history and literature that we wanted to problematize. So, having chosen 1859 for its apparent historical importance, we set out to investigate the year as neither an end nor a beginning but a year unto itself. Our aim in doing so was to test the implications of reading texts and the textual records of events, not from the perspective of a recognizable discipline that would treat them as stages in a linear development, but as nodes in a synchronous network of cultural meanings. We called this project, this cross-sectional view of the past, a synchronic history (perhaps, as one of our students claimed in his final paper, "the biggest oxymoron since 'jumbo shrimp'").

In conceptualizing how such a thing might be done, we took as a starting point for ourselves and the class the first chapter of Clifford Geertz's *The Interpretation of Cultures* (1973). Though much has been written since on systems of meaning in cultural formations, Geertz's book is attractive because it offers a basic understanding of culture that emphasizes textuality. Also, in contrast to some more recent work in this area, his prose is accessible to undergraduates. "The concept of culture I espouse," writes Geertz, "is essentially a semiotic one. Believing . . . that man is an animal suspended in webs of significance he himself has spun, I take culture to be those webs, and the analysis of it to be therefore . . . an interpretive one in search of meaning" (5). Our work in England, 1859 was to develop this sense of the necessity of interpreting culture, not only through studying theoretical readings that assert the textuality of culture and the readability of the social text but also, and most important, through building a kind of cultural vocabulary: a body of codes, of tropes, of available narrative and nonnarrative structures for the English in the year 1859.

One of our first assignments was to create a history of the preceding year—in our case 1990. We asked students to generate, in class, a list of events, personages, and artifacts from that year. Next they chose from the list a few items of manifestly different orders (e.g., German reunification, compact disk recording technology, retro fashion, Lucky Charms cereal) and developed, for the next class, these items' involvements with one another. This assignment produced potential ways of relating different synchronic phenomena—from the naive (Lucky Charms and the leveling of the Berlin Wall exist at once only coincidentally) to the paranoid (the success of Lucky Charms is a small instance of the success of consumer capitalism in general; thus, in a sense, Lucky Charms caused the leveling of the wall).

In another class session we modeled a close reading of the codes in a single contemporary text: the movie *Star Wars*. Students listed and then discussed the values promoted and conventions deployed in the movie—a discussion that was extremely successful because the class could easily amass a fairly intricate set of meanings and identify them as cultural codes: binary oppositions such as that between human (rebels) and machine (Empire), plot trajectories like Han Solo's gradual socialization, celebrated values such as individuality (but of a certain kind: the conformism of the clone Empire is rejected, but so is the renegade behavior of the unsocialized Han). Whatever the value of these particular readings, they were, in fact, readings. The importance of both this exercise and the history of 1990 exercise was that they encouraged students to treat all social phenomena as texts in need of interpretation and as potential repositories of meanings that transcend the limits of an individual author's (film director's, cereal box designer's) imagination. Such a view of social reality as inherently textual and of texts as inherently social goes a long way toward eliminating the text-context distinction and replacing it with a workable concept of the social text.

The great difficulty after these initial assignments was moving from texts that were familiar to students to texts essentially alien, texts from 1859. Our solution was to employ a methodology that might best be described as archaeological. We asked our students to treat texts, events, and objects from 1859 as artifacts and to consider those artifacts in relation to one another and to an evolving sense of mid-century Victorian culture. Many of these artifacts were chosen by us (our list of primary readings). A significant number of them, however, were chosen by the students themselves. The artifact assignment, as it came to be called, required each student to research and present a unique aspect of the culture of 1859 and relate it to that year as we were coming to understand it. Student interests as displayed in this assignment were diverse: one chose Victorian mourning rituals, another researched the London sewer system, while a third discussed Victorian women in the workplace. The cumulative effect of these projects was what we had learned from Geertz to call a "thick description" of our year (6). None of us knew at the outset that female mine workers often wore trousers and were defiant enough about it to pose for London photographers; nor did any of us suspect that Londoners themselves were inordinately proud of their sewer, a public work that in their eyes placed the British among the most civilized of peoples (just as Rome's Cloaca Maxima did for the Romans). As we struggled to relate these seemingly unrelated artifacts—to ask, for example, what pride in sewers, working-class women in trousers, and Wilkie Collins's sensationalism had in common—the need for new models of history became apparent. In this way our theoretical texts were called into play by our strange juxtaposition of primary texts.

In his "Theses on the Philosophy of History," Walter Benjamin writes that "what we perceive as a chain of events [the angel of history] sees as one single catastrophe which keeps piling wreckage upon wreckage," producing only a "pile of debris" (257–58). Admittedly, a pile of debris offers little in the way of clear historiographic methodology. Nevertheless, this particular passage turned out to be one of our students' favorites and contributed considerably to their ability to see beyond a conception of history as a series of related events leading logically to the present. To highlight our own—often unwitting—complicity with specific conceptions of history, we began our explicit discussion of theory by asking students to sketch out, quite literally, different possible shapes for history: circles, spirals, interlocking gyres (someone had read Yeats), a line with a point at one end and an arrow at the other, a line with arrows at both ends, a jumble. (Some students complained about being limited to a two-dimensional medium, blackboard and chalk.) This classroom project took us to Marx, Benjamin, Raymond Williams, and other theorists who offered models of history equally susceptible to this kind of spatial representation. Through asking the question "What shape is history?" we had in effect laid bare the theoretical problem at the heart of our project; whatever shape one preferred, it was clear that history could offer no fixed backdrop against which to measure literature but is, rather, a problem itself, equally in need of interpretation.

In his discussion of "dominant," "emergent," and "residual" cultural practices, Williams offers a model through which to understand diverse elements within a culture not as left over or as ahead of their time in relation to some monolithic conception of that culture but as active participants in a complex, cultural process. This model also provides a useful contrast to the relatively mechanistic model offered by Marx in the preface to his *Contribution to a Critique of Political Economy*. In a short section from *Truth and Method*, Hans-Georg Gadamer discusses the dilemma of the historian who desires an assessment of the past on its own terms without denying his or her own historical subjectivity. "The hermeneutic task," writes Gadamer, "consists in not covering up this tension [between the text and the present] by attempting a naive assimilation but consciously bringing it out" (273). By recognizing that we ourselves were responsible for shaping the history we were writing, we were in fact bringing that tension to the fore. With each reading, we added new terms to our critical vocabulary: Gadamer's "horizons," Williams's "dominant," "emergent," and "residual," Geertz's "thick description," Benjamin's and Marx's "historical materialism." Not every student used these terms in the way those authors had intended, but a common critical vocabulary helped make accessible to class discussion the problems we were working with.

As we have stressed, part of our project involved breaking down the distinction between primary text and background material. *The Woman in White*, with its layering of aristocratic and bourgeois values, thus offered more than a fictional instance of Williams's dominant, emergent, and residual interacting in a single text. It also served as both an example of a Victorian commodity (we discussed the consumption of sensation fiction in mid-nineteenth-century society) and a basis for further theoretical reflection (the artist and principal narrator, Walter Hartright, is both a participant in and a writer of history). In a similar way, we could read Samuel Smiles's *Self-Help* both as a textual artifact in itself and for the theoretical practice implicit in that book's compulsive amassing of innumerable minibiographies. "Is Smiles practicing a kind of 'thick description'?" we asked. "If so, what does that tell us about Smiles's treatment of history? about Geertz's? about our own?" We took each text through what might be seen as a threefold process: we asked questions aimed at contextualizing it in relation to what we had already read, we reconsidered earlier readings in the new context provided by this most recent reading, and we examined ways in which that text might inform our theoretical practice.

To encourage this process, with each week's assignment we gave students a take-home study quiz aimed at moving the focus beyond the isolated text and toward a kind of intertextual critique. One type of question addressed the social narratives and social values implicitly promoted or denigrated by our text for that week. We asked students, for example, to discuss the implications of Darwin's request in *On the Origin of Species* that his readers "regard every production of nature as one which has had a history" (485). In this way we were able to look at the importance of narrative in general, and of specific narrative structures, in a variety of seemingly unrelated texts. Next on the Darwin study quiz, we asked students to examine the relation between one's personal history and one's identity in Darwin as well as in Smiles's *Self-Help*, George Eliot's *The Mill on the Floss*, and Collins's *The Woman in White*. In another set of questions, we asked students to compare the barbarians described by Mill in *On Liberty* with the several Italians found in *The Woman in White* and with the Gypsies in *The Mill on the Floss*. As the course progressed, we were able to identify in a diverse range of texts distinct conceptions of history, narratives of individual development, and sets of values through which these texts could be usefully related.

In this way we treated all our texts as components in the construction of a larger, more complex textuality—what we have been calling a social text. Unlike Scholes's students, who (at least in his book) receive this social text from the teacher as a supplement to the primary readings, our students built their own both from readings on the syllabus and from their work in the library stacks. The text thus produced seems particularly useful to students for two reasons. First, such a text leaves no room for concepts to appear in the abstract, in formulations like "the Victorian response to Darwinism" and "the place of women in nineteenth-century society." Such general concepts do appear, but always in some specific place (a preface, an advertisement) and always in the performance of specific textual-cultural work (providing evidence or a sense of closure). Second, a social text of this sort helps to narrow the teacher-student divide. While various pedagogies have suggested ways around the conventional role of the instructor as privileged mediator between text and student, the introduction of a "given" historical context cannot help but maintain it. By replacing the idea of a context with that of a student-produced social text, our approach by necessity called into question the authority both of the instructor as mediator and of history as fixed backdrop.

For some students, the most exciting part of the course was the periodical project, in which, divided into groups, they pursued social and intellectual analyses of a variety of publications from 1859. As an introduction to this project, we read and discussed Richard Altick's and Jon Klancher's work on the social history of reading in the nineteenth century. (We also spent a class period going over some of the indexes and research methods useful for such an investigation.) For the next week and a half, each group of students studied three periodicals of its own choosing, analyzing the role the journals themselves might have played in the culture of England in 1859 and relating that analysis to the treatment of a single specific issue. By comparing prices, layouts, and probable audiences, we came to see periodicals not only as vehicles for intellectual culture but as artifacts of material culture as well. Working with periodicals also exposed the students to both the excitement and the difficulties inherent in any work involving uncollected primary materials.

Options for the final project varied greatly, but for most students the project offered an opportunity for an extended examination of a single issue through a variety of seemingly unrelated artifacts. For one student, Smiles's *Self-Help* and Christina Rossetti's "Goblin Market" together contributed to a subtle sense of the public image of women in 1859. While this assignment avoided any sense of applying a theory to a text, the difficulty of the project itself demanded attention to certain theoretical problems involving the historicity of texts and the textuality of history. It was from this perspective that students approached key notions from our theoretical readings: Geertz's webs of significance, Benjamin's historical materialism, and Gadamer's notion of horizons.

In the end, the course turned out somewhat differently than we had planned. As any good group of students will do, ours set its own goals, made selective use of the materials we presented, and forced certain changes in both the focus and format of the class. What this meant in terms of our initial aims was that students never reached the level of theoretical abstraction we had hoped they would. While the best students did envision and execute new ways of reading cultural phenomena, most of the class learned primarily to ask new questions. Their answers tended to fall back into the predictable modes of linear history (causality) or human nature (essentialism). Learning to ask new questions is no small achievement, and we were pleased that by the semester's end all our students were working on problems they might not have conceived before the course. Nevertheless, we feel compelled to consider why most failed to follow through on the theoretical project we had envisioned and what course revisions this failure might suggest.

One problem we encountered which hindered the class's progress toward our original theoretical goals was that "history" turned out to be simply too large a concept to grapple with. As the course progressed, we found ourselves focusing almost exclusively on small, clear objects. It became apparent early on that students had a much more rigid set of assumptions about the term *Victorian* than we had anticipated. Class discussions on topics such as adultery, working women, and homosexuality were frequently brought to a standstill by assertions that one or another of these behaviors was just "not Victorian." So it was a small triumph when the student who had been most vociferous on this account was able, in her final project, to push past her preconceptions about the period and let "the Victorians" think and say things she had not allowed them to think or say in her earlier assertions. This local success suggests that the monolithic concept of history may best be broken down through interrogating smaller, more manageable monoliths: Victorian, modern, and so on.

This point brings us, though, to the second probable cause for students' difficulty in following through at the level of theory. As should be evident, much of the class's work involved deconstructing received concepts: breaking down complacent text-context distinctions, decanonizing theory, chipping away at the wall between teacher and student. We were able to accomplish each of these aims to some degree. But because of this success and because we put relatively little emphasis on reconstructing (reacquiring models, retooling methods, re-placing distinctions), students were left only with new ways of juxtaposing texts, new ideas about where to find history, and some sense of what kind of questions to ask. What they lacked was a workable methodology by which to make sense of those texts and answer some of the questions. To borrow a few of the semester's terms, they had succeeded in compiling a thick description but had been unable to construct the semiotic web that could have made it more than a pile of debris. In considering the reason for this shortcoming, we found it helpful to examine the work of a student who wrote more extensively than the others on the class itself. It bears repeating, however, that the work of making possible new questions by taking apart familiar ways of thinking about history and literature is work worth doing.

This student, Tom, whose contributions and enthusiasm throughout the semester had made him an invaluable member of the class, offered to write as his final paper a theoretical critique of the synchronic methodology we had been pursuing. Cautioning him that this would be harder than some other, less theoretical topics, we nonetheless encouraged him since we felt he would be among the students most likely to succeed in such a project. He concluded that "synchronic study is the perfect complement to diachronic history. Therefore, they should be used together." On one level we could hardly agree more; synchronic and diachronic history are not two opposing methodologies but, rather, two mutually informative theoretical constructs. Clearly each construct has its limits, and we had hoped Tom would use some of the theory we had encountered to test the limits of synchronic history, exposing its blind spots while using its insights to explore the shortcomings of more-conventional approaches.

Also disappointing was Tom's principal suggestion for a course revision: namely, a week of lectures at the beginning of the semester summarizing the events leading up to 1859 so that "by the end of the course, a student should be able to say, 'Such and such happened in the 1840s and that's why this certain writer of 1859 thought the way he thought and consequently wrote such and such.'" While our initial response might be to dismiss this suggestion as a naive attempt to grasp at familiar and fixed content, the desire it expresses is not one we either can or should ignore. As Scholes points out, one's ability to read depends on one's knowledge of codes that, even as they operate synchronically, can only be fully understood if their diachronic component is taken into account as well. Students brought to the class a popular sense of history as causal, linear, and marked by great events; they also brought a notion of the Victorian era as a time of great repression, when sex was never discussed and women all spent their lives in petticoats in drawing rooms. Had this sense of history been grounded more firmly in relevant texts and events of the period, the students would likely have been better equipped to critique those presuppositions by examining synchronically a single year.

There are, of course, many ways to address this problem, though a week of general history lectures would hardly leave students with any usable long-term knowledge. Further, students' interests, presuppositions, and intellectual needs vary tremendously from one class to the next. During this course, we occasionally offered brief lectures on the history behind some of the ideas we were discussing (e.g., Darwinism, women's rights, Marxism) or clarified relevant historical points. In another semester, we might use such minilectures more extensively as opportunities to model the way diachronic ideas can inform a more synchronic approach. Integrating the final papers more fully into the work of the class from early in the semester could also have helped each student develop a more work-able synchronic methodology.

How successful was the course, then? Insofar as the students failed to achieve the level of theoretical sophistication we had hoped for, the answer would have to be not entirely. Insofar as they explored alleyways of history and asked questions they could not have imagined before, the course was indeed successful, and we would both be willing to teach a similar course again. Our students will take a new kind of critical reading into future classes and into all kinds of situations involving cultural inter-pretation. This success is not a small one, and it points toward a further implication of our project: our break from conventional pedagogical models by which theory is taught as so much intellectual content to be acquired demanded that we also change the way we judged our students' progress. In a conventional course, teachers evaluate students on how much of the course content they have mastered; the most successful stu-dents master between ninety and one hundred percent. Such a system presupposes a distinct limit on how much a student can get out of the course. In our course, however, the aim was not to offer a body of material to be mastered but to open new ways of thinking, of asking questions, and of confronting a text. In doing so, we offered students the materials and the guidance to accomplish far more than might be expected of most undergraduates. Recognizing the sophistication and seriousness of the materials they were working with, our students worked hard, learned a lot, and had a good time. If they accomplished only half of what the course made possible, they achieved some significant success. Perhaps, then, if we want to challenge our students, the answer is not to scale down our classes into conveniently assimilable chunks (although the apparent success of such an approach can be gratifying to the frustrated instructor) but, rather, to encourage the kind of serious critical inquiry that treats students as fellow intellectuals addressing questions for which we, too, are seeking answers.

Indiana University

Notes

We would like to thank Kathryn Flannery both for providing the original inspiration for our course England, 1859 and for helping us to prepare this paper; Collins Living-Learning Center at Indiana University, Bloomington, for providing a venue for the course; and all our students, for their patience, perseverance, and hard work.

[1] While this kind of intertextual reading has been most closely associated with Renaissance studies, examples from studies of the nineteenth century include Gillian Beer, who considers Darwin in relation to the nineteenth-century novel; Catherine Gallagher, who analyzes texts from the realms of religion and industrialization

as well as literature; Rachel Bowlby, who offers readings of novels alongside readings of nineteenth-century commodity culture; Patrick Brantlinger, who relates Victorian literature to imperialism; and Peter Stallybrass and Allon White, who discuss a wide range of discourses—public health, advertising, psychoanalysis, and popular literature.

[2] Recent textbooks designed for use in teaching theory to undergraduates provide ample evidence of this instrumental attitude. In *A Handbook of Critical Approaches to Literature* (Guerin et al.), an older book, the second edition of which is still in print, the authors offer four literary works as samples on which they perform a variety of readings. Ross C. Murfin's edition of *Heart of Darkness*, the first in a series of new readers put out by St. Martin's Press, confirms that the pattern found in *A Handbook* has yet to be outmoded. Conrad's novel is printed in the front of the book and followed by short introductions to and exemplary readings from five theoretical schools (deconstruction, feminism, new historicism, reader-response criticism, and psychoanalysis). As useful as the book may prove in the classroom, its implications for the status of both theory and literature are disturbing. In this context, the novel *Heart of Darkness* provides what Jane Tompkins has called an "occasion for interpretation"—little more than a test subject to which theories are to be applied (206). And the theories themselves cease to be what they ideally are, powerful intellectual fields in which new questions can be asked and innovative answers posed. Instead, they become content areas to be mastered, techniques to be employed, moves to be made.

Works Cited

Altick, Richard. *The English Common Reader*. Chicago: U of Chicago P, 1957.

Beer, Gillian. *Darwin's Plots: Evolutionary Narrative in Darwin, George Eliot, and Nineteenth-Century Fiction*. London: Routledge, 1983.

Benjamin, Walter. "Theses on the Philosophy of History." *Illuminations*. Trans. Harry Zohn. New York: Schocken, 1969. 253–64.

Bowlby, Rachel. *Just Looking: Consumer Culture in Dreiser, Gissing, and Zola*. New York: Methuen, 1985.

Brantlinger, Patrick. *Rule of Darkness: British Literature and Imperialism, 1830–1914*. Ithaca: Cornell UP, 1988.

Darwin, Charles. *On the Origin of Species*. Cambridge: Harvard UP, 1964.

Gadamer, Hans-Georg. *Truth and Method*. New York: Crossroads, 1986.

Gallagher, Catherine. *The Industrial Reformation of English Fiction: Social Discourse and Narrative Form, 1832–1867*. Chicago: U of Chicago P, 1985.

Geertz, Clifford. *The Interpretation of Cultures*. New York: Basic, 1973.

Guerin, Wilfred L., et al. *A Handbook of Critical Approaches to Literature*. 2nd ed. New York: Harper, 1979.

Jameson, Fredric. *The Political Unconscious: Narrative as Socially Symbolic Act*. Ithaca: Cornell UP, 1981.

Klancher, Jon. *The Making of the English Reading Audiences, 1790–1832*. Madison: U of Wisconsin P, 1987.

Murfin, Ross C., ed. Heart of Darkness: *A Case Study in Contemporary Criticism*. New York: St. Martin's, 1989.

Scholes, Robert. *Textual Power: Literary Theory and the Teaching of English*. New Haven: Yale UP, 1985.

Stallybrass, Peter, and Allon White. *The Politics and Poetics of Transgression.* Ithaca: Cornell UP, 1986.

Tompkins, Jane. "The Reader in History: The Changing Shape of Literary Response." *Reader-Response Criticism: From Formalism to Post-structuralism.* Ed. Tompkins. Baltimore: Johns Hopkins UP, 1980. 201–32.

Williams, Raymond. *Marxism and Literature.* Oxford: Oxford UP, 1977.

Institutions, Classrooms, Failures: African American Literature and Critical Theory in the Same Small Spaces

Lindon Barrett

No comment I have encountered from an undergraduate illustrates more acutely the strong sociopolitical, institutional, and intellectual tensions converging on the limited number of classrooms in which African American literature is taught than one offered rather confidently from the front row of a lecture hall filled with sixty or so students. I remember the comment as follows: "I'm not sure how I'm going to write the paper for this class, because I've never been a slave and can't fully relate to this experience." This announcement was made in response to my open invitation for questions and comments a few weeks into an upper-division course on African American autobiography. It is remarkable for a variety of reasons. Among other matters, this announcement of an imminent failure to engage meaningfully the terms of African American autobiography codifies what may be the central challenge of courses in African American literature, the task of comprehending—of realizing intellectually—important particulars of African American experiences in the so-called New World. In essence, such intellectual activity stands very clearly in opposition—not apposition—to the traditional materials, monuments, and experiences of American cultural literacy, a term coined by E. D. Hirsch to refer to the general knowledge necessary to reinforce and maintain technical literacy. Students of African American literature—both contrary to and exemplified by my student's appeal to the importance of experience—are placed in a position for which their earlier education has in virtually no way prepared them.

Perhaps this situation ought to be regarded as one not of location but of dislocation. Students of African American literature find themselves —in the materials they are reading and the institutional lives they are leading (even if only for a quarter or a semester)—in a position where the texts they are reading do not resemble literature in terms of its traditional subjects, aims, and consequences and where their classroom does not resemble an institution of higher education in terms of who is allowed to speak and what is allowed to be said. Textuality is always a locus of authority, the fixed site of an author; African American literature, however, takes its place in a cultural system in which authority—self-authority or any other—has been traditionally denied the texts' authors. The situation of students of African American literature, as my student's comment suggests, becomes one in which variant discourses converge and fail to resolve their antagonisms. The situation is one of failure.

One can, with these matters in mind, begin to imagine the relevance and productiveness of pairing African American literature with critical theory in undergraduate education, for the situation of this pairing and the situation of the students who might be introduced to it speak significantly to each other. If African American literature and critical theory appear to fail each other, then this failure itself is highly instructive in pursuing an understanding of both fields. At the very least, the failure provides important definitional information about the contrasted fields, and an instructor conversant with both wants precisely to highlight this peculiar relativity. In fact, it soon becomes clear that their troubled relation reinscribes the governing dualism—the intellectual versus the experiential—of my student's appeal. Theory, on the one hand, is marked by a reluctance to acknowledge itself as a political body of works with *material* determinants and consequences; African American literature, on the other, is characterized by the difficulty of acknowledging itself as anything more than the oversimple redaction of the conditions of a *material* and (by negation) political body. One wants to draw attention to the manner in which their "failed" intercourse raises questions concerning the generally unremarked politics of reading—questions that students of African American literature engage necessarily and directly and at risk to their academic careers. In other words, these texts clearly trouble the tense relation between themselves as texts and the cultural system in which they take their places as texts—so much so that one quickly realizes how unlikely it is that a student would make a similar comment in courses on Renaissance or Victorian literature although the very same circumstances obtain. The materials of these courses necessarily stand outside the student's experience (and I phrased my initial response to my student accordingly). That is, although students have been neither Renaissance courtiers nor besieged gentry swept up in the social and intellectual changes of rapid industrialization, it would be unthinkable to raise the same question in those courses. One must ask why such virtually identical institutional and classroom situations appear dissimilar enough to justify a student's unembarrassed commentary before sixty or so peers.

For what reason does the reading of African American texts elicit appeals to incomprehension based on lack of experience? In exploring the answer to this question and some of the many notable critical errors of the appeal, I restrict myself to two points and, in doing so, attempt to suggest how, by employing theory in the teaching of African American literature, some of those errors might be addressed.

It is first important to note that my student's newly discovered (in)abilities dramatically reverse traditional academic practice. The student abrogates the practice of privileging depersonalized knowledge, which is standard to literary and other academic studies. Whereas one most often repudiates (rather than makes appeals to) personal experience in academic studies, my student conceives it imperative to do exactly the opposite. Bell Hooks provides cogent insight into the dilemma of this student, as well as into the institutional dilemma it redacts. She writes: "[R]acism is perpetuated when blackness is associated solely with concrete gut level experience conceived as either opposing or having no connection to abstract thinking and the production of critical theory. The idea that there is no meaningful connection between black experience and critical thinking about aesthetics or culture must be continually interrogated" (*Yearning* 23). Traditional American cultural literacy not only distorts or, in large part, dismisses African American cultures and experiences but also fosters an inability to consider or engage those cultures and experiences intellectually, thus promoting what amounts to a "literate resistance" to viewing them in any way other than within the terms of vague and dismissable angst or—to repeat a phrase—the oversimple redaction of the conditions of a material and (by negation) political body. This "literate" impulse is mass-produced and widely circulated, as Hirsch specifies in his theory of predetermined cultural cues, elaborated in his book *Cultural Literacy*. Therefore, in order to "write the paper for [my] class," students must encounter the difficult and novel task of reconsidering and revising this impulse. Theory—to repeat a central point—may prove instrumental in this revision, for the situation of theory, like that of my student in her dilemma and that of the literature she confronts, is one of dislocation. Theory knowingly absents itself from that which it represents. It maintains and reinscribes this absence as the measure of itself; the matter from which theory absents itself can be crudely understood as "practice."[1] Theory attempts to be a signifier removed from signifiers. It thus fails (as sign) to be where it is not and also fails (as nonpractice) not to be where it is. Equally, the situation of African American literature, which determines the dilemma of my student in the front row, is one of pronounced incompatibilities and tensions. To be African American amounts to having those discourses spoken most easily and fluently by the dominant culture fail to imagine you, and, conversely, to locate an African American self within those discourses amounts to failing those discourses. In short, if theory in itself is a site of profound incompatibilities, then theory becomes an immense (re)source for presenting and understanding—as recorded in a literary tradition—African American thought and behavior and the strategies and circumstances of African American thought and behavior, also in themselves sites of profound incompatibilities; the same obtains vice versa.

Yet, more to the point, just as instructive as the similarities of the two are their differences. Critical theory stands as an ostensibly depersonalized form of knowledge; African American literature does not. Bringing the two together clearly engages the dualism of knowledge and experience underlying my student's perplexing appeal to a lack of experience. Insofar as the abstraction (i.e., knowledge) of critical theoretical concerns hardly seems capable of admitting or bearing relation to the resolute materiality (i.e., experience) of African American concerns and cultural productions, the pairing of the two addresses the standard "literate" sensibility underlying, however consciously or unconsciously, my student's appeal. In making the two fields conversant, one aims then at allowing students to see the complication of materiality and abstraction (or second-order discourse) even in the most apparently material of conditions (i.e., African American literature) and vice versa, in the most abstract of pronouncements (i.e., theory). Granted that in the moments immediately following my student's comment, this process begins for her far afield of theory; nonetheless, it is a process to which theory can amply contribute both in the discourse of the classroom and in course reading materials—issues to which I will turn presently.

More immediately, there is an unstated corollary of my student's appeal that must also be considered: Complementing her conception of her own impairing lack of experience seems to be a certainty or presumption of *my* experience as a slave—indeed, despite a temporal gulf of more than one hundred years making such experience an impossibility, despite my presence at a lectern marking me as the professor (or authority) in the room, not to mention the obligatory accreditation of a PhD underwriting my presence at the front of the room (a certificate not of experience but of, if nothing else, intellectual perseverance). Prompting the student to see her distorting cultural literacy and even racism begins as simply as stating that I have no more experience of being a slave than she does. As a group, we African Americans are imagined to bear little resemblance to the dominant American community while, conversely, each African American is granted an inexorable representativeness in relation to all other African Americans. My student's act of implicitly looking to her professor for experience as a slave, which she acknowledges she lacks, underscores the startling efficacy of mass-produced and widely circulated cultural cues dissuading most inhabitants of the New World from thinking carefully and insightfully about race. Clearly, no one at the present time possesses the experience of antebellum slavery. My student fails to see that race—and here is the unacknowledged crux—always has been and continues to be foremost an intellectual matter, either within or without the classroom but most plainly so in the classroom. While the issue of experience is not irrelevant, neither does it enter the dynamics of the classroom and its impending academic tasks in the manner my student conceives.[2]

Race is not singularly an experience, and experience is not an innocent register of "reality." Both race and experience are implicated in and overdetermined by economic, political, and social struggles. Personal and even collective experience do not define the parameters of race, which is another way of saying that the only interventions in issues of race are not to be made in terms of either personal or collective experience. The belief that this state of affairs holds sway returns one to the odd revision of standard academic practice already noted. Standard academic practice pursues *facts* (which, despite appearances, are also implicated in and over-determined by economic, political, and social struggles), and if facts are somehow paramount in our institutions and classrooms, the fact of personal African American identity is emphatically not the singular one to be considered in this instance. Indeed, in classrooms of African American literature facts themselves are preemptorily questioned and challenged by attention to situations, the situations of those both within and without the classification *African American*. It is, no doubt, at this point that the remarkable difficulties of my student arise.

Undergraduates are tutored to assume "[t]he technique of what might be called methodological neutrality, of 'getting the facts right' before leaping in with our[?] value judgments, [which their institutions of higher education would have them believe] is one of the progressive achievements of [Western] civilization" (Graff 86).[3] Nevertheless, students in African American literature classes discover opposing sets of facts and attendant narratives that no amount of appeals to neutrality might reconcile. In ways analogous to my student in the front row, these undergraduates find themselves speaking and writing at odds with those in whose "care" and within whose power of evaluation they are placed. They remain at odds with their professors of African American literature, who must in some measure revise the facts or "certainties" of their earlier education; equally, they remain at odds with their institutions of higher education, which virtually everywhere resist such revision. In African American literature courses, the narratives or "stories" of a previous education are revised in accordance with diverse critiques of a New World civilization founded by and abidingly committed to the vision of a "white-supremacist oligarchy" (Painter 127). Neutrality itself takes up a place within one of the opposing sets of facts, with the result that there no longer clearly exists the certainty (or illusion) of "getting the facts right"; the *facts* prove instruments of will implicated in, rather than effecting release from, *experience*, interestedness, and the dynamics of cultural, civil, and other forms of power. The facts appear as the discursive gestures of dominant groups "whose exclusionary behavior may be firmly buttressed by institutionalized structures of domination that do not critique or check [that exclusionary behavior]" (Hooks, "Essentialism" 176). (These lessons cannot remain purely "textual" or "academic" when students find themselves in courses that, for all intents and purposes, are brand-new to American education—heralded by political and social upheaval in the 1960s and met with bureaucratic and journalistic trepidation three decades later. (See D'Souza.)

Although my student's response to the "literate" dilemma presented by the course in African American autobiography forms itself as a misrecognition or revision of the binarism traditionally differentiating experience from "methodological neutrality," her inversion of terms is not the key point to be noticed. More significant is her retention of the binarism itself. Indeed, perpetuating the institutional narrative she has long imbibed, the student summarily dismisses both the dynamics of the course and the academic discourse of the classroom in which those dynamics are played out. She construes both as sites at which intellectual configurations no longer obtain. In effect, to resolve her dilemma, she understands her engagement with African American materials as, rather than revising an education already in place, standing curiously *without* that education. In this way, even inverted, the binarism operates to distinguish that which is institutionally (and culturally) valued from that which is not; her articulation of her situation ironically instates within the discourse of the class on African American autobiography the disqualification or bracketing of African Americans, their cultures, and cultural productions long endemic to the dominant communities of the New World. The force of her comment would have African American autobiography virtually inaccessible intellectually; she removes the course in which she is enrolled from the academic tradition she is attempting to master and from the imperatives of the institution in which she is enrolled. She reinstates the textual materials of the course, as well as the ongoing interpretive activities of the classroom, securely within the material realm that, in terms of the popular American mind, almost solely determines African American existence.

Recall that in its central conflict, the conflict of the marginal and the preferred, the study of African American literature exposes and troubles what Hirsch imagines as a supratechnical literacy, the background information or background knowledge—beyond linguistic competence—requisite to reading. Reading African American literature precipitates remarkable encounters with predetermined cultural cues constructing a predetermined reality—to which acknowledged textuality stands in apposition. The acknowledged textuality of African American literature abrogates, in large part, these predetermined cultural cues of official American experience and reality, therefore supplanting expected apposition with disorienting opposition. The appeal of my student can be understood as an attempt to return opposition to apposition. In terms of the pressures of the course, her impulse to disregard, or revise, the tenet that privileges depersonalized knowledge is not misguided; her peculiar revision, however, fails to respond adequately to either the materials or the imperatives of the course. Opposingly, the revision she fails to undertake involves dismissing, rather than keeping intact, the binarism structuring her lament.

More fully considered, her situation and the analogous situations of the sixty or so other students in the class lead to a recognition of the coimplication of *experience* and the *facts* (or more-traditional academic concerns). Made otherwise aware of their curious situations, an awareness to which the intersection of critical theory and African American literature can contribute, undergraduates may be prompted to recognize that

> when it comes to knowledge of the world, there is no such thing as a category of the "essentially descriptive"; that "description" is never ideologically or cognitively neutral; that to "describe" is to specify a locus of meaning, to construct an object of knowledge, and to produce a knowledge that shall be bound by that act of descriptive construction. "Description" has been central, for example, in the colonial discourse. It was by assembling a monstrous machinery of descriptions—of our bodies, our speech acts, our habits, our conflicts, and desires, our politics, our socialities and sexualities —in fields as various as ethnology, fiction, photography, linguistics, political science—that the colonial discourse was able to classify and ideologically master the colonial subject, enabling itself to transform the descriptively verifiable multiplicity and difference into the ideologically felt hierarchy of value. To say, in short, what one is presenting is "essentially descriptive" is to assert a level of facticity which conceals its own ideology and to prepare a ground from which judgments of classification, generalisation and value can be made.   (Aijaz 6)

Undergraduates, in their new and difficult situations, discover that facts are replaced by attention to situations and, moreover, that although open regard for situations may seem superfluous or, at best, ancillary to undergraduate (or all) education, this principle does not apply here, for if there is a set of concerns that African American literature privileges, among them are not only African American thought and behavior but just as surely the *situations* of African American thought and behavior and the inevitable politics of reading (and announcing) those situations. With little or no preparation, undergraduates in African American literature courses are confronted directly with the situations of reading and, more particularly, their own situations when reading. My student's apprehension of her (in)abilities and their relation to the limits of her experience demonstrate the manner in which students of African American literature cannot help discovering with greater immediacy the political dynamics of what passes as literature and as the (con)textuality or situations of literature.

My student finds herself in a situation and in a classroom in which she fails to intellectualize the course materials as well as her own position vis-à-vis race. Thereby, she extends the widely circulated "ideologically felt hierarchy of value" that, by definition, cannot hold sway in a class on African American autobiography. As of yet, she fails to comprehend the class and, ironically, announces her fear that she fails to comprehend the class. One might prompt her to begin to intellectualize her position by posing a question as simple as why she might assume I have experience as a slave while she has none. The point is to begin to make her deliberately recognize and estimate a superordinate "literacy" that it is the aim of the course materials and classroom interaction to interrogate and revise. The issue is to make her intellectualize *her position*, a feat that, despite her lament, she has not yet begun to perform. And, as she intuits, this feat should not be undertaken wholly at the expense of experience. She is intuitively correct to question and resist "standards of pyrotechnics" claiming "that intellectual excellence requires depersonalization and abstraction" (Fox-Genovese 163) and the attendant descriptive license of those standards (even though her particular line of reasoning fails to pursue that interrogation or challenge adequately). To her credit, she somewhat aligns herself with the materials and imperatives of the course: How, one might ask, can the mandatory dismissal of "particular personal experience" form part of an education also concerned with traditions of language and literature that attempt to revise longstanding processes of depersonalization, traditions of language and literature that begin with "the process of [random Africans] becoming a single people, Yorubas, Akans, Ibos, Angolans, and others . . . present on slave ships to America and experienc[ing] a common horror [marked by] unearthly moans and piercing shrieks" (Stuckey 3)? African American linguistic and literary traditions necessarily find their beginnings here, preserve and revise those initial sounds, and in large part record heroic, or at least involved, attempts to retreat from, or cast off, the enforced depersonalization those initial moans and shrieks protest. How, one might ask again, can African American literature reconcile itself to conditions of the academy and higher education that call for depersonalization? Indeed, the education of undergraduates in African American literature courses is profitably complicated when we examine the way in which incipient concerns of African American literature and culture are reinscribed within the conditions of its presence —its situation—in the academy, as well as their own situations.

This proposition I undertake, in part, by pursuing three categories of theory that can be counterposed with African American texts: canonical theory, institutional theory, and African American (and other subaltern) theory. Canonical theory may be thought of as works such as Aristotle's *Poetics*, Sir Philip Sidney's "An Apology for Poetry," David Hume's "Of the Standard of Taste," Immanuel Kant's *Critique of Judgment*, and Karl Marx's *Capital* that stand as part of a prized tradition of belletristic and philosophical texts. I take institutional theory to refer to the relatively contemporary phenomenon of professional academic writings, such as F. O. Matthiessen's *American Renaissance*, Mary Douglas's *Purity and Danger*, and Michel Foucault's *Language, Counter-memory, and Practice*, that reflexively settle or trouble issues of literature, knowing, and culture. African American (and other subaltern) theory includes texts such as the essays collected by Cheryl A. Wall in *Changing Our Own Words*, Edward Said's *Orientalism*, and Hortense Spillers's "Mama's Baby, Papa's Maybe," which turn the energies of humanistic inquiry predominantly to hierarchies of race, gender, sexuality, and class and their invariable complications of issues pertaining to literature, knowing, and culture. Although these distinctions prove helpful in intellectualizing materials that seem to lie beyond that possibility, it is not necessary that they be introduced to one's students. It is more to the point that they provide ways of structuring discussions. Equally important, the distinctions are neither rigorous nor mutually exclusive; they suggest broad contexts in which to place theory in its fretful relation to African American literature.

Of the three categories, I present or refer to canonical theory first and make most of these references in the introductory meetings of the class. My object is to begin to interrogate (in general as well as personal terms) the immediate problematics of our situatedness in a class devoted to African American literature or other materials and to suggest a tradition of speculation that prohibits or at least diminishes the very activities we are to undertake as a class. I breach most standard notions of critical theory for, to highlight the manner in which a strict—and in no way disappearing—canon of humanist figures and thought takes little (or derisive) account of a tradition of African American thought and behavior and the circumstances of such thought and behavior, I pursue the juxtaposition of broad, historical speculations with African American literature. We may briefly survey works by such European and American intellectuals and leaders as G. W. F. Hegel, Thomas Jefferson, Abraham Lincoln, the noted nineteenth-century scientist Joseph Le Conte (a leading figure of the newly established University of California), and the New Critics (who in standard discussions are generally divorced from their "southern agrarian" incarnation). The notion I want to present, especially in initial meetings, is that, no matter how open or mediated, a disqualification or pathological bracketing of dark-skinned others remains a virtually invariable premise of both the general and learned traditions of Euro-American thought. Indeed, I want to present the notion that examinations of "African American" literature and culture must at some point look necessarily to European males and their New World descendants, since it is precisely these communities and their discourses that have in lasting ways determined the hostile conditions and attitudes in terms of which African American literature and cultural productions must at some point be contextualized.

I prompt my class to consider immediately a history in which respected and prized traditions of Western thought disqualify African Americans a priori from the belletristic and philosophical traditions advertised as universal. The class must begin to think of the educational implications of such histories and predilections and to consider how such implications may or will influence the tasks they have set for themselves by taking up the seats they have chosen for the quarter: Is the institution in which they are enrolled a participant in such histories? Are the educations they have received and will continue to receive implicated? At what point did these histories end, if in fact they did? In what ways, given such histories and widespread predilections, will a course covering African American literature or culture necessarily differ from or challenge the vast majority of the other courses in which the students have been or are enrolled? In short, undergraduates must begin to visualize themselves in a situation of profound contradiction; they must begin to contemplate a second-order, or critical, discourse about their own educational situations as well as about the materials they will encounter.

In the late eighteenth century, Jefferson wrote that "[i]n general, [African American] existence appears to participate more of sensation than reflection" (139). Early in the nineteenth century, Hegel proposed that "[w]e must lay aside all thought of reverence and morality—all that we call feeling—if we would rightly comprehend ['the African']; there is nothing harmonious with humanity to be found in ['the peculiarly African'] character" (97).[4] Lincoln, in the mid-nineteenth century, wrote, "I agree with Judge Douglas [that the African American] is not my equal in many respects—certainly not in color, perhaps not in moral or intellectual endowment" (53). One might draw on a variety of figures and extend the chronology as close to the contemporary moment as one wishes and, in doing so, suggest an enduring theoretical context and problematic for African American literature.

My use of institutional and subaltern theories is not so broadly contextual. I employ these theories, rather, as resources for reading texts chosen for the course. To this end, institutional theory provides general (rather than more culturally specific) speculative concepts, which may be relevant to either individual texts or patterns emerging among a series of texts. Elaine Scarry's *The Body in Pain*, for example, provides a helpful model for considering the "discourse" of pain and physical abuse endemic, particularly, to many early African American texts. Scarry looks foremost to torture and war, suggesting that both are "reality-conferring process[es], in the one [torture] it is the non-believer's body and in the other [war] it is the believer's body that is enlisted in the crisis of substantiation" (150). Her distinction between torture and war is perhaps not crucial in the context of African American literature; I do, however, see as crucial in that context the understanding of pain and physical confrontation as reality-conferring processes. To provide a brief example, the insight is borne out in reading the scene from Frederick Douglass's 1845 autobiography in which Demby is summarily murdered for refusing to take further abuse at the hands of the overseer Mr. Gore. At stake in Demby's rebellion is the "reality" of a system founded on the unaccountable equivocation of dark skin with subhumanity, a system in which African American bodies stand as sites (and sights) against which whiteness is contradicted and therefore also predicated most forcefully. Nothing fixes the meanings of the signs of blackness and whiteness, in and of themselves in New World landscapes. These matters are fixed instead by such acts of violence as those that reduce Demby to a "mangled body . . . [whose] blood and brains marked the water" (47), acts of violence that take on, in the words of Scarry, the significance of "the reality conferring process," "the crisis of substantiation," for a questionable sociopolitical order. In this application of Scarry's formulations, the point of irruptiveness at which established value recovers itself in the American landscape—and most fully asserts itself—is the point at which African American bodies are violated.

Scarry's theoretical speculations seem especially helpful when reading a text such as Mary Prince's "The History of Mary Prince, a West Indian Slave," in which meditations on language, literacy, and culture are clearly subordinate to catalogs of physical abuse and recollections and images of physical pain. Equally, Pierre Macherey's *Theory of Literary Production* seems helpful in considering, say, the opening pages of Toni Morrison's *Song of Solomon*. Macherey is concerned with looking beyond a "false simplicity which derives from . . . apparent unity of meaning" to "those disparities which point to a conflict of meaning" and reveal "the inscription of an *otherness*" in certain configurations; he is interested in "that which happens at [the] margins" of certain configurations (79). In the opening pages of Morrison's novel, the "unity of meaning" that the elected representatives of the white citizens hope to realize and master is relentlessly troubled by the *present absence*, or marginality, of African American communities, whose imaginations are equally at work (re)naming "Mains Avenue" first "Doctor Street" and then, in response to official reprimands, "Not Doctor Street" (4). "[T]he charity hospital at its northern end" (4) is similarly (re)named "Not Mercy Hospital" in the light of its refusal to provide services to African Americans. In a similar manner, the critique of Edmund Husserl in Jacques Derrida's early work *Speech and Phenomena and Other Essays on Husserl's Theory of Signs* may help illuminate the efficacy of the "singing voices" and musical motifs in, say, Ann Petry's *The Street* and *The Narrows* and many other African American texts attentive to the cultural primacy of music. Peter Stallybrass and Allon White's *The Politics and Poetics of Transgression* might be taken up in conjunction with Billie Holiday and William Dufty's *Lady Sings the Blues* to demonstrate how Holiday employs the grotesque as well as the charged values of the body and of urban geography in her critique of the American society that perversely celebrates her talents.

At this point, one begins to see at least one additional issue of failure in proposing such intersections of African American literature and critical theory. One recognizes a failure to acquaint undergraduate students adequately with the histories, factions, and abundance of formulas that compose the relatively heterogeneous field known as critical theory. These intersections yield, in large part, a somewhat random exposure to both concerns—or, at least, to theory. Nonetheless, one should not be daunted by the specter of this failure, for the paramount goal is not to provide undergraduate students with a survey or in-depth acquaintance with the dense expanse of critical theory (a project that I believe is more fully suited to graduate school) but, rather, to place students in the position of theory insofar as this position is both relevant and antagonistic to African American literature. One wants to engage the more pressing failure of an apparent inability of the two to address each other, the apparent failure in classes of African American literature of the traditional academic dualism.

This issue is inherently addressed in the third of the three categories. African American (and other subaltern) theory takes as its focus the co-implication of literary and intellectual activities in social systems of domination and hierarchy—in "the sordid history of colonialist expropriation, material exploitation, and class and race oppression behind European world dominance" (Viswanathan, "Beginnings" 22–23). William Andrews, for example, in the first chapter of *To Tell a Free Story*, "The First Century of Afro-American Autobiography: Notes toward a Definition of a Genre," draws on speech-act theory to delineate the sociohistorical and, therefore, narrative constraints facing early African American autobiographers; Valerie Smith, in *Self-Discovery and Authority in Afro-American Narrative*, interrogates the tensions and incompatibilities of an unreflective privileging of the notions of literacy and literariness in relation to African American lives and texts. Other texts that come to mind as suitable for undergraduate scrutiny include Joanne Cornwell-Giles's "Afro-American Criticism and Western Consciousness: The Politics of Knowing," Mae G. Henderson's "Speaking in Tongues: Dialogics, Dialectics, and the Black Woman Writer's Literary Tradition," and Christopher Miller's "Theories of Africans: The Question of Literary Anthropology." These exemplary texts provide an eclectic sample of recent work conjoining the concerns of African American literature and critical theory. Cornwell-Giles examines the problematics of attaining self-knowledge in a philosophical dilemma perpetuated by the hostile point of view of a dominant discourse; Henderson proposes that the manner in which black women write and speak in modulating multiple voices is a central and distinguishing feature of their discourse; Miller explores some of the ways in which mastery proves unattainable for the Western scholar in pursuit of the African other. Spillers's "Mama's Baby, Papa's Maybe" bears mentioning again. This essay, making such distinctions as that between the "body" and the "flesh," is very difficult but worth the time and close attention it requires. Students need not master the essay in its entirety to cull important and original insights from it. Colonial and postcolonial theories also belong in this category: for example, Homi Bhabha's "Sly Civility," outlining pathological contradictions of colonialist discourse; Gauri Viswanathan's *Masks of Conquest*, detailing the formation of English literary study in British India as a strategy of sociopolitical control; and Jenny Sharpe's "Figures of Colonial Resistance," arguing against the transparency of the intellectual who puts forth narratives of resistance.

It seems clear to me that the incompatibility of the two fields is instructive in aiding undergraduates to "write the paper[s] for [my] class[es]."

The inevitable involvement of each field with failure, as well as the apparent failure of the two fields to address each other, does not constitute grounds for their mutual dismissal; it forms the ground on which undergraduate students can begin to read the fields in concert. At the very least, the *opposition* illuminates analogous tensions that students of African American literature must confront in the texts they are considering as well as in the circumscribed spaces of the institutions and classrooms in which they find themselves. The situation of the pairing, like that of students who find themselves in the position of writing papers on African American autobiography despite their different "experiences," is remarkable but not ludicrous. Once undergraduates are made to entertain the difficulty of reading the two fields in concert (not simply, as one would expect, the difficulty of reading theory), these students are placed (although they may not realize it, until someone points it out to them) in the situation of making "analyses of culture within the relations of power which divide [culture] into preferred and marginal categories" (Carby 42). Such conflicts constitute preeminent concerns, themes, and references for African American literature, with the result that the study of literature assumes its place, more or less openly, within the dynamics of discursive and cultural conflicts. The remarkable pairing queries both a discrete notion of literary studies and the often unremarked dynamics of reading sustained in institutions that privilege ostensibly depersonalized knowledge and the attendant "descriptive" license such knowledge promotes.

African American literature and critical theory are thought to be ineluctably opposed concerns, resolutely incompatible, and in this apparent dissimilarity lies precisely the benefit of considering them in tandem. I propose that no inherent benefit lies in the fact of theory itself; rather, benefits lie in the troubled convergence of the two fields within the classroom. Clearly, there can be no final word on this matter, for that is precluded by the presence of controversy, in which—by definition—final words appear forever elusive. Still, I offer a tentative final word—insofar as such a paradox is allowed. In classes on African American literature one must remain attentive to the tensions and failures arising before and even around one; one must even create some tensions and failures oneself.

University of California, Irvine

Notes

[1] I use the term *critical theory* primarily in agreement with the currency gained by the term as suggested by Gayatri Spivak: "Theory in the United States institution of the profession of English is often shorthand for the general critique of humanism undertaken in France in the wake of the Second World War and then, in a double-take, further radicalized in the mid-sixties in the work of the so-called poststructuralists" (788). Thus, even further, theory is a site of incompatibilities and tension.

² Professors of African American literature who are African American are not the only instructors who must confront in the classroom the issues delineated here. On the contrary, insofar as they must be prepared to engage textual materials, any such instructor, regardless of race, must be prepared to negotiate the variety of ways (some more patent and bald than others, as suggested by my student's comment) in which predetermined cultural knowledge enters the classroom. This student's comment raises a particular issue clearly tied to the race of her teacher. Nevertheless, at the same time, it raises a general issue not nearly so restricted. There are, of course, important issues to be considered concerning instructors of African American literature who are not African American; however, this situation is not the primary focus here. In an extended consideration of the more general issue, I hope to delineate the manner in which my student's announcement suggests a paradigm for bringing together the seemingly inimical pair of African American literature and critical theory.

³ In the light of the work Graff would go on to produce, this passage, published in 1979, is almost unimaginable.

⁴ Hegel continues, "In Negro life the characteristics of point is the fact that consciousness has not yet attained to the realization of any substantial objective existence—as for example, God, or Law—in which the interest of man's volition is involved and in which he realizes his own being" (97).

Works Cited

Aijaz, Ahmad. "Jameson's Rhetoric of Otherness and the 'National Allegory.'" *Social Text* 19 (Fall 1987): 3–25.

Andrews, William. *To Tell a Free Story: The First Century of Afro-American Autobiography*. Urbana: U of Illinois P, 1986.

Bhabha, Homi. "Sly Civility." *October* 34 (1985): 71–80.

Carby, Hazel V. "The Canon: Civil War and Reconstruction." *Michigan Quarterly Review* 28.1 (1989): 35–43.

Cornwell-Giles, Joanne. "Afro-American Criticism and Western Consciousness: The Politics of Knowing." *Black American Literature Forum* 24.1 (1990): 85–98.

Derrida, Jacques. *Speech and Phenomena and Other Essays on Husserl's Theory of Signs*. Evanston: Northwestern UP, 1978.

Douglas, Mary. *Purity and Danger*. New York: Ark, 1984.

Douglass, Frederick. *Narrative of the Life of Frederick Douglass, an American Slave*. Ed. Benjamin Quarles. Cambridge: Harvard UP, 1960.

D'Souza, Dinesh. *Illiberal Education: The Politics of Race and Sex on Campus*. New York: Free, 1991.

Foucault, Michel. *Language, Counter-memory, and Practice*. Ithaca: Cornell UP, 1977.

Fox-Genovese, Elizabeth. "To Write Myself: The Autobiographies of Afro-American Women." *Feminist Issues in Literary Scholarship*. Ed. Shari Benstock. Bloomington: Indiana UP, 1987. 161–80.

Graff, Gerald. *Literature against Itself: Literary Ideas in Modern Society*. Chicago: U of Chicago P, 1979.

Hegel, G. W. F. *Lectures on the Philosophy of History*. Trans. J. Sibree. London: Bell, 1914.

Henderson, Mae. "Speaking in Tongues: Dialogics, Dialectics, and the Black

Woman Writer's Literary Tradition." *Changing Our Own Words: Essays on Criticism, Theory, and Writing by Black Women*. Ed. Cheryl A. Wall. New Brunswick: Rutgers UP, 1989. 16–37.

Hirsch, E. D. *Cultural Literacy: What Every American Needs to Know*. New York: Houghton, 1987.

Hooks, Bell. "Essentialism and Experience." *American Literary History* 3.1 (1991): 172–83.

———. *Yearning: Race, Gender and Cultural Politics*. Boston: South End, 1990.

Jefferson, Thomas. *Notes on the State of Virginia*. Ed. William Peden. New York: Norton, 1954.

Lincoln, Abraham. "First Joint Debate, Ottawa, August 21: Mr. Lincoln's Reply." *The Lincoln-Douglas Debates*. Ed. Robert W. Johannsen. New York: Oxford UP, 1965. 37–74.

Macherey, Pierre. *A Theory of Literary Production*. London: Routledge, 1978.

Matthiessen, F. O. *American Renaissance*. New York: Oxford UP, 1941.

Miller, Christopher. "Theories of Africans: The Question of Literary Anthropology." *"Race," Writing, and Difference*. Ed. Henry Louis Gates, Jr. Chicago: U of Chicago P, 1986. 281–300.

Morrison, Toni. *Song of Solomon*. New York: NAL, 1977.

Painter, Nell Irvin. "Race Relations, History, and Public Policy: The Alabama Vote Fraud Cases of 1985." *America in Theory*. Ed. Leslie Berlowitz, Denis Donoghue, and Louis Menand. New York: Oxford UP, 1988. 125–37.

Prince, Mary. "The History of Mary Prince, a West Indian Slave." *Six Women's Slave Narratives*. Introd. William L. Andrews. New York: Oxford UP, 1988. 1–44.

Said, Edward. *Orientalism*. New York: Vintage, 1979.

Scarry, Elaine. *The Body in Pain*. New York: Oxford UP, 1985.

Sharpe, Jenny. "Figures of Colonial Resistance." *Modern Fiction Studies* 35.1 (1989): 137–55.

Smith, Valerie. *Self-Discovery and Authority in Afro-American Narrative*. Cambridge: Harvard UP, 1987.

Spillers, Hortense. "Mama's Baby, Papa's Maybe." *Diacritics* 17.2 (1987): 65–81.

Spivak, Gayatri Chakravorty. "The Making of Americans, the Teaching of English, and the Future of Culture Studies." *New Literary History* 21.4 (1990): 781–98.

Stallybrass, Peter, and Allon White. *The Politics and Poetics of Transgression*. Ithaca: Cornell UP, 1986.

Stuckey, Sterling. *Slave Culture: Nationalist Theory and the Foundations of Black America*. New York: Oxford UP, 1987.

Viswanathan, Gauri. "The Beginnings of English Literary Study in British India." *Oxford Literary Review* 9.1 (1987): 2–26.

———. *Masks of Conquest*. New York: Columbia UP, 1989.

Wall, Cheryl A., ed. *Changing Our Own Words*. New Brunswick: Rutgers UP, 1989.

Theory as Translation:
Teaching "Foreign" Concepts

Simon Gikandi

> *Even though I wanted to break with French Literary*
> *Traditions, I did not actually free myself from them until*
> *the moment I decided to turn my back on poetry. . . . I*
> *became a poet by renouncing poetry.*
> Aimé Césaire, *Discourse on Colonialism*

For the teacher of literary traditions that are defined as oppositional or noncanonical—postcolonial, ethnic, or marginal literatures—the deployment of critical theory is both inevitable and highly problematic. It is inevitable because critical theory, as Homi Bhabha has observed, makes us aware "that our political referents and priorities—the people, the community, class struggle, anti-racism, gender difference, the assertion of an anti-imperialist, black or Third World perspective—are not 'there' in some primordial, naturalistic sense. Nor do they reflect a unitary or homogeneous political object" (11). It is problematic because critical theory is accompanied by what I consider to be the anxiety of cultural translation: how to use concepts developed within the Western tradition to explicate texts and cultures that have, in many instances, risen to resist this tradition. My primary concern, then, is how theory can renounce its conditions of possibility so that it can function as an agent of translating meanings across cultures, classes, and geographical spaces. And if I seem to deploy theory in the classroom by appealing to the authority of what many puritans would consider to be untheoretical categories—reality, experience, and history, for example—there are two reasons for this nontraditional approach: first, one has to start with concepts that students take for granted and often use to resist the impetus toward a deconstructive pedagogy; second, as Aimé Césaire asserts in my epigraph, we sometimes need to renounce theory in order to affirm the historical and epistemological contexts in which literary texts emerge and evolve.

I always begin my deployment of theory by articulating the position of scholars who, like Barbara Christian, argue that theory is a theological practice using an abstract language to obscure the historical conditions that have produced postcolonial literatures such as those I teach. I find this inaugural renunciation of theory an important pedagogical strategy not only because my students find it easier to understand the arguments presented by the opponents of theory—who tend to use a more intelligible prose—but also because such critics use concepts like *history, experience,* and *literary language* in their "everyday sense." In this approach, I run the risk that students will identify with the nontheoretical position because it appears to be the path of least resistance, but my idea is to invite them to enter the field of literary theory in the company of familiar and comforting terms. Since my goal is to enable my students to become, as early as possible, full participants in the discourse on theoretical concepts as it emerges in the classroom, I help them reconstruct such terms before we begin to deconstruct them.

At the same time, I want to avoid the tendency to impose my own ideological positions on the subject under interrogation; I want my students to become full partners in mapping out the terrain of theoretical struggle; opening the semester with Christian's essay "The Race for Theory" seems to work well. In reading Christian our primary concern is not her claim that theory, because of what appears to be its current hegemonic position in the academy, has become the preserve of a few intellectuals, cultural policemen in the intellectual field; rather, we tend to focus on what the author considers to be the antithetical relation between theory and the marginalized discourses whose position it is supposed to secure. Christian's argument here is easily explicable: theory negates the distinctive elements of oppositional literatures—the nature of meaning and value, the intersection of "language, class, race, and gender," and the authority of experiential reality (39). In the discussion that follows the reading of this essay, many students will echo Christian's sentiments; the terms she valorizes are, after all, important to the students, who are keen to understand how language, class, race, and gender determine literary practice and our interpretation of texts.

Although I am eager to make the counterargument that a self-conscious theoretical position is indispensable to a sustained reading of non-Western texts, I know that I must be cautious in articulating my own attitude toward Christian's essay; I do not want students to turn against her just to share my privileged professorial stance. Indeed, over the last few years, in which critical theory has been the source of numerous controversies that have trickled down to the students even before they enter my classroom, one of the most important tactics I have learned to adopt is an ambivalent posture toward theory itself. I know, in private, that I need to deploy theory because it allows me to deconstruct the imperial narratives of Western culture and their epistemologies, but I want my students to sense a certain skepticism toward our techniques and objects of analysis; I want them to realize that theory is not a philosophical position they are expected to endorse but a critical method that they can deploy in various ways.

The important point, though, is that the Christian essay has given the students substantive issues to talk about early in the semester. Once they have developed a good sense of what the primary issues are, I begin to change my priorities and focus; now I move my students away from their intuitive identification with the nontheoretical position and persuade them to question the cultural categories they have taken for granted. Our discussion of Christian's essay, for example, becomes much more complicated the moment we begin to confront it with its own contradictions.

The first step in this process is to raise the question of nomenclature: what is literary theory, and how is it different from what Christian is trying to do in her essay? Here, I use René Wellek and Austin Warren's differentiation of theory and criticism: literary theory is concerned with "the principles of literature, its categories, criteria," while literary criticism and literary history are concerned with the study of "concrete literary works" (39). This distinction is in itself suspect (my use of concrete texts in the course already negates the Wellek-Warren postulation), but within the parameters established by the above definition, the students are quick to see how Christian's essay is itself theoretical. But this assertion does not tell us much in itself; to term all readings of literary texts *theoretical* is to negate the specialized ways in which theory is currently being deployed.

My second step, then, is to raise the stakes by citing Paul de Man's definition of literary theory as a practice predicated on a radical dissociation of literary texts and their historical and aesthetic categories. "Literary theory," argues de Man, "can be said to come into being when the approach to literary texts is no longer based on non-linguistic, that is to say historical and aesthetic considerations" (7). The self-consciousness of literary theory, from a de Manian perspective, depends on the use of a linguistic terminology that "designates reference prior to designating the referent," a language that "considers reference as a function of language and not necessarily as an intuition" (8).

While I might explain key terms such as *reference* and *aesthetic considerations* in the above definition, my strategy is to let the students struggle with de Man's argument on their own. I know that this task is often difficult, given the complexity of "The Resistance to Theory," the essay I am using here; I also know that this is the kind of essay that might easily reinforce my students' fear of the esoteric language of theory, about which they heard Christian complain. But I have developed a way of detouring around such problems: instead of asking the students to read the whole essay, I provide them with short excerpts, which they can read several times until they have a clear sense of the argument the theorist is making. It is important to resist the temptation to tell the students how de Man is defining theory, so I let them toil over the passage until they have come up with a consensual understanding of the definition.

When this understanding is achieved, our discussion moves on to a third step: a confrontation between the two views of reading—and hence of literary language—promoted by Christian and de Man. Several questions guide this discussion: What does Christian mean when she says that literature, which is primarily concerned with experience and reality, is the formal "integration of feeling [and] knowledge" (42)? Why does de Man reject historical and aesthetic categories? Why does Christian valorize experiential reality, a reality that is felt and represented in a literary language that affirms "that sensuality is intelligence, that sensual language is language that makes sense" (47)? Why does de Man have problems with this commonsense view of language and reality?

As the students debate the merits and demerits of both positions, they often turn to me for arbitration. My contribution to this debate, however, is ambivalent or deliberately provisional. From a de Manian perspective, I tell them, we are being asked to believe that we can understand the crisis of history that generates the novels we will be reading in class—works such as Chinua Achebe's *Things Fall Apart* and Michelle Cliff's *Abeng*—only by abstracting them from their epistemological conditions. Similarly, we must discuss the crisis of representation that overdetermines the colonial subjects in George Lamming's *In the Castle of My Skin*, but we are not to consider the discourse of empire that constructs them and the semantic categories that enable them to resist it. We are even to read Joseph Conrad's *Heart of Darkness* without worrying about the materiality of what it signifies, without bothering about the deployment of the Africa space in this text of empire. Turning back to Christian, however, we are asked to believe that "people of color" are a transparent collective entity that does not theorize or use abstract language, because it experiences the world sensually; she tells us that people of color produce literatures in which the self exists in a harmonious relation with its culture, history, and language. Unless we accede some authority to the referent, I ask, what are we going to do about the great epistemological questions raised by these novels—questions about history, language, and the discourse of selfhood? If we accept Christian's perception of "writers of color," how do we explain that these writers not only theorize about these issues but also write primarily about colonized selves whose relation to history, culture, and language is often brutal?

Raising questions is, clearly, one of the most important weapons in my pedagogical arsenal. Even when they are purely rhetorical, such questions are important not only because they generate discussion (and hence allow the students to scale the wall that surrounds theoretical concepts) but also because they help teachers avoid the temptation to impose their views and interpretations on the students. At the same time, however, such questions are effective only when they are framed by some didactic positions that will reassure students in moments of doubt. It is not unusual, then, for me to state why critical theory is an indispensable tool for teaching postcolonial literatures: theory makes us self-conscious of the problematic institutions and histories that generated such literatures.

But reflections on the theoretical tendencies that surround postcolonial literatures are not enough in themselves, so I usually spend about an hour providing a nontheoretical context: a positivist history of colonialism and its culture. This form of contextualization may appear naive to some teachers, but I have found it to be an important way of connecting students to references and frameworks that make the reading of texts "worldly" and hence meaningful. By the same token, to counter what I consider my students' ethnographic drive—their desire to read, in literary texts, objects whose origin and intelligibility is to be found in the world of experience, historicism, and nature—I constantly question the way such background enters literary texts. I cannot, for example, afford to let them assume that just because we live in a world in which people are defined by race, the concept of race is self-evident, natural, and sanctioned by their own experiences. I want then to resist this dangerous biologism in order to see how race, as it emerges in works like W. E. B. Du Bois's *The Souls of Black Folk*, is socially constructed. The metaphor of race must therefore be rigorously deconstructed.

But I also know that the visual authority of race and racism—the students' experience and knowledge of both—cannot be excluded from their modes of reading; in this respect, as S. P. Mohanty has observed, a deconstructive pedagogy is always in danger of hypostatizing a mode of reading that simply reveals our inability to have any knowledge about cultural experiences: "In the classroom this can devolve into a predictable maneuver: text after text would be revealed in its subtextual play of emptiness, for an unceasing and unchanging allegory of textuality always 'Reads' itself to reveal the hand in the new God in all Its creation" (166). To avoid this "allegory of textuality," I deploy my pedagogical tactics in two directions at the same time: I gesture toward some deconstructive philosophy—a concern with absences and gaps, the instability of historical categories and of the consciousness that shapes the unspoken and unrepresentable elements of discourses—but I also strongly advocate referential meanings in literary texts.

In other words, I always begin by establishing the discursive field of the literary text as one in which meanings are constantly being produced and contested. In teaching Conrad's *Heart of Darkness*, for example, I draw my students' attention to how cultural positioning determines the kinds of meaning we adduce to this text. I remind them that the traditional criticism of this book has derived its authority from negating the epistemological and historical conditions that overdetermine Conrad's textual practice: by ignoring the novelist's relation to the culture of imperialism—and its attendant discourses—we can fall back on its semantic ambiguities and read it, with Lionel Trilling, as an apolitical yet radical critique of Western civilization (18). It is because we become easily engaged with the mesmerizing novelistic language of the text, I argue, that we are able to negate the concreteness of its African setting.

The best way to make these points, I believe, is to confront students with Chinua Achebe's essay "An Image of Africa: Racism in Conrad's *Heart of Darkness*," a dramatic reading of the novel that unceremoniously breaks the spell of classicism surrounding many interpretations of this novel and, at the same time, foregrounds questions of race and gender. Achebe's reading of Conrad can be compared and contrasted with any canonical interpretation of the novel, such as Trilling's essay or the works of Ian Watt. The purpose of this critical confrontation, however, is not to privilege one mode of interpretation over another but to discuss the issues one critic foregrounds and another suppresses. In this way students can finally begin to isolate the categories and presuppositions that govern the practice of theory.

I remind my students that whatever modes of reading we adopt, questions about literariness (de Man) and experience (Christian) are ultimately questions about the status of the referent in critical theory. I find Mohanty's stricture important in this regard:

> If we refuse to consider the referent as a "real object" guaranteeing the artificial circumscription of every semiotic operation and providing a theological security to interpretation, then *referentiality* suggests a larger question, one that deals with the *social determination* of signifying practices, linguistic and otherwise.   (158)

In teaching *Heart of Darkness*, then, I want to insist that the deployment of Africa in the novel, though important to Conrad's epistemological intentions, should not be construed as the real object against which the accuracy of novelistic representation will be judged. After all, I like to remind my students, at issue here is not the "real thing" (Africa) but its imaginary construct in Africanist discourse.

In this sense, I want to get my students away from their intuitive desire for a real Africa against which Conrad's "heart of darkness" will be vilified and denied. To defamiliarize the notion of the referent as an entity that is synonymous with the "real object," I appropriate the techniques of the negative pedagogy I rejected earlier: I argue that what Africa is can never be known precisely because the object is a figure constructed in European discourse, a projection of the Western desire for the other. I point out several excellent examples of this projection and show how it blocks any knowledge we might have about African peoples: the famous scenario in which Marlow sees his journey up the Congo River as a form of temporal regression; the unforgettable homoerotic moment when the African boatman dies and is embraced by Marlow as an acknowledgment of the dialectical relationship between self and other; and the image of the African woman who functions as the embodiment of primitivism, sexuality, and death.

That we have no way of reconstructing Africa as it functions in imperial discourse inevitably leads to our questioning the norms and values in this narrative. At this juncture, I tread carefully, to sustain a crucial dialectical relation with the referent: I want, on the one hand, to argue that Africa as it is represented in Conrad's novel has meaning only within the norms and values established by the novelist's culture and the imperial episteme; what is at stake in this novel is the European deployment of Africa as a mechanism of coming to terms with Europe's own cultural crisis. On the other hand, I am aware of the performative power of Conrad's text: it gestures toward a primitivist image of Africa that pre-dates it but that the novel confirms through hints and suggestions. Conrad's text is going to be read as an image of Africa, and this reading is difficult to negate precisely because the novel confirms what other discourses have established as a reality.

The theory of intertextuality helps us deal with this problem up to a point: by teaching *Heart of Darkness* side by side with Achebe's *Things Fall Apart*, I allow one text to question the other. I try to show how Africa is represented in the colonial text as both a blank space and monstrous presence, a landscape dominated by phantasmal images, and as an unhis-toried body without self-conscious subjects. I then discuss the ways in which Achebe's novel tries to counter such images by instituting an alter-native cultural practice, a historicity, and a set of coded cultural norms (see Gikandi 24–31). Here, as previously, the shift from theoretical para-digms to literary texts is governed by an implicit pedagogical strategy: the text is the exemplar for the theoretical concept, providing concrete evidence of such terms as *intertextuality* (or *primitivism* and *imperialism*); at the same time, the theoretical concept clarifies the meaning and status of the text in its cultural context. I have found this shift from "pure" concepts to "concrete" texts to be one of the best ways of satisfying the students' desire for exemplars.

Yet none of the above tactics seem to be of any use when it comes to deploying theory to teach cultural differences. The problem here, not surprisingly, is compounded by the very referent that I adopted to help me ground theory in the world of the text. Whereas I spent time earlier exploring the unique cultural and historical experience in which the texts emerged, I now find myself trying to discourage students from reading this "background" either as a body of values against which the actions of characters in the works will be judged or as the "source" that weaves itself into the text. I am eager, for example, to show that we cannot com-prehend the cultural grammar that dominates Achebe's novels without understanding his Igbo culture, but I also want to insist that these novels are not ethnographic texts that proffer objective knowledge in a context in which the texts of the other are easily consumed as fictionalized accounts of exotic cultures.

To deal with this problem, I quote Edward Said's differentiation of representations and experiences: what is commonly circulated in a cul-ture and what is at stake in cultural exchange, he says, is not truth but representations; "there is no such thing as a delivered presence, but a *re-presence*, or a representation" (21). I clarify this distinction with a dramatic example—a reproduction of Pablo Picasso's *Guernica*. As a representation of the horrors of the Spanish civil war, the painting provokes strong reactions in us, but when we examine it, we find no visual evidence of the war itself, only symbolization; the work is an artistic translation of the bombing of Guernica, not an image of the original event.

But if "the original does not exist for the reader's sake," as Walter Benjamin wonders, "how could the translation be understood on the basis of this premise?" (70). If I translate Achebe's cultural texts by Americanizing them (finding analogies and parallels in American culture), I will have negated the notion of cultural relativism that was intended to validate Igbo cultural practices; I will then have opened the door for an unrelenting feminist attack on Okonkwo's relationship with his wives, an attack that defeats the novelist's tragic intentions and arises from a certain ethnocentrism. Indeed, any gesture toward the doctrine of cultural similitude akin to Benjamin's theory on the kinship of languages (73) will only end up fixing the other as inferior and primitive. The valorization of cultural difference, however—and the insistence that "their" cultural practices are valid in "their" time and place—may lead to a simplistic identification with the other, an identification that glosses over complicated questions and, inevitably, reduces it to an exotic or erotic space.

As I deal with such problems of cultural difference, my "trick of the trade" is simply to bring the problems of reading and translation out into the open: I tell the students that since we are not Nigerians, we can read Achebe's text only in our own terms; we need to realize, however, that our terms are inadequate either because they emerge from our (ethnocentric) cultural position or because our relativism negates the conflicts and contradictions that have generated the novel in the first place. I am not, of course, sure that this strategy works in any significant way. My pedagogical tactic may be a simple way of acknowledging, with Benjamin, that "all translation is only a somewhat provisional way of coming to terms with the foreignness of languages" and their cultures (75). My goal is modest: to try to develop tactics that will make the issues more intelligible without making them transparent or simplistic. In this respect, difficulty can sometimes be turned into a strategy of deploying theory in the classroom.

Our students are always complaining about the difficulty of theory, but when literary concepts come loaded with conventional and reductive meanings, our challenge is to problematize them by making them more difficult. Consider again, for example, the concept of race. Our students enter the classroom with what they view as an immutable understanding of this term; they often come to class expecting us to confirm their a priori notion about how this concept has emerged and how it functions in narrative and cultural practices. Within an American context, as I noted earlier, students take for granted that race is a biological construct whose resonance depends on whether, in the great theater of racism, one has been a victim or a victimizer; the concept is thus imprisoned in its visual representation.

In reading Du Bois's *The Souls of Black Folk*, for example, students would like to discuss the affective nature of racial oppression in the Reconstruction South and the binary structure that sustains racial doctrines, its metaphors and metonymies. But race, for Du Bois, is something more than its presence; it emerges within a specific tradition, and it belongs to an extensive intellectual genealogy; it hovers, in his thoughts and reflections, somewhere between its biologism and its social construction. How, then, do I address race in Du Bois's text? How do I rescue this complexity from the overwhelming shadow of biology?

I begin by conceding to the familiar and experiential: in view of the weight Du Bois gives to experiences that are structured by race and to the metaphorical representation of the racial cognito as the overdetermining category of African American culture, I spend time exploring the affective nature of race through Du Bois's metaphor of the veil and the shadow and his concept of "double-consciousness." Such readings of race seem to confirm the students' expectations. But not for long: my second lecture begins by questioning Du Bois's understanding and deployment of race; I problematize the issue by noting how what appears on one level to be his positivization of the black self is, on another level, dangerously dependent on racist discourse. I conclude with Anthony Appiah's affirmation that race, as it emerges in Du Bois's work, is a structure without a referent; "there are no races: there is nothing in the world that can do all we ask 'race' to do for us" (35).

I have to confess that my second lecture is deliberately provocative, and I sometimes hate to see the troubled looks on the faces of my African American students, who may feel that I have betrayed the race or that my nationality has not prepared me for the kind of racism Du Bois is writing about; but as I will soon discover in subsequent discussions and papers, they are ultimately fascinated by the complexity of race in *The Souls of Black Folk*. Many of them have been in classes where the book was taught by instructors who were content to isolate proclamations that were turned into platitudes repressing the difficult issues the book raised; I have the satisfaction of hearing my students say that although they disagree with my views on race, they are able to understand the book and its complex enabling condition much better because of my problematization. I have achieved my pedagogical results here by making issues that appeared self-evident more difficult.

We need to recognize, however, that because there is always the implicit understanding that the function of the teacher is to make things simpler and clearer, making things difficult creates its own ambivalence. My students want me to translate philosophical concepts—to serve what

George Steiner calls "the intent of communication"; they want such concepts to be translated into a language that is not resistant to "immediacy and comprehension" (18). My desire, however, is to show how the fluidity and essential untranslatability of such terms has to do with language itself and the organization of knowledge. The promise I make to frustrated students is that once we put such terms into operation—that is, relate them to texts and actual cultural practices—we will have a model that will make them sensible. But this process only leads to another difficulty, a second level of translation: the texts that promise us a model in which, to paraphrase Steiner, pragmatic experiences can cohere with a semantic system sometimes confront us with textual meanings that threaten institutionalized knowledge.

An excellent example of this kind of contingent difficulty arises when I try to explore the concept of historiography in relation to postcolonial or even American literature. My goal here is to differentiate what Edouard Glissant calls the "notion of a single History"—which he defines as "the most disturbing consequence of colonization . . . and therefore of power" (93)— and history as a narration of contested events. Glissant's primary text is Faulkner's *Absalom! Absalom!* His argument is that the relation between history and literature in Faulkner's novel is concealed in the *"longing for the ideal of history"* (70). While Faulkner's text adopts a narrative mode that exemplifies the ways in which history is contested in its narrativization, it also seems to proffer so many reserves of information that students are easily tempted to read it simply as a novel of the Civil War; they fall back on a secure history rather than envision a disturbing historiography.

To deal with this problem, I argue that Faulkner's novel appears to reject the superhistorical romantic perspective which Miss Rosa would prefer, that it uses dispersed focalization to foreground the diversity of time and experience, and that its narrative mechanisms are generated by the series of displacements that history itself engenders. But this argument runs counter to the modalities that the students have inherited from American history—their superhistorical vision of the Civil War and what Michel Foucault would call its "apocalyptic objectivity" (152). At this juncture, I realize that I can make the distinction between history and historiography only by drawing on the students' own sources of knowledge: film and television. Is the Civil War we see in *Gone with the Wind* or Ken Burns's PBS series *The Civil War*, I ask, the same event in Faulkner's text? By discussing the different narrative strategies that emerge in the three texts, the students can now see why the meaning of history depends on its modes of representation, not on its objectivity.

But a greater difficulty is posed by what Steiner calls "ontological difficulties" (41). Because we take it as axiomatic that the function of theory is to mediate the crisis of values in modern Western culture, we often fail to realize that our students have come to us with a fundamental investment in the romantic grammar of this culture. Several years ago, for instance,

I was using Jamaica Kincaid's short story "Columbus in Chains" as an example of the anxieties colonial history generates in colonial subjects and of the techniques postcolonial writers adopt to displace this history. The story revolves around an episode in a West Indian history textbook in which Columbus, after his ill-fated fourth voyage, has been arrested by Bobadilla and sent back to Spain in chains. Since I had assumed that my American students were familiar with this episode, my focus was not on its historical meaning or significance but on the colonial subject, Annie John—how she defaced the colonial narrative of history and deprived it of its theological meaning, as a way of releasing herself from hegemonic meanings. I was in the middle of explicating the triadic relation between history, the colonial subject, and representation when several of my students asserted that before we discussed the politics of representation in the story, we needed to explore a preliminary point: why had Kincaid made up this story about Columbus in chains, and why did she relate this fiction as if it were a fact?

At first I was surprised to discover that my students thought Kincaid was playing an interesting game of signification, but then I realized that the historical referent I had taken for granted had been omitted from the textbooks that invented Columbus for them. In these circumstances, the only way I could counter their iconized history of Columbus was to fall back on the very empirical demonstration—and, some may say, naive historicity—that I was trying to counter: I had to refer them to the appropriate sections in the *Encyclopedia Britannica* that describe Columbus's fall from grace and his deportation to Spain. In effect, I could deploy theory only by valorizing the objective knowledge it was supposed to question. Like Aimé Césaire, who created a postcolonial poetics by rejecting the inherited tradition of poetry, I could deploy theory only by renouncing some of its assumptions. To explain the Columbus episode in Kincaid, I had conceded to positivism, the dreaded enemy of critical theory, because I had come to realize that the function of theory was not merely to negate the diagrammatic representation of knowledge and to denounce existing regimes of meaning but also to construct alternative interpretants for different cultural practices.

University of Michigan

Works Cited

Achebe, Chinua. "An Image of Africa: Racism in Conrad's *Heart of Darkness*." *Massachusetts Review* 18 (1977): 782–94.

Appiah, Anthony. "The Uncompleted Argument: Du Bois and the Illusion of Race." *Critical Inquiry* 12.1 (1985): 21–37.

Benjamin, Walter. "The Task of the Translator." *Illuminations*. Trans. Harry Zohn. Glasgow: Fontana-Collins, 1973. 69–82.

Bhabha, Homi. "The Commitment to Theory." *New Formations* 5 (1988): 5–24.

Césaire, Aimé. *Discourse on Colonialism*. Trans. Joan Pinkham. New York: Monthly Review, 1972.

Christian, Barbara. "The Race for Theory." *The Nature and Context of Minority Discourse*. Ed. Abdul R. JanMohamed and David Lloyd. New York: Oxford UP, 1990. 37–49.

de Man, Paul. *The Resistance to Theory*. Minneapolis: U of Minnesota P, 1986.

Du Bois, W. E. B. *The Souls of Black Folk*. New York: NAL, 1969.

Foucault, Michel. "Nietzsche, Genealogy, History." *Language, Counter-memory, Practice: Selected Essays and Interviews*. Ed. Donald F. Bouchard. Ithaca: Cornell UP, 1977. 139–64.

Gikandi, Simon. *Reading Chinua Achebe: Language and Ideology in Fiction*. Portsmouth: Heinemann, 1991.

Glissant, Edouard. *Caribbean Discourse: Selected Essays*. Trans. J. Michael Dash. Charlottesville: U of Virginia P, 1989.

Mohanty, S. P. "Radical Teaching, Radical Theory: The Ambiguous Politics of Meaning." *Theory in the Classroom*. Ed. Cary Nelson. Urbana: U of Illinois P, 1986. 149–76.

Said, Edward. *Orientalism*. New York: Vintage, 1979.

Steiner, George. "On Difficulty." *On Difficulty and Other Essays*. New York: Oxford UP, 1978. 18–47.

Trilling, Lionel. *Sincerity and Authenticity*. Cambridge: Harvard UP, 1972.

Wellek, René, and Austin Warren. *Theory of Literature*. New York: Harcourt, 1970.

Gray Is Theory (Except in Black and White or Color); or, The Paradoxes and Pleasures of Film Theory

D. N. Rodowick

"Film needs theory like it needs a scratch on the negative." Attributed to Alan Parker, a contemporary film director (Lapsley and Westlake), this quotation expresses a resistance to theory often characteristic of both filmmakers and film students.[1] Lurking behind this resistance is the idea that theory is destructive of both art and pleasure. When a film's negative, or what is often called the original, is damaged, it is ruined; no more copies can be produced. A process of repetition, of endlessly copying a known and cherished pleasure, is definitively interrupted.

For the dedicated film teacher, however, Parker's gibe seems strange since film studies has been so heavily identified with "theoretical approaches" to the study of mass culture. Strange perhaps, but not unfamiliar, for the history of teaching film in American universities is characterized by a curious paradox. Emerging only in the last twenty-five years, film studies has been on the cutting edge of attempts to integrate semiotic, psychoanalytic, Marxist, feminist, and multicultural perspectives on cultural criticism. Yet nowhere is the resistance to theory met so forcefully than in the film classroom, especially in introductory classes. This paradox is endemic to the medium. Even Sergei Eisenstein, one of the greatest and most prolific film theorists, cites Goethe's *Faust* in complaining, "Grau ist die theorie . . ." (2).[2]

Parker's comment is facetious. Nonetheless it represents a paradox that historically has placed films and theory in an agonistic relation. The idea is that a "popular culture" requires no interpretation; that films, for example, are immediately and transparently intelligible to their audiences. Implicit in this dig is also the idea—which I will call Parker's law— that an inverse ratio defines the relation of the "natural" intelligibility of films to the obdurate nature of film theory; that is, the more transparent and consumable the film, the more recondite the theory required to explain it. Parker's law also implies two corollaries: that films are responsive to a mass, democratic expression while theory is obfuscating and elitist and that films are pleasurable and life-giving while theory is dry and moribund.

Some students may also hold these opinions in unconscious or inarticulate ways. Their resistance, however, is often fed by the old adage "Familiarity breeds contempt." Successive generations of college students have become more and more visually acute. The television generation that invented film studies has long since been succeeded by the Macintosh and MTV generation. Because our students have been immersed throughout their lives in an audiovisual universe, they feel they already "know" it since it so thoroughly permeates their daily experience and their ways of thinking. A group of first-year students might begin a class on African literature with a completely open and enthusiastic mind if they have had little or no previous exposure to it. The same students will begin their first day of Introduction to Film Studies with the conviction that they already know all there is to know about film.

Now even if Eisenstein lamented the "grayness" of theory, his dismay did not inhibit him from producing in volume some of the most erudite, cross-disciplinary reflections on film aesthetics yet published. While Eisenstein's considerable aesthetic writings are certainly difficult, they are nevertheless pleasurable, in fact imbued with a great sense of fun as well as a certain pedagogical emphasis. Eisenstein was also a teacher of renown, and his dual emphasis on pleasure and pedagogy in film is instructive for us today. Even his filmmaking was meant not only to entertain but also to inform and to encourage the realization of socialist ideals.

Aesthetics and theory were complementary rather than opposed areas of work for Eisenstein and equally pleasurable, though in different ways. Scattered throughout his late writings is a psychoanalytic explanation for these differences. The apparently spontaneous pleasures of creation as well as spectatorship are the result of complex unconscious trains of thought; the role of theory is to work through and give conscious expression to otherwise subterranean processes. A great many of his writings recapitulate his films to understand how they signify, becoming meaningful and pleasurable for his audiences. Certainly Eisenstein saw theory as a way for making better films and for teaching others how to make better films. But he also understood that there was an important philosophical issue at stake: that the object of theory was *to understand how films are understood*.

This phrase was actually coined by Christian Metz in his early essays on film language (*Film Language* 145). In my view it has always provided the most eloquent and concise response to the questions of what film theory is and what film theory does. I return to this idea below. First, however, I want to address the paradoxes devolving from the historical appearance of film theory in the university classroom.

When I began teaching film, I proposed a seminar titled Textual Analysis in Film and Literature. The Course of Study Committee refused this class with the question "How can films be *texts*?" Alternatively, they cheerfully approved the class when its title was changed to Textual Analysis in Film and Literary Theory. Obviously, both literary and film *theory* could be analyzed as texts since they were written. Films could not. This dichotomy is the mundane expression of a logocentrism entrenched in Western philosophy since at least the Enlightenment. I am thinking in particular of an iconoclastic anxiety that arrived with the birth of aesthetics, in our modern sense of the term, in the eighteenth century (see, e.g., Mitchell; see also Rodowick, "Figure," "Reading," and "Impure Mimesis"). Concerned with the self-identity of art and of the various representational media, this line of thought is marked by a hierarchical distinction that elevates the poetic arts—as closest to speech and therefore thought—in relation to the visual arts. Systematized by Gotthold Lessing in his *Laocoon*, though with a long philosophical genealogy, this position considered linguistic and plastic expression as ontologically opposed categories: speech, and its representative writing, would henceforth be the language of philosophy since linguistic expression was closely identified with thought and rational processes. By the same token, "images" were considered to be without language and thus irrational. This opposition supported evaluative hierarchies in which, from Hegel to Heidegger, poetry is the highest art because, in its relation to speech, it is closest to thought. In the same movement, the practice of criticism is valorized as a necessary but supplementary act. Through writing, it restores concepts to art, especially music and the visual arts, since through this opposition they are considered to be "speechless" and therefore without concepts.

This problem is not merely philosophical. Recapitulated in the university classroom, it had important consequences for how the visual arts, especially film, were addressed and taught. For example, film studies began to make its appearance in university curricula in the 1960s, largely in the context of literature departments. The first instinct of many teachers was to adopt literary methods of classroom organization. As one might teach a novel a week, so too did one show a film a week. But many economic and technological problems became apparent. Whereas students were expected to buy and read a novel before they came to class and to notate and work through a reading on their own, films had to be projected, either using up time that would otherwise be available for discussion or effectively doubling the hours required for a class session. Unlike a book, a 16mm film cannot be owned and projected by an individual student. Now even when a university is able to build up a film collection, prints are fragile, and students are often justifiably discouraged from using them individually. In the classroom, teacher and student alike have to confront both the ephemerality and the temporal tyranny of the medium. Technology is cranky and unpredictable, and films can wear out. Organizing clips and incorporating them as "citations" within class discussion is often a harrowing experience. Film thus presents considerable technological barriers to an effective pedagogy.

The 1960s witnessed an explosion in the publishing of film criticism and analysis equaling the rapid expansion of film studies curricula. This explosion was the response not only to a genuine interest in the study of film but also to a concrete pedagogical problem that created a market for "texts" in the classroom. Robin Wood's superb studies *Hitchcock's Films* and *Howard Hawks*, for example, treated those directors' films with the thematic seriousness of literary works and, being books, were assigned and treated as such in the classroom. Critics wishing to treat film seriously found ample opportunities to publish in journals such as *Film Quarterly*, *Movie*, *Film Comment*, *Sight and Sound*, and *Film Culture*, as well as a host of smaller magazines and journals. Critics were also able to assemble their film analyses into books. Simply speaking, instructors taught film by, each week, screening one film and assigning one essay or chapter of criticism. At a fundamental level, film watching and classroom learning were considered, by teacher and student, as separable activities.

This method, which is still the norm in many film classrooms today, conceals various unanalyzed anxieties and assumptions about what counts as knowledge and the transmission of knowledge. The use of videotape and laserdisc has ameliorated somewhat the technological problems of the teaching of film, but technology cannot provide the solution for a philosophical and theoretical problem, that is, the feeding of cultural biases about the image and the moving image that have deep historical roots. Film's relation to time is tyrannical in a way that is unique to this art. The passage of the film through the projector and onto the screen is constant, linear, and irreversible. Made possible by a constantly shifting beam of light focused in a darkened movie theater, the power and pleasure of film watching derive from intangible and dreamlike qualities that Metz defines as a double absence pursued by the spectator: the hallucinatory projection of an absent referent in space as well as the slipping away of images in time. Moreover, film images present a powerful impression of reality (*Imaginary Signifier* 58–66). Their movement, perceptual intensity, and automatism—their mechanical, nonhuman, and thus apparently objective rendering of reality—tend to suppress awareness of their constructedness as complex semiotic and discursive systems. Film's powers of identification thus present a genuine problem for film theory, film teaching, and the place of theory in the classroom. However, the literary mode of film teaching, which uses the written text as supplement in both the literal and philosophical sense, responds to this problem without addressing it theoretically.

The teaching of film immediately poses a problem of theory that, although it has consequences for the teaching of literature or any other form of cultural expression, nonetheless is more serious for film. I am not arguing for restoring the purity of cinematic experience by banishing texts from the classroom. On the contrary, contemporary film theory has seriously challenged our ideas of what can be called a text and counted as discourse, as well as hierarchies of value opposing written and visual communication. Moreover, it has called into question the view of aesthetic experience as a pristine encounter between the spectator and the work of art. For me, the goal of film theory, and of introducing theory directly or indirectly to the classroom, is *to shift fundamentally the conditions of spectatorship itself*. This goal entails not only introducing students to a certain discourse *about film*—for example, what Christian Metz, Jean-Louis Baudry, and Laura Mulvey have to say about the technological, psychological, and ideological underpinnings of spectatorship—but also addressing how films themselves are discursive, semiotic systems and how the meaning of films shifts when the contexts for reading them are changed.

What made film studies exciting in the 1970s and 1980s was its innovative strategies for understanding how cultural artifacts make meaning, give pleasure, and are understood. Film studies in the 1970s reintroduced to the classroom the question of what it means to read in response to a medium whose founding ideology was that of universal intelligibility. For me, teaching theory effectively means focusing not only on reading as an activity but also on transforming the positions of spectatorship to which students are accustomed, in the classroom as well as in the movie theater. In this respect, I believe that the teaching of film theory involves three challenges. The first challenge requires changing materially how films are presented and appropriated in the classroom. The second involves finding ways to present theory historically—in essence, as positions of reading, subject to debate and transformation, that can shift how texts become meaningful and pleasurable to their audiences. The third involves teaching theory as a process of empowerment with respect not only to understanding how one thinks but also to enlarging possibilities of meaning and pleasure.

In his book *The Imaginary Signifier*, Metz argues convincingly that the film industry trades economically on a phantom and intangible commodity—the production of pleasure. Film presents an intensely psychological experience unlike the experience presented by any other art. What keeps theaters full and the industry developing apace is that spectators exchange money for nothing more substantial than what Metz calls *"an orientation of consciousness, whose roots are unconscious, and without which we would be unable to understand the overall trajectory which founds the institution and accounts for its continuing existence"* (93). As a mass-produced experience of the imaginary, the cinema must modulate between several regimes of desire. The darkened theater and temporal irreversibility of the cinematic experience encourage passivity and interiority and discourage intersubjective responses, while the movement and quasi-hallucinatory presentation of images and sounds sustain conditions of watching and hearing akin to fantasy or dreaming. Feminist theorists like Laura Mulvey add that the narrative form of many commercial films reinforces this situation through point-of-view structures encouraging voyeuristic and fetishistic fantasies based on a patriarchal appropriation of images of the female body.

Discussion of these hypotheses is one way of introducing theory to the classroom. But discussion is ineffective if it does not serve to restructure how films are screened and used for teaching and learning, so we return to the problem of citation. Raymond Bellour has referred to film as "le texte introuvable," a text that is "unfindable" because it is so difficult to cite. Unlike the specificity of literature, which seems undisturbed when translated into the written language of criticism, the specificity of film is entirely transformed when critical reading reproduces it in the form of film stills, charts, and written descriptions. "In this," Bellour writes, film "is particularly unquotable, since the written text cannot restore to it what only the projector can produce: a movement, the illusion of which guarantees the reality" (82; my trans.).[3] Both the limitations and fascinations of the textual analysis of film, then, derive from disturbing factors of movement and time that are essential to the cinema's powers of representation and identification.

As I argue in the last chapter of *The Difficulty of Difference*, this paradox is neither an obstacle to nor a liability for film theory and analysis. Only by interrupting the film's time and movement can we facilitate critical reading and theoretical knowledge. Similarly, the citability of literature in the language of written interpretation guarantees neither that a critical reading will take place nor that, in Roland Barthes's terminology, a text will be derived from an originating work. While textual analysis may be thought of as synonymous with close reading—critically detailing the film scene by scene and shot by shot—it must not simply stop with description and commentary. What the activity of textual analysis implies is a reading that *transforms*. As Barthes demonstrated time and again, for the text of a work of literature to be reproduced—as an analytic model of its obdurate inner movements, its complex symbolic processes, and its relations to desire—the originating object must be reconstituted in a new context and in a new form. In no way does textual analysis seek to repeat the experience of a film. Instead, by strategically fragmenting and rewriting its object, this form of close reading reconstructs otherwise unconscious processes of signification and reading, rendering them explicit and intelligible. Strategies of close analysis do not necessarily attempt to repeat what a film means. Rather, they present opportunities for constructing positions from which films can be read in new and sometimes unforeseen ways.

Therefore, while Metz identifies the orientation of consciousness organized by the fiction film with regressive fantasy, he also insists that neither the form of the narrative film nor the context of reception can determine this experience; they merely stage, more or less successfully, the conditions under which it may occur. In fact, in his view repetitive moviegoing has less to do with the desire to see particular films than with the desire to reexperience this condition of wakeful dreaming. Alternatively, Metz stresses that one can adopt a variety of positions of meaning and desire before any film and that the film theorist in particular chooses to stand "outside the institution" (*Imaginary Signifier* 138). This emphatically positive and productive view has often been overlooked in contemporary film theory. The resistance to theory sometimes found in beginning film students is often the unconscious expression of an anxiety wonderfully characterized by one of Pierre Janet's patients as being afraid to read for fear of getting the books dirty (Blanchot 91). Indeed, when students read Mulvey's argument for undermining the "satisfaction, pleasure, and privilege" (68) of Hollywood films, they might find their worst fears about film classes confirmed. However, undermining one particular if widespread form of identification and pleasure might itself be a liberating act, not only in the knowledge it produces but also in its creation of new contexts for reading and new forms of pleasure.

The best way to introduce students to theory, then, is to stress that while it will change them as spectators and will, one hopes, encourage them to interrogate the pleasures they have found in moviegoing, theory also introduces them to new pleasures derived from wresting control of the spectatorial experience away from the projector. Every practical classroom strategy, in this respect, returns to the problem of citation, if for no other reason than to discourage students from making judgments based on impressionistic memories of last night's screening. I find it extremely useful to ask students to keep informal diaries where they record their thoughts and impressions with respect to watching films screened for their classes. When kept consistently, the journal encourages a process of self-reflection about the spectatorial experience, gets students in the habit of making arguments and taking positions on what they have seen, and often provides a useful way of initiating class discussion.

Even more important is the assignment of film analysis along with theoretical readings. I find two kinds of exercises very productive: one involves segmentation—the breaking down of a film into its scenes or sequences as a way of understanding basic patterns of narrative organization, and the other involves performing a shot-by-shot breakdown of an individual sequence as an exercise in understanding how film form, on even the most minute levels, can contribute to the purveyance of meaning.[4] What I consider most important here is introducing students to a process that is fundamentally alien to traditional moviegoing. Through analysis exercises, the irreversible time of projection is replaced by strategic interruptions: repetitive viewing; slowing, stopping, and reviewing the film; comparing and contrasting diverse sections such as beginnings and endings; and so forth. It is also useful to have students perform these exercises in small groups. This practice engages them in a process of discussion and debate that makes clear how divergent opinions, arguments, and readings may be inspired by the same sequence of film. The main idea, however, is to break down the unilateral determinations of meaning and pleasure set by the seemingly irreversible flow of film time while multiplying the kinds and nature of discursive interactions that can take place around a film.

The size constraints of lecture classes usually force a teacher to impose a choice of film for these assignments. For segmentation exercises, I usually select the opening ten minutes of a Hollywood film. Narrative construction is often clearest and most visually rich in the openings of films; moreover, students need not rely on prior knowledge of the film to write about them. The choice of a scene for a shot-by-shot breakdown is somewhat trickier; teachers must rely here on their own knowledge of film history and the literature on close analysis. For both assignments I prepare study guides in advance with suggestions on what to look for or think about. Class time is set aside for both assignments so that I can be present to answer questions and resolve problems, though students feel free to continue work at home or at campus video carrels if they are available. Screening the relevant clip three or four times in class usually suffices for these assignments. In close analysis seminars, students should make their own film choices. In this context, however, I encourage them to segment an entire film and often to choose a scene for a shot-by-shot breakdown from that film. Again, having them work in self-chosen groups of three or four enhances the learning process.

This process relies, of course, on the maintenance of a video library as well as video carrels where students can work outside class.[5] It also requires that the teacher incorporate model citation strategies in class through the use of video clips and frame enlargements. Visual citations, if chosen well, also provide a focus for discussion that can render esoteric ideas more concrete while encouraging students to challenge interpretations given in their reading, or by the teacher, with their own point of view.

Classes on close analysis use theory to transform the material conditions of spectatorship as a way for students to control and understand images in ways occluded by normal film projections. Alternatively, the film theory survey class should present the process of theoretical inquiry as a historical and critical reflection on positions of thought and reading in relation to film. With this objective in mind, I tend to organize theory surveys around two questions: How do we know what we know *through* films? How do we know what we know *in relation to* films?

I often organize surveys of film theory as four areas of investigation: representation, signification, spectatorship, and ideology or social meaning. The first two areas involve problems of reference and meaning. More simply, I am talking about questions of iconography and image construction on the one hand and of narrative structure on the other. Every theory of film and photography—from the neo-Kantian and proto-Gestalt formulations of Hugo Münsterberg and Rudolf Arnheim to the semiotic formulations of Christian Metz and Umberto Eco—presumes that *how* we construct meaning *through* images involves complex and largely unconscious perceptual and cognitive processes. Considering the powerful influence of visual communication on our current lives as well as on the history of the twentieth century, a teacher's first task is to encourage students to reflect on how little they think about images despite the amount of social communication they receive through them. The second goal of many otherwise different film theories is to critique the apparent immediacy and naturalness of mechanically reproduced images, emphasizing instead their discursive nature and formal complexity. This approach includes defining the range of subjective choices that must be made concerning subject matter, framing, scale, camera angle, perspective, lighting, and the use of sounds, movement, and duration as semiotic processes that construct meaning rather than transparently reproduce a preexisting reality. Obviously, film analysis exercises also contribute to this question and can be incorporated into a survey class.

Studies of spectatorship continue this line of inquiry by examining how positions of meaning are organized through various formal and technological factors: from what point-of-view editing accomplishes, for example, to how an impression of reality is produced by camera and projector. Finally, questions of ideology complete the shift from an emphasis on film form or language to models of reading. Such discussion covers competing models of viewer psychology drawn from Freudian and Lacanian psychoanalysis, Gestalt psychology, and cognitive science. Equally if not more important, I present how theoretical inquiry facilitates the examination of potential biases of sex, class, and race coded in narrative films in unconscious as well as overt ways. Another important issue is how alternative filmmaking practices—as well as critical strategies developed in the context of Third World and other nationalist film movements and by feminist, gay and lesbian, and multicultural approaches— have challenged more-conventional kinds of spectatorship.

Particularly in chronological surveys, one runs the risk of reducing the historical complexity and contradictoriness of various debates by presenting the history of thought on cinema as a linear progression toward ever more perfect theories of film. But every theory has a history. By focusing on the historical breadth and diversity of models of reading, the theory survey suggests that there is no single truth concerning film but, rather, a process by which positions of meaning emerge through debate as well as social struggle. By presenting theories of cinema as competing critical positions, I find it easier to demonstrate that presumptions of thought change through time and that they can be challenged, critiqued, and innovated. This approach is not simply one of a critical pluralism that attempts to widen students' interest in diverse points of view and different kinds of filmmaking. It also requires a classroom strategy that addresses theory as a process that effects not only what one thinks but also how one thinks. We must therefore break down whenever possible the consumerist approach to learning, by which the teacher is selling something that students may or may not buy. Instead, the history of theory should be presented as an ongoing debate in which the students are encouraged to participate.

The students should engage in critical dialogue with the material presented and with the teacher, as well as with one another. Since some are shy about presenting their ideas or challenging the teacher in lecture situations, seminars without fixed seating are always a preferred format. If the course is taught in lecture format, the teacher should encourage dialogue in class whenever appropriate and, if possible, arrange small groups of discussion sections in addition to lecture times. I prefer to break up lecture classes into three fifty-minute sections: an introduction session sets the context for a screening to follow that evening; then I give another fifty-minute lecture, after which the students divide up into small discussion sections or pursue individual and group work at our Film Study Center.[6]

For written work, I find that several short, informal papers encourage this process better than do one or two longer seminar papers, even in graduate classes. In the course of a semester, I usually require students to write four papers of about five pages each as well as to keep a diary. As with film diaries, diaries on readings and discussion enable students to keep a personal record of their responses and to develop ideas that they can expand in their papers. Diaries also provide a useful launching pad for discussion in sections and in class. For the most part, I believe that the organization and structure of diaries should be personal, providing students a place to work out their own personal strategies for approaching the material. In assessing their work, I regard style as less important than process; I assign grades only on a plus, check, or minus system indicating relative levels of satisfaction. What I look for is the effort to produce an argument or a point of view, even in the most fragmentary form. Equally if not more important is the effort to formulate questions. As a rule of thumb, I ask students to try to record in their diaries at least three questions a week that they can share in class. In the best cases, this assignment increases their confidence about speaking up in class as well as their sense of democratically influencing what should be discussed. It also gives me a relatively clear idea about how to focus my performance in terms of clarifying problems or exploring issues that the students find particularly thought-provoking. Diaries thus encourage a habitual process of critical dialogue with the lecture material, readings, and films. They also help teachers monitor their performances.

While students should be encouraged to develop their own ideas for papers through the keeping of diaries, providing some guidance for papers through suggested topics or approaches is always helpful. I usually prepare study guide questions for both introductory and survey classes. I distribute these guides before giving the lecture or assigning the reading material they cover. They serve as suggestions for developing paper topics and also give the students a sense of what I find important. Some guidance is necessary, I think, as a way of encouraging students to focus on specific questions, topics, and passages suggested by the readings. Let me add, however, that study guides are merely suggestions for discussion; their role is to encourage and enable a process whereby students begin to formulate their own questions and topics or their own critical dissections of rhetorical and philosophical assumptions in the readings. The papers, then, continue a process that ideally begins with the diaries. While good writing is always important, the main issue for these papers is the process of working through an argument or formulating and clarifying a set of questions. Once again, the most important goal is to devise pedagogical strategies that encourage students to view theory as a process of critical empowerment rather than as passive submission to authoritative ideas.

Finally, I want to address the question of theory as a process of empowerment. When taught well, theory can be a process of liberation with all its attendant pleasures, as opposed to a dry intellectual exercise.

I have insisted that a general reflection on theory is necessary for working out the practical consequences of teaching film theory in the classroom. This reflection is necessary because theory is not a thing—a group of ideas, an identity or an attitude—that can be acquired or discarded; rather, I would call theory that process of reaching self-consciousness about how we know what we know. Theory may be taught badly or well, but there is no classroom where it is wholly absent. By the same token, theory is ever present in our daily lives. Whenever we make judgments of knowledge or value, we invoke, consciously or not, a system of assumptions, definitions, concepts, and beliefs: in short, a theory. When this process is unconscious, we risk becoming slaves to habit or prejudice. Teaching theory as a process means encouraging students to liberate themselves from habits of thought, not only through self-criticism but also through a process of active creation and imagination. This process is what Tania Modleski has called, in relation to feminist theory, the performative function of critical thought. In her view, critical thought does not merely ascertain and clarify received meanings but also aims "at bringing into being *new* meanings and *new* subjectivities, seeking to articulate not only what is but 'what has never been.' In this respect, it may be said to have a performative dimension—i.e., to be *doing* something beyond restating already existent ideas and views . . ." (14). Theory may thus also have a utopian dimension in the best sense of the word. Through theoretical inquiry not only do we define what and how we know, but in liberating ourselves from old habits of thought we also imagine and create new possibilities of knowledge, desire, and meaning. In this liberation resides the pleasures of theory.

University of Rochester

Notes

[1] Lapsley and Westlake's *Film Theory: An Introduction* is a superb introduction to contemporary film theory. My book *The Crisis of Political Modernism* might prove useful for more-advanced students. Teachers may also find Cook helpful for preparing courses or for use in class. The best anthologies of contemporary film theory are Penley; Nichols; and *Screen Reader 1* and *Screen Reader 2*.

[2] My comments on Eisenstein's pedagogy are inspired by Aumont.

[3] An alternative English translation is "The Uncitable Text." I give a fuller account of this problem in the last chapter of *The Difficulty of Difference* (117–40).

[4]Bordwell and Thompson provide a basic introduction to and bibliography for the methodological problems and procedures of close analysis. Their chapter "Narrative as a Formal System" (54–88) introduces questions of segmentation, providing a good follow-up bibliography. They also provide a basic bibliography on close analysis (368). See also Lehman.

[5] Andrew discusses the pedagogical importance of the film study center. Teachers must also keep in mind that the use of 16mm film, video, laser disc, and frame enlargements introduces not only aesthetic and methodological problems but also legal ones. For a discussion of the aesthetic issues, see Usai. See also "Statement on the Use of Video in the Classroom" (Society for Cinema Studies).

[6] I should also reemphasize that, depending on the focus of the class, the format of "a film a week" may or may not be appropriate. In a close analysis seminar one might choose to work on a single film for an extended period, even a whole semester. Alternatively, a course or a part of a course that concentrates on trends or general issues may work better with a series of films that adds up to more than one a week. This freedom of choice is one advantage of having access to a good videodisc and laser disc library. My impression is that even experienced film teachers exercise too little pedagogical imagination in this respect. While one is always bound by economic and technological resources, my advice nonetheless is to try never to be bound by convention.

Works Cited

Andrew, Dudley. "An Open Approach to Film Study and the Situation at Iowa." *Film Study in the Undergraduate Curriculum*. Ed. Barry Keith Grant. New York: MLA, 1983. 39–48.

Aumont, Jacques. *Montage Eisenstein*. Trans. Lee Hildreth et al. Bloomington: Indiana UP, 1987.

Barthes, Roland. "From Work to Text." *Image-Music-Text*. Trans. Stephen Heath. Glasgow: Fontana, 1977. 155–64.

Baudry, Jean-Louis. "The Apparatus: Metapsychological Approaches to the Impression of Reality in Cinema." Rosen 299–318.

———. "Ideological Effects of the Basic Cinematographic Apparatus." Rosen 286–98.

Bellour, Raymond. "Le texte introuvable." *Ça cinéma* 7-8 (May 1975): 77–84.

———. "The Uncitable Text." *Screen* 16.3 (1975): 19–27.

Blanchot, Maurice. "Reading." *The Gaze of Orpheus*. Ed. P. Adams Sitney. Trans. Lydia Davis. Barrytown: Station Hill, 1981. 91–98.

Bordwell, David, and Kristin Thompson. *Film Art: An Introduction*. New York: Knopf, 1985.

Cook, Pam. *The Cinema Book*. New York: Pantheon–British Film Institute, 1985.

Eisenstein, S. M. *Non-indifferent Nature*. Trans. Herbert Marshall. Cambridge: Cambridge UP, 1987.

Lapsley, Robert, and Michael Westlake. *Film Theory: An Introduction*. New York: St. Martin's, 1989.

Lehman, Peter, ed. *Close Analysis*. Gainesville: U of Florida P, 1990.

Metz, Christian. *Film Language: A Semiotics of the Cinema*. Trans. Michael Taylor. Chicago: U of Chicago P, 1991.

———. *The Imaginary Signifier: Psychoanalysis and Cinema*. Trans. Ben Brewster et al. Bloomington: Indiana UP, 1982.

Mitchell, W. J. T. *Iconology: Image, Text, Ideology*. Chicago: U of Chicago P, 1986.

Modleski, Tania. "Some Functions of Feminist Film Criticism; or, The Scandal of the Mute Body." *October* 49 (Summer 1989): 3–24.

Mulvey, Laura. "Visual Pleasure and Narrative Cinema." Penley 57–68.

Nichols, Bill, ed. *Movies and Methods*. Vols. 1 and 2. Berkeley: U of California P, 1976, 1985.

Penley, Constance, ed. *Feminism and Film Theory*. New York: Routledge, 1988.

Rodowick, D. N. *The Crisis of Political Modernism: Criticism and Ideology in Contemporary Film Theory*. Berkeley: U of California P, 1994.

———. *The Difficulty of Difference*. New York: Routledge, 1991.

———. "The Figure and the Text." *Diacritics* 15.1 (1985): 34–50.

———. "Impure Mimesis; or, The Ends of the Aesthetic." *Deconstruction and the Spatial Arts: Painting, Film, Architecture*. Ed. Peter Brunette and David Wills. Cambridge: Cambridge UP, 1993. 96–117.

———. "Reading the Figural." *Camera Obscura* 24 (1991): 11–44.

Rosen, Philip, ed. *Narrative, Apparatus, Ideology*. New York: Columbia UP, 1986.

Screen Reader 1: Cinema/Ideology/Politics. London: Society for Education in Film and Television, 1977.

Screen Reader 2: Cinema and Semiotics. London: Society for Education in Film and Television, 1981.

Society for Cinema Studies Task Force on Film Integrity. "Statement on the Use of Video in the Classroom." *Cinema Journal* 30.4 (1991): 3–6.

Usai, Paolo Cherchai. "The Unfortunate Spectator." *Sight and Sound* 56.3 (1987): 170–74.

Wood, Robin. *Hitchcock's Films*. New York: Castle, 1965.

———. *Howard Hawks*. London: British Film Institute, 1981.

Teaching Cultural Criticism in Denver, Colorado

Jan Gorak

Many teachers will agree that the survey course still fulfills a useful function in undergraduate education. Students bustle from topic to topic or from author to author at such a pace that they have no time to become obsessive or bored; teachers are too busy keeping up with their own reading assignments to peddle too many favored agendas. Be that as it may, a teacher entrusted with presenting a survey of modern criticism from Matthew Arnold to Michel Foucault in a ten-week quarter confronts special difficulties: much of the material is difficult, although no more so than *The Waste Land* or "The Dead," two other staple features of the undergraduate curriculum. The overall pattern that holds the separate difficulties together, however, has yet to emerge: it will be some time before the separate critical projects of Foucault, Stanley Fish, and Northrop Frye—to name but three important voices in modern criticism—resolve themselves into teachable unity. Moreover, the vocabularies and conceptual frameworks of twentieth-century critics vary greatly: to move from the criticism of T. S. Eliot to the criticism of Jacques Lacan calls for greater conceptual leaps than to shift from the poetry of W. B. Yeats to the poetry of Seamus Heaney, for example.

To give my disparate subject matter some unity, to introduce my students to the working assumptions and vocabulary of one distinct cultural group, and to give some topical buttressing to what sometimes appears to be an abstract endeavor, I devote a four-week period (eight two-hour classes) to my course Cultural Criticism. On a campus like ours, where the chancellor's public commitment to diversity flies in the face of a dauntingly homogeneous campus community, this choice has a clear reference point for my students. And from my own point of view, as someone born and raised in Britain but whose working life has been spent elsewhere, the issue is also important. I cannot remember when I first heard the word *culture*, but in retrospect I can see that it must have been applied to many diverse aspects of my life. For example, I can recall relatives' warning me off the Third Programme because it was "too cultured," national radio broadcasters' praising northern brass bands as authentic "regional culture," and extremely fascinating visits from robed aldermen and waistcoated local dignitaries who our teachers told us represented "civic culture." At college, I learned about T. S. Eliot's culture, which seemed to be something very different from the Euroculture the country's governing party belatedly hoped to join; the "national culture," which one group claimed any such membership would jettison; and the "alternative culture," which some of my contemporaries had already filed down to their sole alternative. In recent years, since coming to the United States, I have encountered barrio culture, print culture, mall culture, and a host of other variations on a word of seemingly endless malleability.

My students always like my stories of oppression from the old country, and they are particularly intrigued by the way my educators, entertainers, and governors all appeared to conceive of culture as an exclusive club. This unanimity and paternalism squares with the representations of Britain that they have encountered: a land of masterpieces, iron ladies, and tiaras. But when we open our first assigned work, Edward Said's *Covering Islam*, uneasy questions about contemporary American culture soon come into the open. Is it not true that American media tend to circulate a few dominant images of Islamic culture? Are not those images—like the images of working-class culture in Britain during the late fifties and early sixties—a mixture of condescension and hostility? Would it not be true to say that in both countries certain stereotypes, constructed in the interests of groups very different from the groups who are the subject of the stereotypes, are all that we see of cultures construed as inferior by powerful sections of our society?

Although most of my students will agree with Said's thesis that a certain drastically limited repertoire of images is all that reaches Americans of Islamic culture, they want—want desperately, I have found—to believe that Islam is static, undeveloped, or less advanced than the United States and that there is a tight correspondence between the televised image and the social reality. They will concede that during Desert Storm Saddam Hussein did appear to spend a lot more time in bunkers than, for example, James Baker, but few of them are inclined to ask why. I tentatively posit a definition of culture as "a recurrent set of symbols and images appropriate to a certain prescribed range of social biographies" and ask my students to recollect the most pervasive images of Islamic males and females. Inevitably, we discuss the shouting mob around Ayatollah Khomeini's funeral casket—people who were actually striking themselves in furious grief, as the students observe with astonishment—and the veiled faces of Islamic women. We agree that whatever else these images signify, they point to social biographies not American and not Western. We begin to understand that cultural images—the worker's cloth cap in East Lancashire, the perpetual veil of the Iraqi women, the corporate logo that sponsors Eric Clapton or Pete Rose, and a hundred homecoming celebrations on our own campus—stand for a particular kind of collective lifestyle, and the representation of these images on our television screens stands not just for "the way it was" in 1926 or 1991 but for a precise, invisible decision about "the way it was" framed according to particular constructions of the world.

But whose constructions of the world? Said leaves us in no doubt that State Department priorities determine the media representations of groups perceived as hostile to American interests. My students are usually reluctant to accept this vision and sometimes resist it fiercely—or they accept it equally fiercely and plunge into conspiracy theories, finding a military junta behind the Super Bowl. We try to explore the interests behind media representation of women, minorities, hostile nations, even "the American way." I point out how unlikely it is that any one group can control the plethora of representations that bombard an American living room every evening, but I also point out that in a society where local television stations are nationally described as "markets," it is unlikely that these images correspond to raw, unmediated reality. We consider the usefulness of the term *hegemony*, defined as the division of culture into dominant, emerging, and subordinate groups, and we ask ourselves whether "our" communications media consolidate or challenge these divisions. I refer the students to Raymond Williams's useful discussions of media ownership and control in *Communications* and *Television: Technology and Cultural Form*.

We now consider possible counterbalances to State Department dominance of the media in times of war, not least the vast number of foreign journalists involved in any international conflict. In a discussion about the Gulf War, however, one student remarked that American briefings outnumbered briefings by other nations about threefold, that the American media "covered" the conflict more exhaustively than any foreign competitor, and that American generals (one general in particular) enjoyed far more airtime than their "alliance partners" did. At this potentially disturbing stage in the course, I at least am forced to concede that when addressing any international issue in which the United States declares an interest, our electronic culture effectively becomes the executive arm of United States foreign policy. Where F. Scott Fitzgerald held that "culture follows money," my class decides that culture follows power, that the matrix of symbols available in our culture always serves a particular interest, especially in times of national crisis.

At this point, we move to the work of Michel Foucault. For a long time, I wondered how best to introduce an undergraduate audience to Foucault. Absolutely indispensable, he remains relatively bewildering to many students: his subject matter is recondite, his style difficult, his intellectual machinery frightening. The interviews collected as *Power/Knowledge* are easier to read than his more theoretical texts, but not ultimately very helpful unless one has immersed oneself in some of the major work.

This year I elected to teach Foucault's *I, Pierre Rivière, Having Slaughtered My Mother, My Sister, and My Brother* (some of his students contributed to the book). Perhaps because the work originated in a year-long seminar with Foucault's students at the Collège de France, it appears far more accessible than his more famous works. I have always been greatly taken by C. Wright Mills's observation that every culture issues forth in representative biographies and significant roles: in this sense, Foucault's case of parricide in the nineteenth century offers a thoroughly compelling plot, for in murdering mother, sister, and brother, Pierre brings on his head the fears, the knowledge, and the recrimination of his century. Early reports, significantly, describe him in terms that might have been applied to a Reformation witch: he is a monster, a madman, a wild animal. These same reports, relayed by the regional newspaper, the *Pilote du Calvados*, also try to soothe the shredding nerves of a small community threatened by an unapprehended multiple murderer; they quite unwarrantedly speculate that Pierre is probably dead ("the wretched man has killed himself" [17]) yet simultaneously reassure their readers that the police will shortly make an arrest. Our class contrasts this response with the likely reactions of contemporary media, which more often attempt to deepen anxiety than to allay it, and we ponder the likely reasons for this shift. One student wondered whether the size of the audience for contemporary newspapers is significant, noting dryly that a newspaper serving a frightened rural community is unlikely to want to scare its few readers to death. Another thought that the challenge of television may have raised the stakes of sensationalism; we focus again on the interests served by coverage, the way any representation inevitably gives so much more than Mr. Gradgrind's famous facts.

When we collect the separate representations of Pierre that appear in the *Pilote* (an incidental delight of the book is that, like a novel by B. S. Johnson or William Burroughs, it allows its readers to assemble it all over again for themselves), we learn to modify the argument of *Covering Islam*. Yes, the media circulate stereotypical images of potentially hostile groups and persons, of what Said terms "transgressions." Yes, they are reluctant to change these images even in changed circumstances. But Pierre's image does change for the readers of the *Pilote du Calvados*; one student noted how, once Pierre is incarcerated, the editors of the newspaper offer space to correspondents who see him as a rural victim as well as those who see him as a peasant-demon. My cynical rejoinder that once a dangerous criminal is in prison, his human qualities can afford to come into prominence for a relieved audience brings a swift rebuttal: the case of Ted Bundy did not provoke any sustained inquiry into the legitimacy of capital punishment, and the horrific fate of Randall Adams (the subject of the movie *The Thin Blue Line*) did not provoke United States legislators to investigate the relation between regional justice and its out-of-state beneficiaries. In some ways, one student firmly submitted, the readership of Pierre's society was better served by its media than we are today, when the pressure to write a gripping story or to cast the glamorous, harmless Mark Harmon as the glamorous, deadly Ted Bundy cuts across more complex questions of guilt, justice, and sentencing.

Yet I also remind the students that Pierre enjoyed little autonomy either before or after his crime. To live in a culture is to be circumscribed by its various reference groups, and we contrast the Pierre of village lore (an idiot, a boy who overloaded carts and beat horses) with the Pierre of scientific research (his "bilious-melancholic temperament" [123] and his descent from a long line of lunatics figure prominently here). And we also note that the foundation for a scientific verdict about Pierre was built on the shaky structures of local rumor, so that scientific knowledge and criminal judgment depend, however distantly, on what Pierre's neighbors will leak out about his early upbringing and adolescent behavior. Next, we note the course of judgment on Pierre from countryside to provinces to capital. When I ask the students whether such subordination to a central power still persists in our own "global" culture, someone reminds us of the special authority lent to the 1991 "Pentagon briefings" on the Iraqi conflict.

Our last class on this topic focuses on Pierre's own testimony. I use this class as an exercise in what Clifford Geertz has called anthropological understanding, which he sees as "attempting to determine how . . . a people define themselves as persons, what goes into the idea they have . . . of what a self is . . . the symbolic forms—words, images, institutions, behaviors—in terms of which, in each place, people actually represent themselves to themselves and to one another" (58).

How does Pierre represent his mother? What is the difference between Pierre's self-understanding and the way in which his local community understands him? How do Foucault and his students translate Pierre's actions into comprehensible terms for a twentieth-century audience? Does their translation do any less violence to Pierre's own testimony than that of the scientists who originally examined him? Why do many groups feel that they can explain Pierre and his actions better than he can explain himself? My aim at this point is to help the students not only to understand how some groups and regions seem fated to be "spoken for" by other, more privileged or more professional groups but also to comprehend the elaborate classification systems that shape even how we read an apparently raw, autobiographical narrative.

At this stage of the course, the class can conceive of culture in terms of a prescribed set of roles and symbols (veils are acceptable in Teheran but not in Tennessee, philosophy in the nineteenth century was for Parisian scientists but not for adolescent peasants), a systematic set of exclusions and marginalizations (the "body count" of the Gulf War remained largely invisible; we have no first-person narrative of Pierre's years in prison: in each case, the subject effectively vanished once a dominant set of interests ceased to focus on it), and a cluster of shifting interests that effectively create their objects of attention (I recall the celebrated case of Margaret Mead's Samoans, a group that seemed custom-made to answer the needs of American anthropologists yet which vanished from the literature when those needs transferred elsewhere). But do these conclusions mean that culture pushes always in one direction, that it represents only the powerful and their interests?

We now move to Mikhail Bakhtin's *Rabelais and His World* to contest this view. But first, we strengthen it, for Bakhtin describes in great detail how an official canon of representations controls our perceptions of how we ought to behave and speak and even how the human body ought to look (a point as important in the days of MTV's Madonna as in the days of Raphael's Madonna, I am quick to add). He systematically describes the fixed images inside that canon, so that the students can see that "covering Venus" is, in its way, as rule-governed as "covering Islam." Finally, he links this repertoire of images and system of rules to a value system that he defines as Christian humanist culture. Students and teacher now come to see the separate episodes of their education knit together into a common basis, but where such common concerns once led to much self-approval in the hands of former Secretary of Education William Bennett, many of my students—thanks to Bakhtin—start to question that unity, to wonder whether culture demands too much uniformity, reverence, and conformity. Bakhtin is an enormously well-read critic, and he draws on many obscure sources, forcing readers to visit old monuments and new territory with great freshness and forming a valuable stepping-stone toward a genuine education in his own right.

For a teacher of cultural criticism, his importance will probably lie in a different direction. My course so far has offered few pockets of resistance to the dominant power bases of family, church, state, and science. In the fairs and marketplaces of Rabelais and later in the world of Dostoevsky, however, Bakhtin finds evidence of a popular culture—a culture collective, anarchic, body-centered, and dynamic, whereas official Christian culture is individual, orderly, spiritual, and quiescent. As we follow Geertz's advice and listen to the voices from Bakhtin's popular culture—digressive, rebarbative, theatrical, and even nonsensical—we note how its logic and locutions differ from the valuations of polite Christian society. We imagine its recurring images of swarming collective bodies and contrast them with the images of individually finished perfection in classical sculpture. We acknowledge (some of us recoil from) the physicality of Rabelais's language, and we contrast it with the contemplative thrust of *Utopia* or *The Winter's Tale*. By degrees, we come to see Rabelais's popular culture as a different world, a world whose repertoire of actors, images, situations, and locutions has formed itself in direct, almost point-for-point opposition to official culture. We are now in a position where we can see culture in terms of a struggle between power and its disenfranchised shadow. We can now extend the range of social biographies that form the basis of culture to include testimonies from the margins as well as the center.

At the end of the course, I ask students to consider any "alternative" cultures they have encountered in their studies or beyond. One student thinks of Huck Finn with his apple barrel, patched jeans, vernacular speech, and black companion; another reminds us of the circus people in Dickens's *Hard Times*, and we remember that Mr. Sleary's otherness, like Huck's or Gargantua's, takes on a verbal form (he lisps). We consider the role of language, gesture, and dress in alternative cultures. We then move to discuss the fate of alternative cultures in our own period: when a student brings up the case of sometime transgressors like Lou Reed and Roger Daltrey and their efforts for Honda and American Express, I think it is time for the course to end. And in confirmation of our adage that culture follows power, by the power vested in me by the University of Denver, the course *does* end.

Courses like the one I describe are often attacked for sacrificing hard knowledge for still harder politics or for lacking a historical dimension. I think I have devised a syllabus that answers some of these objections, since I clearly present politics as a major component of any given culture but by no means as the sole one. I am also interested in representation, communication, image, and knowledge. In focusing very closely on the historical rhetoric of cultural representation (the way a particular culture convinces us that its preferred images are natural and even eternal), I am of course focusing on an art that, unlike poetry, notoriously makes things happen. But when I read the case of Pierre Rivière with my class, I feel no need to make any excuses for this choice. The history of culture has its anonymous victims as well as its canonical monuments, and as a teacher of the humanities, I clearly owe responsibility to both groups. The course I have devised is one way of discharging my obligations to the former. I teach other courses that will leave my audiences in little doubt about my affection for the latter.

University of Denver

Works Cited

Bakhtin, Mikhail. *Rabelais and His World*. Trans. Hélène Isowlsky. Bloomington: Indiana UP, 1984.

Foucault, Michel. *I, Pierre Rivière, Having Slaughtered My Mother, My Sister, and My Brother*. Trans. Frank Jellinek. Lincoln: U of Nebraska P, 1982.

———. *Power/Knowledge: Selected Interviews and Other Writings, 1972–1977*. Trans. Colin Gordon et al. Ed. Colin Gordon. New York: Pantheon, 1981.

Geertz, Clifford. *Local Knowledge: Further Essays in Interpretive Anthropology*. New York: Basic, 1983.

Said, Edward. *Covering Islam: How Media and the Experts Determine How We See the Rest of the World*. New York: Pantheon, 1981.

Williams, Raymond. *Communications*. Harmondsworth, Eng.: Penguin, 1962.

———. *Television: Technology and Cultural Form*. New York: Schocken, 1975.

Index